JACK CARNEAL
DESTROY YOUR SAFE AND HAPPY LIVES

JACK CAR

DESTROY YOUR SAI

NEAL

E AND HAPPY LIVES

RARE BIRD
LOS ANGELES, CALIF.

This is a Genuine Rare Bird Book

Rare Bird
453 South Spring Street, Suite 302
Los Angeles, CA 90013
rarebirdbooks.com

For more information, address:
Rare Bird Subsidiary Rights Department
453 South Spring Street, Suite 302
Los Angeles, CA 90013

Set in Dante
Printed in the United States

10 9 8 7 6 5 4 3 2 1

Library of Congress Cataloging-in-Publication Data

Names: Carneal, Jack, author.
Title: Destroy your safe and happy lives / by Jack Carneal.
Description: First trade paperback edition. | Los Angeles, CA :
Rare Bird Books, [2019]
Identifiers: LCCN 2019012262 | ISBN 9781644280300 (pbk.)
Subjects: LCSH: Carneal, Jack. | Drummers—United States—Biography. |
Rock musicians—United States—Biography. | LCGFT: Autobiographies.
Classification: LCC ML419.C336 A3 2019 | DDC 786.9092 [B]—dc23

LC record available at https://lccn.loc.gov/2019012262

For Aram, Jason, Ned, Paul, Will & Willie
and
Chris, Maxwell & Tabb

Inwardly torn asunder as I was, without any expectation of leading a happy earthly life…without hope of a happy and comfortable future— as it naturally springs from and lies in the historical continuity of family life—what wonder then that in desperate despair I grasped at nought but the intellectual side in man and clung fast to it, so that the thought of my own considerable powers of mind was my only consolation, ideas my one joy, and mankind indifferent to me.

—Søren Kierkegaard

If a man knows not and knows not that he knows not, shun him.
If a man knows not and knows that he knows not, awaken him.
If a man knows and knows that he knows, follow him.

—Arab proverb

FOREWORD

By Will Oldham

It's important to think about the past. We are encouraged to let it go, to let it all go, and face today and imagine that we are facing tomorrow with fresh eyes and learned lessons. But I have forgotten many things that I should have learned. And there is far too much about my own past that I never knew in the first place. It's a rare opportunity to be able to throughly revisit an earlier period in one's life.

Jack Carneal here collects anecdotes and reflections about some terrific times we shared playing music and living life. His memories are his own, certainly; I remember that the Tibetan Buddhist monks at the water park outside of Cincinnati wore orange Speedo bathing suits, where Jack recalls them swimming in their traditional red robes. And many of his recollections are from the drummer's point of view, a position I have never envied.

I grew up in the theater, doing plays and a little bit of film and television pretty solidly through the end of my teens. In the off hours I focused on music, but not as a practitioner. My friends made music and I watched them rehearse and went to their shows. When I started making music, I brought much of what I'd learned from the theater into the making of music. Each tour and production was cast separately, more or less. We start fresh with a new approach to a new situation.

This book is as strong an argument for certain ideas of ensemble building as I could hope for. When you build an ensemble for a tour or a recording, you primarily take into consideration what each prospective member of the ensemble might be willing and able to bring to the table. You bring folks together who you know have the potential to strengthen the adventure. You cross your fingers that they'll be open and willing enough to do so. It's a leap of faith on everyone's part. And just as each participant is chosen as an individual, each has their own unique incentive or set of incentives for casting their lot with you. Some need to know they'll get paid. Some look to accumulate definitive experience in their chosen field. Some only require the prospect of the adventure itself. And then some just dream.

But each brings the mass of their life into the whole affair. We bring our musical tastes and abilities, our musical histories and compatibilities and conflicts. In assembling these groups—casting these ensembles—you look to work with and spend time with people who will inform, expand, and challenge not only what we embark upon musically but also what we enter into personally. Making records and doing shows aren't outside of life, of course.

The mass of our lives is defined by our pasts and our futures. Did I know that Jack Carneal would one day write a book about some of our shared experiences? Not in such specific terms. I did count on Jack carrying on in life in such a way that the music would benefit from his experiences yet to come, that the music would get bigger and deeper and wider through its reflected relationship to Jack's evolving biography, as it does with each participant's.

Recordings are captured moments. If there is spontaneity and improvisation in the recording process, you might be lucky enough to capture, in a reliveable way, a frozen moment of the essence of a given musician's thought processes and character. And you can witness, again and again, the interplay of a group of musical humans with the unique dynamic of exactly that group. And if your listenings continue into subsequent eras of your own life, that recording can shift and change for you as well, in the same way that an objective actual event in your past is never the same, changing each time it is remembered, like a monk's Speedo, or was it a robe? And any given listener's entry point into their awareness of a recording will be informed by time that has passed since the recording was made. Those involved with the making of the music can enhance and/or deflate the power of the music.

Prior to the existence of this book, we had: some photographs, some recordings, and memories. It's marvelous now to have this deeper exploration of our significant shared ride.

Part One

To learn, above all, to distrust memory. What we believe we remember is completely alien to, completely different than what really happened. So many moments of irritating, wearisome disgust are returned to us years later by memory as splendidly happy episodes. Nostalgia is the lie that speeds our approach to death. To live without remembering may be the secret of the gods.

—Álvaro Mutis, The Adventures and Misadventures of Maqroll

1

I'd Be Riding Horses If They Let Me

ON OCTOBER 9, 1994, during a Palace Music show at the Fri-Son club in Fribourg, Switzerland, I watched from behind my drum kit as the rhythm guitar player and singer in our band finished singing a verse of the song "Horses," took a single step to the left, leaned over, and hocked a yolk-sized gob of spit into the thinning hair of a middle-aged man standing in the front row.

Far from being an aggressive act of punk rock provocation, singer Will's decision to drop a loogie in the guy's hair came instead from what appeared to me, from my perch behind the band, to be some deeply thoughtful place, which made it all the funnier. Will had been standing at the mic in something like a yogi's tree pose—one leg folded, his foot flat against his calf, knee pointed across the stage at guitarist Aram—as two burly men standing in front of him brayed at one another in sharp Teutonic voices while Will tried to sing. Their beers rested on the stage at Will's feet.

Besides the two men, there weren't many people in the audience, which was disappointing. We'd been told that the Beastie Boys had sold the club out the week before, we'd seen their graffiti on the walls of the club's band room, and we'd expected, perhaps arrogantly, a similar crowd. Instead, the ends of our songs echoed for what sounded like minutes before anyone in the tiny audience had the nerve to break the tense air with a clap. We happened to be playing the Jon Langford, Sally Timms, and Brendan Croker-penned "Horses" especially quietly as a birthday present to Tonny, our Dutch tour manager, who stood behind the soundboard. The super slow and quiet version of Mekons' "Horses" emphasized even more awkwardly the noise coming from the two men in the front row.

Then, without appearing the least bit perturbed by the men's interruptive guffaws, Will finished singing a line, breathed in deeply through his nose and gathered something worthy of spitting from his throat, took a step, then folded his body in a way that allowed him to position his mouth over the man's head, almost tenderly. He pursed his lips and let the gob shape itself—like a golf ball dangling in a sock—as it lowered onto the man's thinning pate.

After he spit in the man's hair, Will stepped back behind the mic, restored tree pose, and continued to sing.

To this day I remember the fond look on the man's face as he peered up at Will and clapped, the spit sitting in his hair like an egg. He had no idea he'd been defiled by the very man he'd paid to see.

SIX MONTHS EARLIER, I wasn't touring the world in a rock and roll group watching the singer of my band spit on a dude in the front row. In fact, I wasn't in a band at all.

Instead, I was struggling through a typical day as a clerk at Plan 9 Records on the University of Virginia's campus in

Charlottesville. Plan 9 was enjoying a moment in the spotlight because Bob Nastanovich, percussionist of indie rockstar group Pavement, had worked there while an undergrad at UVA. The notion that one of my musical heroes worked at the same store I did, had stood at the same counter answering the same stupid questions, gave me a puzzling sense of satisfaction, as if even that vague proximity to Bob made me a more interesting person.

My job at Plan 9 consisted primarily of selling "Whoomp! (There It Is)" cassingles, trading scatological Raymond and Peter barbs with my coworkers, and likely sipping an exotic coffee drink that two brothers who'd just moved from Seattle were selling from their cart outside our door. Incidentally, these addictive and expensive coffee drinks, made from black, glistening beans as pungent as skunk weed, weren't normal coffees but instead creamy confections called *lattes*, which we record store clerks pronounced as if the word rhymed with *bats*, and with their extra doses of syrup tasted not unlike high-octane melted ice cream.

In June, I'd completed an MFA in Fiction from the university's English department. One slow afternoon in spring the store's phone rang. I answered. It was my friend Ned Oldham, the loogy-hocking singer's older brother and former classmate of mine at UVA, who was calling me from his new home in Birmingham, Alabama, with exciting but strange news.

"It's crazy," Ned said, "but Will has asked you, me, Aram, and Jason to play two weeks of Lollapaloozas as the next Palace Brothers."

"Us?" I said. "Lollapalooza, like, with Nirvana and Perry Farrell? Is this a joke?"

Ned explained that Will, who also lived in Birmingham, had asked Ned if the odd studio band we'd put together with our friends Aram and Jason Stith would want to join him as the next incarnation of the Palace Brothers, the band Will had founded in the Oldhams' hometown of Louisville.

In addition to the Lollapalooza shows, said Ned, there were going to be some club shows along the way, and there might be a month-long tour in Europe in the fall.

MY FIRST RESPONSE, AS one might expect, was brainless giddiness. I hung up the phone, turned to my coworkers and crowed that I would soon be delivered from the Dickensian drudgery of our record store clerkships. I'd never have to answer another stupid question about where the Metallica CDs were ("Do you know what a CD looks like? How about the order of the letters in the alphabet?"), or to guess the identity of the mysterious young rapper—whose first name, according to a measurable percentage of customers in that era of pre-internet enlightenment, was *Notrious* [sic]—who'd just appeared on yet another mixtape.

Just as importantly, I'd never have to make another sundried tomato and artichoke spread wrap at my second job at HotCakes while being berated by a brassy, splay-footed chef who stormed around the kitchen like Rip Taylor from Hollywood Squares.

Instead I'd soon be traveling the wider world as a working musician in a famous indie-rock band. Never mind that I'd never done it before, I'd been discovered, transported, and my life, as I understood it in my limited capacity to understand anything, would soon be better than it had been before.

MY PURE IF CALLOW joy was the reflexive, nearly chemical reaction to the deep existential despair that had haunted me since finishing my degree. I was failing as a writer and Will's invitation struck me as that of a beneficent god rescuing me from the depths of my despair. It was only later that night that I'd wrestle with the darker elements of my good fortune. In the quiet and deep dark of the night, lying next to my girlfriend (now wife) Chris, I acknowledged to myself that I was terrified at how little our non-band deserved its good fortune.

It was a valid fear: Our nameless band wasn't real. We were friends and we all happened to be able to play musical instruments, but we didn't even live in the same town and had never, not once, all played together in the same room at the same time. I lived in Charlottesville, Ned in Birmingham, Jason in southwestern Virginia, and Aram in Charleston, South Carolina; we played music through the ancient medium of the four-track tape machine, sending tapes through the mail. None of us knew Will very well. And now we were being asked to go on a national tour with him, an artist who was gaining enough attention to be asked to play at a national festival like Lollapalooza with bands like Nirvana, the Beastie Boys, Pavement, and Smashing Pumpkins.

The Lollapalooza crowds, in my fevered, hour-of-the-wolf visions, would be acned conglomerations of bared teeth and greasy hair spreading out from the stage in an endless nightmarish cascade, a Bosch or Goya painting come to life, and filled with wretched demons whose role during the time we spent on stage would be to watch the drummer's every move, judge his every decision, and keep a tally of his screwups on their hash-stained fingertips.

I'd soon find out that no one, and I mean no one, cared a single whit about the drummer, but at the time, especially during those early morning visitations of dread, I was clueless enough to consider my role in the ensuing drama an important one.

AT THE TIME, WILL's band the Palace Brothers had released one full length record and a couple of seven inches, all of which had been gaining critical adulation and, more interestingly to me, were being purchased by my favorite customers at Plan 9, the true music fans.

As I saw it, we were on similar paths, me, Ned, and Will. He, too, wanted to make art for a living. He'd been a trained actor and by all accounts, including those of his brother Ned, he was damn good at it. But he'd bagged the acting stuff, deciding instead to focus on the writing and making of music, so maybe he was a little farther down the path than we were. But, again as I saw it, not much farther. Ned and I had been writing songs and playing them steadily for two years, and I was recognizing that I liked playing the drums with Ned better than I liked sitting in front of my computer pretending I could write fiction. Ned's songs were tight rockers with smart, funny lyrics. We'd sent a promo tape out to a few labels: nada. Meanwhile, Will was, in the vernacular, gaining traction. Drag City, a fantastic record label based in Chicago, on which bands like Pavement, Smog, Silver Jews, and Royal Trux had released records, was putting out Will's records, and to this record nerd, that was a big deal.

My tenuous connection with Will allowed me to feel an odd and weirdly possessive connection with The Palace Brother's debut album *There Is No One What Will Take Care of You*, which had been released the previous summer, almost concurrent with Ned and I receiving our MFA degrees. *There Is No One...* was an amalgam of rock, white gospel, and traditional British folk, and consisted of glorious, stoned chanteys with seasick, nodding tempos that often sounded in danger of collapsing, while a plaintive banjo wobbled in the background. I was a big fan of the Flatlanders' *More a Legend Than a Band* and found some resemblances in the records' simple acoustic arrangements. But if Flatlanders was somewhat slickly produced, *There Is No One...* was not. That the musicians had decided to leave in the banjo clams and off-kilter tempos without seeing the need for another take or two reflected the early Do-It-Yourself/*first thought, best thought* credo of the punks, but, unlike the punks, this record had the peculiar kernel of lyrical genius. It was sui generis.

The edgier music our manager would allow us to play on the store's stereo ran the gamut from Beck to Pavement to Urge Overkill to Smashing Pumpkins to Morphine, and maybe, for a bit of racial balance, Guru's *Jazzmatazz, Vol. 1*. On really wild days he might let us play a song or two from My Bloody Valentine's *Loveless*.

Rap was absolutely off the menu. "Even De La Soul has curse words!" the manager would exclaim peevishly.

Said manager, a tall, bird-like man with a fluty voice not unlike one of the Muppets, scowled whenever I tried to put the Palace Brothers on the house system and scrambled to eject the CD before anyone in the store was tainted. The lyrics were highly literate and thoughtful but equally strange, dark, and funny. These included those for the only indie-rock song up to that point written, it seemed to me, from the perspective of an elderly man as he admonished his elderly wife for her potentially cuckolding wanderings. The tragicomic title, "I Tried to Stay Healthy for You," made me chuckle every time I heard it.

AFTER NED HAD TOLD Will we'd be his band, I received in the mail a cassette of spare, spooky songs. The envelope contained no note, only an unmarked tape, like something a CIA agent might drop behind a bench in an obscure state park in rural Virginia.

The music on the tape, only Will and a nylon string guitar, left the impression that it had been made in a hurry. Left on the tape were the sounds of Will's rings knocking against the fretboard of his guitar, the slight wow and flutter of the tape as it ran through the recorder, and the dramatic and eerie sound of a thunderstorm as Will played and sang. It was a dub of Will's second yet-to-be-released album on Drag City, which we'd be touring to support, called *Palace Brothers* and later renamed *Days in the Wake*. Will had first recorded the songs on a portable Marantz in order to give copies of the tape to the musicians he'd asked to help him make the second record, so they could learn the songs. After a few false starts with the musicians, and some sense that it wasn't really working out, Will decided to release the practice tape as his follow-up to *There Is No One…* in all its lo-fi glory.

As a lifelong basher who'd grown up kneeling at the altar of classic rock drummers like Moon, Ringo, Watts, Bonham, Mitch Mitchell, and Neil Peart of Rush, and who also loved the driving, straightforward style of drummers like REM's Bill Berry, Cheap Trick's Bun E. Carlos, X's D. J. Bonebrake, Jody Stephens of Big Star, Stan Lynch of the Heartbreakers, Derrick Bostrom of Meat Puppets, and the Feelies' Stan Demeski, finesse and nuance had never been my strong suits. I enjoyed sitting on my throne and driving the chariot into the breech, without having to think too much. There were drummers I loved, guys like George Hurley from the Minutemen, Can's Jaki Leibezeit, or famed session drummer Bernard Purdie, who I recognized were far better than I'd ever be, but it's important to establish that I was a basher, a tasteful basher I think, but a basher nonetheless.

All of these unsettling factors gave me night sweats. Will's request for us to back him had come so far out of the blue that the story—our humble non-band would soon play onstage near not only Nirvana, Beastie Boys, and Smashing Pumpkins, but also Nick Cave's Bad Seeds, Pavement, George Clinton, and A Tribe Called Quest—had the unsettling qualities of a half-remembered dream, or maybe something that would soon be revealed as a joke.

What did he see in our band, whom he'd never seen and barely heard?

In any case, after talking to Chris, it became an easy decision: I'd work at the record store through May when the lease ended on our house in downtown Charlottesville, then Chris and I would spend a month with my parents in Richmond, after which I'd spend the rest of the summer, and perhaps my life, living the dream of playing in a rock band.

The Way That
He Walked

THE PREVIOUS SUMMER, JUNE of '93, Will and his girlfriend Dianne accompanied Joe and Joanne Oldham from Louisville to Charlottesville to celebrate Ned's commencement which, of course, was my commencement too. After a few martinis at my place, we all went to a classy local restaurant called the South Street Inn, a former whorehouse on the edge of what was then one of Charlottesville's rougher neighborhoods. Seated around us were dazzling young UVA graduates, coiffed and suited, wearing sport coats and ties, bathed in candle-glow, the future members of golf and country clubs enjoying another rite of passage.

Now that I'd completed the degree I assumed that my career as a novelist would, by rights and decree, commence. In many ways Ned was less serious than I was about our having finished our MFAs. He recognized that our degrees meant nothing beyond a simple certification of having completed a course of work, whereas I was convinced that we were special.

A publishing deal, a huge one, was on the near horizon, so close I could smell it. What did it smell like, you ask? Delicious, of course. Butter and vanilla cake, candy-coated peanuts. My visions of my future as a writer were dappled with summery, leafy shadows, with my walking among crumbling, crenellated towers somewhere in rural Italy or Scotland or England with a notebook and fountain pen in my hand, accompanied by a soundtrack of lutes, shawms, and sackbuts.

As far as I could tell, Will had been served the cake, but maybe hadn't enjoyed it as much as I imagined I would. As a youngster, he'd trained in Louisville's lauded Actor's Theater, then starred in John Sayles's movie *Matewan*, then dropped out of Brown University, moved to Los Angeles, gotten an agent and his Screen Actor's Guild card, and made a go at being a professional actor. After being in a few Hollywood movies and apparently being offered a role in *Doogie Howser, M.D.* with Neil Patrick Harris, Will had chosen to quit Los Angeles in order to go back to Louisville.

A few of the musicians who helped Will make the first Palace Brothers record were in a band from Louisville called Slint. One afternoon after classes back in Charlottesville, Ned played me Slint's record *Spiderland*. Ned had been in two bands with Britt and Brian from Slint, and as we sat there listening to the record his old bandmates had made, it was hard for me to square the dour music with the dude sitting next to me, who, as far as I could tell, was a hail-fellow-well-met type, as was I, and who liked listening to Meat Puppets and Big Star and Serge Gainsbourg. The songs Ned and I had written were tuneful rock songs aimed at pleasing the ear. Slint's lurching music was not aimed at pleasing the ear but instead, I assumed, the brain, and my brain was not complex enough to be receptive to Slint's music. Later, Slint's *Spiderland* would be lauded as an essential record of the nineties, as influential as Nirvana's *Nevermind*. While there were zero surface similarities between Will's music and Slint's, that Slint had had a hand in making the Palace Brothers' record with Will was not surprising. Neither record, *Spiderland* or *There Is No One...* cared a whit about the audience. It was music made solely for the edification of the musicians.

Back then, I didn't understand this. It had never really crossed my mind that a band might exist for purposes other than entertainment. I thought that's what bands did, entertain. And if now is the time to posit that your narrator might well be far less intelligent than the guys in Slint, than Will, than Dianne, than Ned, well, let it be written. I was behind the curve. These brilliant Louisvillians were natural-born contrarians. If the tuneful, cute moptops in Pavement were zigging, the intense, odd, birth control glasses-wearing Slint—and Palace Brothers, by extension—were zagging.

I dared not mention it, but I really wanted to know why Will had left LA. Why would he trade what he had—a life in LA, an agent, a budding acting career, a potential role on *Doogie Howser, M.D.*—for, as Ned explained it, recording a few semi-acoustic songs in an unheated farmhouse with his Slint friends?

Why would he refuse the cake?

Why would he want to destroy his career as a young actor in Hollywood?

Why would anyone want to start from scratch?

AFTER A HALF HOUR, I happened to mention The Mekons, a band I loved because of their literate lyrics and sense of humor, but mostly because they wrote and played kick-ass, no-nonsense 4/4 rock songs.

With my mere mention of The Mekons, Will and I were suddenly on the same wavelength. It was exhilarating. I couldn't tell if the martinis had suddenly kicked in, or if the candle-glow of the table and the open bottles of wine had loosened Will's tongue, but a suddenly animated Will praised the band as the apotheosis of a pure ideal. To me, The Mekons were just another band I enjoyed no more or less than the Meat Puppets, Sonic Youth, or Dinosaur Jr., but to Will the shambling art punk socialists from Leeds were the best band ever to walk the face of the earth. Later in the fall of '94, Will would release a song called "For The Mekons et al," which would be included on a sampler compilation called *Hey Drag City*.

The aim, according to Will's interpretation of The Mekons' pure punk ethos, was to devote one's entire being to working hard at one thing, with little to no interest in money, happiness, or comfort. The corporate structure and commodification of music was not only to be avoided but actively undermined. The notion of easing into and pursuing a career in music, or anything, I suppose, was anathema. It was better if things were hard.

I'd always thought a line from my favorite Mekons song was delivered with winky-winky irony, but listening to Will after too much gin and too much wine, fat and happy and full after an exorbitantly priced meal being bought for me by someone else, surrounded in the restaurant by future hedge fund managers, attorneys, and Wall Street capitalists dressed in Brooks Brothers and Duck Head, smug in my own achievement, having recently attained an advanced degree from the august University of Virginia, I considered that maybe they were serious:

Destroy your safe and happy lives, before it is too late!

THE FOLLOWING WEEK, NED and Jennie moved to Birmingham, Alabama, where Jennie would soon start medical school and where Ned would begin teaching English at Samford University. Immediately I missed my friends. Girlfriend Chris was still living in New York, and here were Ned and Jennie moving on up the rungs of life's great ladder, leaving me behind.

Stuck in Charlottesville with the blues, and working two jobs at Plan 9 and HotCakes Deli, I was determined to become a best-selling and critically acclaimed author in the vein of Cormac McCarthy, whose 1992 novel *All the Pretty Horses* had introduced much of the reading world to an author I'd worshiped for years. I'd had a prematurely white-haired professor in the 1980s at Sewanee named Tam Carlson who'd bought out Ecco's remaindered stock of McCarthy's book *Child of God*, published in 1973, and taught it to a handful of undergrads who, most likely, had never read such an empathetic portrait of a homicidal necrophiliac. The book jolted my pot-dulled and incurious undergraduate brain in a way I'd never before experienced and made me want to become a writer. It may have been a stretch, but I considered that Will and McCarthy were mining similar territory down in the deepest and muckiest caves of human behavior and warped spirituality.

Thinking of McCarthy, of Thomas McGuane, and of Will, I'd sit at a desk every morning trying to begin a novel that would, I hoped, descend into my mind as mystical visions offered by benign muses. To manipulate this exchange with anything like discipline or thought was to ruin it.

I continued to listen to *There Is No One...* almost daily, finding Palace a perfect soundtrack to a far-from-perfect summer. Every week I'd put in my hours at the record store, stuff manila folders with the dot-matrix printed short stories I'd written during grad school and send them to various magazines. Weeks later, returning from work, I'd see the SASEs in my mailbox with my handwriting on the front. I didn't even have to open them.

My downstairs neighbor was a disturbed MBA student with hyperthyroidism and a drinking problem, who also happened to be a lesbian. She'd often storm upstairs, bang on my door, her bulging eyes flashing manically, and blame me for the mouse infestation in our house, or to complain that I was too loud, or to accuse me of stealing her parking place on the street again. Then her anger would dim, she'd invite herself in, lean against my wall, let her long bangs flop into her face, adopt a butch James Dean pose, and tell me for the twentieth time in her raspy voice that she'd been struck by lightning not once but twice.

"Two different times," she'd say. "Not the same day."

"And it's rare enough to be struck once—"

"Do you have a beer?" she'd interrupt, pointing to the one I held.

"I thought you were an alcoholic," I'd say.

"It's just a beer, geez."

"Er, no, this happens to be my last one. Sorry."

Even though I barely had a penny to my name, I bought an expensive *djembe* and began to take lessons from a dreadlocked drummer who tried to imbue in me the old-school West African code of the *djembe-tigi*, the swaggering, dick-swinging master drummer. During our lessons he'd tell me in his quiet but theatrically intense voice that throughout the long night of whipping the dancers in the local African dance troupe into a frenzy of lustful thrusting and grinding, he'd pop so many capillaries in his hands while thrashing the concrete-hard surface of the drum that he'd spend the rest of the night pissing blood.

When I wasn't working at Plan 9 or HotCakes or writing or riding my bike, I'd sit in my empty pad in my underwear and try to remember the mathematically complex beats he was trying to teach me, thinking about how awful it would be to see blood coming out of my schlong, recognizing as I got lost again and again in the maze of beats that I was no master drummer.

THINGS GOT BETTER WHEN Christine decided to leave Manhattan midsummer and to join me in Charlottesville. Chris and Jennie had been in the Peace Corps together, in the Central African Republic, and I'd met Chris at Ned and Jennie's wedding in Baltimore. Originally from Rochester, she claimed that her wild life in early nineties Manhattan had run its course, and she wanted something quieter, more bucolic. Charlottesville fit the bill. It helped that we got along. And yes, it helped that we were in love.

At HotCakes I worked on the sandwich line, a job made slightly less painful by the flamboyant head chef and the periodic visits by local celebs Sam Shepherd and Jessica Lange, who loved HotCakes' sacher tortes. One day I arrived to find that the chubby, baby-faced dishwasher had returned from a stint in the state pen in Richmond. There'd been a murder; he and/or his boyfriend may or may not have killed a drag queen the dishwasher may or may not have been seeing on the side.

The newly sprung dishwasher stood sullenly at his sink, sulking, his arms invisible in soap suds, as the chef hurled barbed jail shower jokes at him, to the great delight of my fellow employees. Horace, a middle-aged black man and one of my coworkers on the sandwich line, laughed as much or more than anyone. Horace had burn scars all over his upper body and neck, and I was reminded that I'd once worked in a restaurant in Coronado, California, years before where my manager, a Native American woman, also had burn scars on her face and neck. She and Horace shared the same caramel-colored strands of ropy tissue on their shoulders and necks that pulled their mouths down at the corners.

In a rare moment of gravity, Edwin, the chef, took me aside one afternoon and told me never to ask Horace how he got the burns.

As MY WRITING CAREER languished, there was, through the fall and winter of '93 and '94, a gathering energy around the Palace Brothers.

More and more customers began walking into Plan 9 asking if we'd ever heard of this band from Louisville whose singer had been in *Matewan* and whose members were also in Slint. A few articles and reviews began to appear in the stacks of above- and below-ground zines we displayed next to the front door of the shop, all of them raves, with *Spin* magazine calling *There Is No One...* "defiantly cracked" and also naming it one of the best releases of 1993. Two more Palace 45s had been released by Drag City, "Come In"/"Trudy Dies" and "Horses," with the flipside "Stable Will." The singles disappeared soon after arriving, clutched in the hands of our store's most fervent music fans.

In December of '93 I chose *There Is No One...* as my Employee Record of the Year, barely beating out Stereolab's *Transient Random-Noise Bursts with Announcements.*

THIS MIGHT STRIKE SOME readers as an unneeded digression, but the following anecdote plays an essential role in warping my expectations of the Palace experience, which of course hadn't happened yet.

In November 1993, a few months before Ned called Plan 9 to share the good news about Will asking us to join him as the Palace Brothers, a young Charlottesville singer-songwriter brought a box of his own self-produced CDs into the record store. When the lad wasn't warbling his earnest acoustical pop songs at a few local clubs, he was a bartender at Miller's, one of the bars where I drank endless pints of Guinness and Bass with Ned and our writer friends. This was during the floppy disc era, well before computers had CD-R drives, and when it cost big money to have a single CD burned, much less thirty, and I recall feeling bad for the elfin bartending songwriter, standing there with his box of CDs, recalling the tiny tips I'd left on the sticky bar. He couldn't have had a whole lot of money to waste paying some professional studio to burn them, and that I considered his music insipid pap only made the exchange that much more awkward. My sense of patronizing record store clerk superiority was only diluted by the prospect of the *schadenfreude* I knew I'd feel as soon as the CD tanked.

He and his band played a few times a week, either at a bar called Eastern Standard or at a local club called Trax, sometimes down in Richmond at the Flood Zone. I'd seen them, sure: slicker than a peeled onion, very well-practiced, and technically proficient. But the dominant ethos and intelligence behind the songs and their performances struck me as reheated jam-band noodling overlaid on free-verse soppy adolescent reveries, even when the band was joined by a couple of hotshot C'ville jazzbos, including the most ridiculously skilled drummer I'd ever seen.

The singer appeared, in his modest way, to be ambitious, and even that bothered me. How dare he actually try to be good!

A story I'd written for the *C'Ville Review*, a weekly rag, was highly critical of the band, the thesis being that they "did not rock." But someone had to like them, right? The shows at Trax were often SRO, crammed with well-coiffed sorority girls and stocky frat-lads in tie-dyes and Birkenstocks, stinking of pot smoke and beer breath, doing their palsied chicken dancing.

The store manager took the box of CDs from the kid, sighed, and said we couldn't pay him anything up front. Instead we would have to put the CDs in the consignment section saved for Charlottesville's local artists, mostly folk singers with halitosis and overweight, dandruffy bluegrassers in overalls. The consignment area was sure commercial death. I hadn't sold a single consigned product since I began working at the store. We'd pay him as his CDs sold, which was to say he'd never get paid. The young musician shrugged his shoulders, thanked us politely and walked out.

As I watched him walk down the sidewalk, not thirty seconds after leaving, the store's phone rang. I happened to answer it.

"Hey, do you have that new Dave Matthews Band CD?" the excited caller asked.

"The one he just dropped off, you mean? What, are you standing outside the door? Did he pay you to call us?"

"So, you have it?"

I picked up a copy and looked at the cover, one of those eye-tricking autostereograms from the nineties.

"Uh, yes, I happen to be holding it in my hand."

"Can you send it to Ann Arbor?"

"Ann Arbor, as in Michigan?"

I had to ask my manager, who was already looking at me in stunned amazement, if we could take phone orders for a consignment product, and how much to charge for shipping. While I was finishing up the phone call, a group of students came in and bought more copies. Ten minutes later, another call, this one from Los Angeles, then another call from Syracuse, one from Chapel Hill.

We sold the full box of CDs in a half hour, and within another five minutes we'd put in another order to Dave.

There was no internet then, no cell phones. How on earth were these kids learning about the new CD? In any case, in the coming months, right up until I left the store, my primary job at Plan 9 became being the dispenser of Dave Matthews Band CDs. We could not keep them in the store. Some afternoons, standing at the counter waiting for more DMB fans to arrive, I'd scribble numbers on scrap pieces of paper. The dude was making thousands and thousands of dollars…

It would be misleading for me not to admit that the Dave Matthews Band's inexplicable success was on my mind as the departure date for the Lollapalooza shows' rehearsal approached, and would continue to haunt me throughout my years as a musician. The way I saw it, the future of Palace was a simple syllogism: we were going to be a better band than the DMB, led by a singer/songwriter with genuine talent, a real poet, ergo our success, both critical and financial, would be all but guaranteed.

ON APRIL 5, '94, two months before Will, Ned, Jason, and I were all to meet at Aram's home in Charleston, South Carolina, to begin practicing for Lollapalooza, Kurt Cobain shot himself. Nirvana had been slated as Lollapalooza's headliner before Cobain had tried to commit suicide earlier that spring, when the band withdrew from their shows and decided they needed to focus on making sure Cobain was okay.

And now he was dead.

I'd been slow to get on the *Nevermind* bandwagon—"Smells Like Teen Spirit" sounded like top 40 doofus hard rock to me—but I enjoyed *In Utero*'s dark corners and was looking forward to watching Nirvana perform. What drummer wouldn't want to watch Dave Grohl play every day for two weeks?

A few days later, on April 8, Chris and I left Charlottesville for New York City. While she hung out with some old friends from her Manhattan days, I went to a Liz Phair and Raincoats concert. The Raincoats, a band Kurt had championed before his death, were visibly upset onstage, and it was a somber evening. I was affected by how starkly Cobain's death cast shadows across the cultural landscape, and in my hyper-sensitive state his suicide meant no less than the rising of Yeats's blood-dimmed tide, the ceremony of the innocence of the nineties drowned.

Walking around Manhattan the day after the show, it was easy to sense that something had ended with Cobain's death, and something new was beginning. It was a cloudy and dull Manhattan afternoon, with the smell of pretzels and coppery subway exhaust thick in the cool air, and as excited as I was to begin the adventure of being the Palace Brothers' drummer, hidden in the shadows of Cobain's suicide were intimations of my own mortality. I was no longer young, almost the same age as Cobain had been when he'd shot himself, the same age as Brian Jones, Pigpen, Jimi Hendrix, Jim Morrison, Janis Joplin, Basquiat: I'd turn twenty-seven in August. I was submitting my short stories and getting rejection after rejection and instead of increasing my resolve, the constant disappointment was becoming exhausting. In Times Square, Cobain's kohl-eyed sad-face stared down at Chris and I from a giant screen, as if in sympathy.

What was wrong with my stories, you may well ask? One of my stories ended with two homeless men supergluing themselves by accident to the doll they shared. Another story ended when a recently head-injured protagonist and his mother (who stood more than six feet tall, weighed over two hundred pounds, and was dressed like Carmen Miranda, complete with fruity cornucopian headwear) start a fire by mistake at his gay brother's Halloween-themed art opening. The third story involved an elderly farmer who helps a young man try to find the wedding ring lost when his wife was killed in an airplane that crashed into the old man's soybean field. Presumably her finger, with wedding ring still attached, was still in the field somewhere. There was lots of folksy wisdom packed into that one, I tell ye, wisdom about patience and perseverance and stubbornness…and the joys of hoecakes and whiskey and beans cooked all day with a ham hock, that sort of thing.

If any of these scenarios sound fascinating to you, you were probably not an editor at the *Paris Review* in 1993.

A friend from Richmond, the drummer in a band called Technical Jed, had sent me a VHS tape that included a short PBS documentary produced in West Virginia, and I became obsessed with it. Sure that no one could ever have seen the tape besides my friend and me, I set about writing a novella based—stolen, really—on the main character, who happened to be an eccentric glue-sniffing clogger from the mountains. The novella was a feel-good paean to empowerment through home ownership called *The Next House I Paint Will Be My Own*. When I described the plot to another friend, a dude who had no interest in the hipster tape-trading scene, he said without hesitation, "Gosh, sounds an awful lot like Jesco White, the Dancing Outlaw." For reasons I'll never be able to explain, I'd spent a year and a half on this novella, countless hours wasted.

IN THE WAKE OF Nirvana's having to cancel their Lollapalooza gigs we'd also learned that Pavement wouldn't be playing on the Lollapalooza tour either, possibly because Malkmus had sung a jokey verse in his song "Range Life," a song from Pavement's winter release *Crooked Rain, Crooked Rain*, that disrespected the new headliners Smashing Pumpkins. Rumor had it that Billy Corgan had thrown a fit and demanded Malkmus and Pavement be removed from the bill. Another disappointment.

Meanwhile, in June, after I'd quit my jobs at HotCakes and Plan 9 and Chris and I had left our house in Charlottesville, none other than *The New York Times* had reviewed Will's solo show at the Thread Waxing Space in Lower Manhattan. A review in such an august publication was not only a validation that my decision to quit my jobs was not idiotic, but an example of something I found truly exciting: Will's career as a musician was gaining more traction. This was good for me. It was good for Will, sure, but also it was good for me. It was good for Aram, for Jason, for Ned as well. We were vacationing with my extended family (a vacation during which mother, father, sister, uncles, aunts, cousins, and Chris and I had all crowded around a small black and white television in our beach house while watching O. J. Simpson driving his white Bronco down an LA freeway), and I was able to show everyone the review in the Gray Lady with something approaching pride.

"This is the band I'm joining," I said. "The band I'm in. Or will be playing in soon."

"What's happened to the old band? Are they being fired?"

"Well, no, there's not really an old band. There was, but I'm not sure what happened… Anyway, it's pretty much just this guy in the paper, the main guy."

"But they were called the Palace Brothers, plural. What happened to the other brothers?"

"I'm not sure. I still haven't talked to Will about any of that."

"I'd tell you not to quit your day job," my Dad muttered, "if you *had* a day job."

Dad was wrong, and he knew it. In truth I did have a day job, and was making pretty good dough as a landscaper whose specialty was squaring off privet hedges with electric shears so sharp you could shave on their edges.

Whither Thou Goest,
I Will Go

THERE WAS AN EARLY holiday glow: our first practice in a roach-, mosquito-, and flea-ridden industrial bunghole deep in the only part of Charleston, South Carolina, that is not beautiful allowed Aram, Ned, Jason, and me to know that we did a good job of electrifying the Palace catalogue. The first song we played together was "Ohio River Boat Song." It was an exciting but somehow muted afternoon, and, in retrospect, a significant few hours in our lives. Whatever path we'd been on up to that point had diverged, perhaps been erased, and we were now on another, heading in an entirely different direction.

We're all still on it, truth be told.

At practice, as Ned, Aram, Jason, and I smiled and otherwise engaged in the vocal exchanges and body language that reflected what one might term excitement or happiness, high fives and the like, *Hey, we're good*, Will betrayed few emotions. There were smiles, I remember, a bit of laughter, sure. This was going to work,

I knew, and I relaxed. My take on our mission was fundamentally naive: we'd go out, have a bunch of laughs, play some tunes, travel around, make some money, and be lauded. I forgot that Will was in the early phases of building a career. Will didn't relax much and I only understood later that it was him who'd have to stand up there in front of everyone singing his songs, not me; I got to sit in the back and pound away on the skins.

MUCH LATER, I'D READ what John Coltrane once said about Miles Davis and be reminded of those early days of our nascent Palace experience: *(Miles) rarely discusses music. You always have the impression that he's in a bad mood, that he's not interested in, or not affected by what other people are doing. It's very hard in a situation like that to know exactly what you should do. Maybe it's because of that, that I just started to do what I wanted.*

EVEN THOUGH THE MUSIC Ned, Aram, Jason, and I had written up to that point was mostly post-punk rock and roll, our range of musical tastes allowed us to touch on psychedelia, country, straight rock, blues, blasts of noise, even reggae. Overall, we had the searching qualities of a sixties or seventies rock band like The Band, Crazy Horse, or the Grateful Dead, a comparison with which Ned, Aram, Jason, and I, Dead fans all, were content.

In retrospect, our electrification of Palace's mostly acoustic songs laid the foundation for a lot of music that would be made in the coming years, a recontextualization or reevaluation of the music made by singer/songwriter bands of the sixties and seventies, which many punks in our generation had been taught to loathe. As a drummer, I was thinking about famed session musician Kenny Buttrey's drumming on Young's *Harvest*, especially the way he begins to split the kick drum couplets after the first verses of the song "Out on the Weekend," which is similar to the straight, no-nonsense 4/4 of "Heart of Gold" and "Old Man." Derrick Bostrom copied these robotic beats somewhat on *Meat Puppets II*. I'd loved Buttrey's drumming on songs like Dylan's "I Am a Lonesome Hobo" and "As I Went Out One Morning" and thought that there were moments during those early practices when Jason and I clicked together like Buttrey and session bassist Charlie McCoy. The contrast between Buttrey's straightforward kick couplets in the beginning of songs like Young's "Out on the Weekend" and the more playful and loose kick as the song progresses creates the sense of the song being loosened as it's played. Just as James Brown asked his drummers to emphasize the first beat in a measure, "the one," almost as if to surprise the dancer waiting for his cues, Buttrey's playful popping bass drum gave what many thought was prototypical white-man country-folk music the spine-sliding, sly humor of funk. Levon Helm of The Band knew some secrets, too, and I listened closely.

Later, I heard drummer Dave Mattacks' work with Fairport Convention, Richard and Linda Thompson and Steeleye Span, realizing that I was doing many of the same things he did, without having ever heard him: trying to fill the empty ¾ spaces with tight, rolling snare fills or quick roundels of tom strikes in order to make sure that the songs swung instead of lurching back and forth between the one and the three like waltzes. I'd also been playing what was something like a sloppy flam between bass and snare, which I'd heard one of the Palace Brothers' drummers, maybe Britt Walford (although a few guys played drums on that first record, including Todd and Brian), doing on a few songs on *There Is No One What Will Take Care of You*. Later, when I heard Mattacks using the same techniques I wondered if Britt hadn't listened to him before.

With Will's fundamentally brilliant songs and voice, Jason's soulful bass playing, Aram's genre-defying guitar wizardry, and

Ned's subtle and intelligent rhythm guitar, his spiky, probing leads and genetically-matched vocal harmonies with his brother, we sounded less like we were plumbing the traditions of Appalachia and instead exploring more of a kind of country-soul-British folk-rock mashup, if such a thing can be imagined. It was not difficult to sense from the start: we were a skilled but unpolished rock band, and with Will's dramatic songs and front-man demeanor we were, if nothing else, not going to be boring.

After practicing for a few hours in the roach spray–reeking room in North Charleston with plum-colored shag on the floor and no natural lighting, we'd emerge from the stanky gloom of the practice space into the glory of a South Carolina summer and head to Folly Beach or Sullivan's Island to meet Christine, Jennie, Dianne, and Aram's wife, Mclean, for a late afternoon swim. I'm pretty sure it was during this glorious period of our lives when both Will and Aram began their lifelong love of surfing. I recall having a borrowed surfboard or two with us as we swam. We spent hours trying to stand up in the mild Atlantic surf, and Chris was the only one to achieve any success. Afterward we'd stop at a market, a liquor store, return home, and cook fresh fish and drink beer and wine, always joined by Chris, Dianne, Jennie, and Mclean—who bore a resemblance to Nico: tall, high cheekbones, white-blonde hair.

Raven-haired Dianne would join us on the tour as the tour manager, the person responsible for doling out our per diems, and as the person who would soon control the cashbox, she took on the nom de tour "Numbers," and will be identified as such in the next few chapters.

If it hasn't been made clear already, both Aram and Ned were married while Will and Numbers were going steady; Chris and I would be married within a few years. Jason was the only single man in the band. This domestically stable portrait of an archetypally unstable unit—the touring rock band—was a fundamental part of my understanding of our mission;

I suspected we'd avoid many of the rock band clichés upon beginning our tour, namely sex with groupies. I was correct.

At night, after supper, we'd often watch VCR tapes of Bruce Brown surfing movies like *Barefoot Adventure, Surf Crazy,* and *Slippery When Wet,* and the pure freedom expressed in the footage, and that the movies were about travel as much as surfing, lent our tour an air of the surf adventure, even though there would be no surfing. It was about the journey as much as the destination, and each destination on our tour, just like each surf break, would have its own inherent challenges.

THROUGH THE HONEY-COLORED FILTER of fond recollection, I remember that one afternoon during a break in rehearsal, we dared Will to eat one of the pink pickled eggs kept in a cloudy jar of mucosoidal liquor on the counter of a local gas station where we often bought dollar hot dogs. You could also buy an American cheese sandwich for $1.69, which seemed expensive to me for American cheese and white bread. The pickled eggs appeared to have been sitting in the jar since the Civil War. Will accepted the bet without hesitation. I recall him removing the egg with the supplied tongs, a wide smile splitting his face as Aram, Jason, Ned, and I began to crack up, the liquid, thus disturbed, swirling with eggy excrescence, looking not unlike a lava lamp, then Will popping the egg whole in his mouth and rubbing his belly as he chewed and swallowed. He may have eaten a second one. There was no money involved. Will just wanted to prove to us that he wasn't afraid to eat the foul-looking eggs.

Jason took on the nom de tour Selma Lagerlof, a Swedish author he was reading at the time, so we became used to addressing him as Selma as often as we called him Jason, just as we'd call Dianne Numbers more often than Dianne. Jason's musical roots were planted firmly in a world far different from my own. While my middle-school band haunted the perimeter of Richmond's punk/new wave scene, he'd played bass in high school for the ESVA's own Black Elvis (an African-American fellow from Virginia's Eastern Shore named Clearance Giddens who sang Elvis songs at weddings, Rotary Club events, county festivals). While I listened to bands like Uncle Wiggly, Trumans Water, and Archers of Loaf, both Aram and Jason might discuss selections from jazz bassist Stanley Clarke's oeuvre at length, or how Jaco Pastorius's bass playing in Weather Report was the pinnacle of musicianship. They were extraordinary musicians, as was Ned, as was Will, and could communicate in that guitar-speak that I just never understood. I was the drummer, the working class member of the band. It was my job to shut up and keep the beat.

One afternoon we were riding back to town in the bed of a pickup truck with the surfboards, hot South Carolina breezes caressing us, when Will mentioned that he wasn't sure if he wanted to be a singer in a band anymore.

"What would do you do instead?" I asked.

"Go to law school," Will shrugged.

As we were setting up for our first show at Lounge Ax in Chicago on July 15, 1994, we got a request from Nick Cave's people to put Cave and the band on the guest list. Will refused.

"I've paid to see him before," Will said as he uncoiled a guitar cable and as I unpacked my cymbals. "I've bought his records. He can pay to see us. He can afford it."

I didn't think it was a big deal to extend a courtesy to an influential artist like Cave, but to Will the generous gesture would be loaded. Maybe it would betray Will's sense of control or indicate submission. Perhaps Will's refusal to let Nick and his band in for free would create an understanding that like any great artist—Dylan, Chilton, James Brown, Thelonius, Picasso,

Herzog—the young Kentuckian Will Oldham did things his way, kowtowed to no one, and knew that being brainlessly nice was to surrender control of your world and to show your ass. As I got older I appreciated Will's unbending nature and resolved to adopt some of his tactics myself.

At the time, however, I thought, *Come on, dude, lighten up. It's Nick Cave!*

(Much later, I'd filter a lot of Will's attitude through an understanding of Brown and Levinson's research into what they called *negative and positive face*. The aim of someone expressing positive face is to create a bond through a sort of social submission, to be seen as friendly, as a non-threat. That was me, what with my somewhat hippyish, *it's all-good* tendencies. Those expressing *negative face* are emitting an almost simian, passive but threatening vibe: I do not want to be your friend. Do not bother me. You will have to earn my trust. Negative face is obviously more punk.)

I also noted that the poster for the show had us billed as Palace Band and not Palace Brothers. It made no sense. Why were we not billed as the Palace Brothers?

"Because the Palace Brothers were the people that made that one record," Will said. "We're not them."

The show that night included Chicago's Plush, the San Francisco Seals, and Louisville's Pale Horse Riders. PHR featured the youngest Oldham brother, Paul, and usually Pavement's Bob Nastanovich, who didn't play that show because Pavement was out on the road. Additionally, this would be the first time I'd meet not only Paul but Paul's bandmates, a few of whom, like drummer Peter Townsend, will appear later and will play an increasingly important role in this epic narrative. San Francisco Seals member Barbara Manning had been in World of Pooh, a pop band I liked during my Plan 9 days. It was a great show, a sold-out success—and there was Cave, his spectral face rising bluely above the crowd. Later, standing on the roof of Drag

City's offices after eating late-night steak burritos and drinking horchata for the first time with Drag City honcho Dan Koretzky, looking out over Chicago's skyline, I allowed myself a moment of triumph.

I'd arrived and was living the dream.

Whatever anxieties I had had about playing music in front of people, about our band generally, had disappeared. My hour-of-the-wolf worries dissipated and floated up into the Chicago night. The distant, scattered lights of the city became an evocation of glamour, of success, and came to represent the fulfillment of a single small dream. This would be gravy. Being in a rock band could not be easier or more natural, I thought.

I was wrong.

Our debut Lollapalooza show at the World Music Theater in Tinley Park outside of Chicago the following day was disastrous and sad-tromboned/slide-whistled any sense of confidence gained from the previous night's triumphant show at Lounge Ax. The lead roadie was a huge white-haired Swede named Foley who bore a resemblance to seventies wrestler Ric Flair. One of the stagehands, an older guy who looked not unlike rockabilly artist Charlie Feathers with poorly dyed, Brylcreemed hair, and a pack of smokes rolled up in his shirtsleeve, bitched at me during load-in for putting my drums at the top of the stage ramp.

"Or do you even care?" he said unevenly, his eyes unfocused, head loose on his neck.

"Of course I care," I answered to his non sequitur, moving my drums. "I'm new here. Sorry, pal. Happy to move them, just tell me where."

"Of course you care," he hissed.

Later I saw him trembling, staring into the distance. Soon he was under a tree, on his side, his hands between his knees.

Aram, Jason, Ned, and Will were all using a natural crystal deodorant that summer that didn't work, so the interior of the van had begun to take on a uric reek not unlike the primate house at a zoo. We'd spent a part of the morning before the show with Dan K and Rian from Drag City in our smelly Ford van parked in the Lollapalooza parking lot listening to a cassette of the vocals-only mix of the Beach Boys' *Pet Sounds*. Stunned by the beauty and skill of the singing, I carried a honey-colored, optimistic California vibe to the stage for our first Lollapalooza performance. But as soon as I stepped onto the wide, black surface of the Lollapalooza platform I felt a vertiginous, telescoping "dolly zoom" effect as Aram, Ned, Jason, and Will appeared to slide away from me. The stage at Lounge Ax the night before had been comfortable and tight, I could see into the eyes of my bandmates, smell their crystally pits, but this stage was as wide and impersonal as a football field.

Then, just as Will turned to me, nodded his head, and I counted off our first tune so that Ned, Will, and Aram could begin to pluck the dulcet lead guitar notes of "Ohio River Boat Song," a fabulous song and one of my favorites to play, and a great choice for a show opener, we were greeted by an insane pounding, howling, and skronking from the main stage just across the asphalt lot in front of us. It was the Boredoms, from Japan, also scheduled to start at 1:00 p.m. Anyone familiar with the early and inaccurate reputation of the Palace Brothers as sensitive, touched indie-rock musicians might appreciate the humor inherent in our performance's juxtaposition with the Boredoms. The Boredoms pummelled audiences into submission with a hippie dada wall of math-skronk. We were supposed to give the crowd chills with our hushed, intimate folk fables. Palace would battle the Boredoms daily for the next two weeks. Our friend Bobby Arellano (more on him anon) would much later make a film of the strange juxtaposition of the two bands.

Second, the Boredoms' nullifying din notwithstanding, it didn't take long to get the sense that the sound we were producing that distant afternoon on that Lollapalooza stage outside of Chicago sounded more like improvised free jazz than the songs we'd been practicing. I'm not sure what we did to displease the muses. There were many times that afternoon when I was lost, afloat on a sea of echo, trying to find my way through a drone of sound-hash, bashing away at the kit without any idea of where we were in the song.

There's something particularly nightmarish about bombing onstage in front of an audience, but to describe my sense of utter and complete bafflement that afternoon is nearly impossible. I wanted so badly to be doing well; instead I could not have been doing worse. During Will's powerful song, "You Will Miss Me When I Burn," we turned the beat backward, began to confuse the one and three, the very foundation on which the song rests. Bassist Jason (aka Selma) and I exchanged embarrassed glances, trying to read one another's lips as we attempted to steer the ship back into the pocket, trying to find the beat and pair it to the melody, and failing. Nothing we tried could right the ship.

The audience still clapped and whooped.

As we shlumped off the stage after our horrendous first Lollapalooza show and my entire body tingled with humiliation, I recall one fellow musician nodding his head sagely and telling us how awesome we were, and how odd it was that we didn't sound at all like Slint, or like the Palace Brothers' record.

Awesome? I thought. *Had he been paying attention? Was he deaf, or otherwise impaired, perhaps with some form of a mild but diagnosable neurological condition?*

He continued with a string of questions: You're Britt, the incredible drummer from Slint, right? Who'd also been on a Breeders record, credited as Mike Hunt? And which one of you guys plays the banjo? Speaking of the banjo, where is it? The acoustic guitars? The fiddle and mandolins? Where are they, in another van, maybe? If the conversation didn't run exactly like the following, it was damn close:

"We don't have any banjos or fiddles or mandolins," Aram said. "I don't think there are any fiddles on any of Will's records."

"There are," he stated.

"There aren't," said Ned.

"There's a cello on 'Come In,'" Jason said. "No fiddles."

"Y'all are the Slint guys, right? No?"

"No," I answered. "No, no, no, no. We are most definitely not the Slint guys."

"Oh," he said, clearly bummed.

THE OTHER BANDS ON Lollapalooza's second stage included Luscious Jackson, L7, Girls Against Boys, Guided by Voices, the Flaming Lips, and the Verve, who were a few years away from releasing the now ubiquitous "Bittersweet Symphony."

Before the tour I'd been fond of the Flaming Lips, who'd played an infamously weird show at Sewanee back in the eighties and whose then-drummer and multi-instrumentalist Steven Drozd hit the drums harder than anyone I'd ever seen. As I watched the Flaming Lips on that first afternoon in Chicago after our terrible set, Drozd's playing induced a synesthetic overload, his kick-drum firing like a rib-pounding artillery shot as he crushed his gigantic cymbals, which reverberated and shimmered in the summer sunlight like gongs.

Next up was the all-female band Luscious Jackson, whose drummer Kate Schellenbach was, quite famously, the first drummer for the Beastie Boys. Luscious Jackson's debut *In Search of Manny* had been on regular rotation at the record store for most of my final year in Charlottesville, and I was entertained by their urbane smooth-funk, soothed and fascinated by their laid-back cool-chick auras. Listening to and watching them was a perfect way to spend a sunny summer afternoon while drinking a coldish beer. Though I'd heard some Guided by Voices at Plan 9 and we'd sold a few copies of *Vampire on Titus*, I had no idea how popular their more recent release *Bee Thousand* was and was surprised at how many fans appeared to be at the second stage because of the ramshackle pop machine that was GBV.

Girls Against Boys was a two-bassist band from DC with some serious hardcore bona fides; three of the guys had been in DC's Soulside. They played an interesting synth-based rock music that seemed worlds away from their punk roots. The Verve, with their odd Paul Weller bowl cuts, skeletally thin bodies, and sunglassed English cool seemed not to want to be there at all. They seemed straight out of central casting, languorous, pissed, non-smiling.

If I didn't love every band we shared the stage with, I was still interested in watching, listening to, and learning from them all.

RIGHT AFTER OUR LOUSY first show, we retreated, still in shock, to the special backstage hospitality area set up for us in a fifteen by fifteen foot space in the parking lot. It had a few chairs and a case of Corona beer, with a placard with "Palace Songs" taped to the box of beer. Few words were spoken about the day's relative debacle. It was a great lesson, and to be clear I was still convinced we were going to be a great band. Just like finely tuned athletes who'd just tanked during the season's opener, we knew the only thing to do was to put the loss behind us and move on. We knocked back a couple lukewarm Coronas, then made our way into the main shed to watch Nick Cave and the Bad Seeds for the first time. The day's cruddy show was already in the rearview mirror. Ahead of us? World domination.

On our way to the Bad Seeds show, we were approached by a journalist from Canada, a portable tape recorder slung over his shoulder, who thrust a mic into Will's face and began jabbering—but jabbering politely, like a good Canadian. After asking Will a question about Slint to which Will responded with a shrug and a grunt, the journo aimed the mic at my face and asked me the same question, whatever it was. I was inordinately excited to cross this important threshold. My first interview! Would I be sharply witty, like John Lennon, perhaps improvising a *bon mot* on the spot? Or would I be enigmatic and demure, like Michael Stipe, and offer the journo a psychedelic non sequitur meant to imply that I didn't see the need for letting the journo into my scrambled mindspace for something as mundane as an exchange of simple information?

Instead, upon being asked the question, I pointed my thumb at Will and said, "He'd know the answer to that a lot better than I would."

Thus ended my first interview. It would not be the last rookie mistake I made.

IT WAS A LAZY summer afternoon, the sun shining brightly, as Will, Numbers, Aram, Jason, Ned, and I took our seats for the Bad Seeds' show.

The Bad Seeds strode onto the stage like a pack of wolves. Each of the band members wore pegged black pants, colorful collared shirts, and spit-shined Beatle boots. The contrast between the soft summer light, the harmless reverie of the knuckleheaded Lollapalooza attendees surrounding us, and the intensity with which Cave and the lads consumed and stalked the stage seemed as discontinuous as attending a Saturnalia bonfire on a sunny beach in North Carolina with a bunch of Target managers.

We watched and listened, pinned to our seats, as Cave and the boys delivered a stunning show. It was like they were saying, "This is how it's done, lads! Pay attention."

During those two weeks, when we pretty much watched the Bad Seeds pretty much every afternoon, I began to imitate

Bad Seeds drummer Thomas Wydler and his jazz-oriented style. I think about his tasteful, timely fills to this day. The band was traveling with a set of tubular bells, and during a few songs the dramatic chimes would ring out from beneath the corrugated roofs of humid Midwestern sheds as if from some fantastical medieval cathedral. Who knew that Cave could be capable of such transformative beauty, listening to him and the Bad Seeds make their way through "Nobody's Baby Now" and the leering "Red Right Hand" day after day?

Our stagecraft didn't change much from the style we used when practicing in our warehouse in Charleston: no dancing, no rock star moves, possibly a flourish or two during a crescendo, maybe a slightly bent knee during a guitar solo, but certainly no dancing, no attempts to whip our crowds into anything resembling a frenzy.

In truth, Jason usually stood stock still, wearing his bass comfortably high, his elbows positioned in the same places I'm sure his middle school bass teacher had showed him, while Aram's thin frame hunched slightly over his left-handed guitar.

On hot days a few of us were inclined to wear shorts, the only band members that did so (except for one of the friendly Girls Against Boys boys). At some point along our travels I thought our dumpy-graduate-students-in-the-humanities looks were causing image problems, so I bought two blousy dress shirts at a thrift store. My first time donning one of them—pumpkin orange as I recollect—the rest of the band laughed openly and shook their heads. The shirts got shoved deep into my duffel bag, where they remained.

AFTER OUR FIRST BAD Seeds show, another beer or two back at our palatial spot in the hot parking lot, and wolfing down a few paper plates of lukewarm chicken tetrazzini from the catering tent, we submerged ourselves into the great masses filing into the main shed and watched as the stage crew set up for the Beastie Boys. Everyone knew that the Beastie Boys had started as a punk band and had returned to their roots and played the live instruments on their most recent releases *Check Your Head* and *Ill Communication*, but even as a fan it was easy for me to take the low road and suspect that the performances on the records may have been studio-enhanced. At that very moment *Ill Communication* was number one on the charts, and I had taken the cynical viewpoint that the Beastie Boys, as much as I loved their records, would be phoning in the shows by simply giving the audience a stream of radio hits and pumping out soft-serve raps to DJ Hurricane's prerecorded beats.

As the three Boys strutted on the stage to Biz Markie's voice and Ted Nugent's sampled guitar booming out of the mains and as they slung instruments onto their shoulders instead of picking up mics—Mike Diamond seating himself behind the small drum kit—I felt the anxious edge of incipient embarrassment. Full-on record store clerk snobbery, certainly connected to my sense that the Beasties were not only Top 40, for God's sake, but number freaking one, toppermost of the poppermost on the dreaded Casey Kasem pop charts, of all things, the absolute pinnacle of sellout. What could be worse than watching a band that everyone in the United States apparently liked pander to a bunch of pubescent knuckleheads who'd lap up anything the three cute Beasties burped out?

With nary a signal to one another, as Biz's voice and the Nuge's guitar faded into the Chicago afternoon, the Beasties kicked in to "Time for Livin'," and we were treated to a two-minute blast of invigorating and goosebump-inducing American hardcore. The Beasties were flying around onstage like madmen. Within seconds we were all laughing involuntarily. Go and listen to those two songs in a row, right now. Do it. If you don't start laughing out loud and feeling the urge to run into your walls, or call some friends to try to arrange a quick game of touch football or five on five at your local playground, or at least to go sprint around the block a few times, then something is wrong with your adrenal system.

It was awesome! I felt joy, that pure joy that makes your eyes fill.

A FEW DAYS INTO the tour, during Luscious Jackson's set, I said to Will that I liked the group because they were harmless. He shot me a withering stare.

"That's the stupidest thing I've ever heard," he said, or something to that effect. "You like them because they're *harmless?*"

"Well, I mean," I stammered, "it's not like when I hear them I feel some need to hate them or love them, they just are, they exist…"

Food, books, music, movies, Will had extreme and well-argued opinions about everything, a trait he shared with Ned. It was as if they'd both eaten every food ever cooked at every restaurant in the world (including Ned's professed fondness for haggis), seen every movie ever made from Finland to India to Indonesia, and had versions of every song ever recorded stored in the vast hard drive that was their mutually shared sibling brain.

Would you like to hear a snippet of the dialogue from Satyajit Ray's first Apu film *Pather Panchali* performed in an exact-sounding simulacrum of Hindi actor Subir Bannerjee's dialect? How about the chorus from Waylon Jennings's "Ain't No God in Mexico" written, of course, not by Waylon but by Billy Joe Shaver? Woe betide the man that summer who produced a mixtape filled with what passed as the moment's hip tunes—Can, Ween, Ash Ra Tempel, Sonic Youth, Raincoats, Pavement, Sebadoh. They would experience Will banning the tape from the van's cassette player with a humiliating flourish.

If it hasn't been made clear, it was my opinion that Will bore the burden of owning a mind that operated with more complex algorithms than my own.

Most of the time, when I went back and fast-forwarded through another tape on my yellow Walkman, I'd acknowledge that Will was right. Ash Ra Tempel and the Raincoats were unlistenable. Much of my beloved Krautrock was, in fact, silly, acid-twisted wanking. I liked it probably because someone had told me to like it. Meanwhile, Will would slip one of the early Ethiopiques cassettes into the van's player, and I'd be stunned at how much more joy emanated from ten seconds of Ethiopiques than from an entire side of Guru Guru or Tangerine Dream.

We stopped along the Pennsylvania Turnpike and caught an afternoon showing of the then brand-new Bob Zemeckis film *Forrest Gump*, a movie I found clever if not world-changing but which appeared to make Will quiver in anger at its soft-minded idiocy and Tom Hanks's affected portrayal of the simpleton Gump.

Ned shrugged. "Wasn't *that* bad."

"Yeah," Aram added. "Inoffensive."

"The chick was hot," Jason said.

Will would look at us, one by one, like Ren looking at a group of Stimpys. Numbers would sigh.

After only these few short weeks, I'd realized that Will's probing, critical spotlight would often illuminate or uncover something hiding in the shadows that spoke of deeper truths. In other words, he was usually right.

DURING OUR SOUND CHECK before a show near Pittsburgh, Will announced that we were going to play three new songs that afternoon, Dylan's "New Pony," the Allman Brothers' "Midnight Rider," and Bob Seger's "Ramblin' Gamblin' Man." I announced from my throne that I hated Bob Seger, having grown up hearing "Hollywood Nights" and "Old Time Rock and Roll" a few thousand times too many, and would prefer not to play "Ramblin' Gamblin' Man." Bob Seger drove me up a wall and his voice elicited unwelcome images of Tom Cruise sliding across a floor in his tube socks and tighty-whities. My *nay* vote was overruled, so we learned the songs.

We played them that afternoon, to great effect, and it was only later that I realized the decision was very well calculated. Our shows had been going over well, we'd definitely gotten whatever rotten thing was in our system out during our Chicago show, but most of our songs were slow and intense. We were playing a lot of new material from *Days in the Wake* and *Hope*, which were introspective, quiet records. Since we were playing a summer show at one in the afternoon, Will recognized that we needed a few crowd-pleasers.

Leaving town after the concert, on our way to the next show, we stopped at a gas station. Will emerged from the station clutching a cassette of the Bob Seger System's record "Ramblin' Gamblin' Man" he'd purchased inside, and shoved it into the van's cassette player. We listened.

I was forced to admit that I was wrong again and Will was right: it was and is a fantastic record.

There were things out there in the world waiting to be discovered, and we were on a journey to discover them. We were all obsessed with books and had a huge pile of paperbacks in the van with us, books by Charles Willeford, Russell Hoban's *Riddley Walker*, a few of John D. MacDonald's Travis McGee books, *Master and Margarita* by Bulgakov. There were many afternoons when Will and Numbers would occupy the front seats, Will driving, as the remaining members sat in the back, our noses stuffed into books.

4

No More A Workhorse

THE SPRAWLING LOLLAPALOOZA OPERATION was a well-run machine. I was amazed to arrive at some new venue in another suburb of a great American or Canadian city every day to see that the two stages, the lights for both stages, the carnival of tents, two enormous sound systems, essentially an entire small town, was all in place and ready to go. I probably should not have been surprised that a professional touring company like Lollapalooza had figured out how to make a tour happen without incident, but this is another example of my own inaccurate expectations about how my Lolla-adventure might pan out. I suppose I expected more of the behavior that I saw on that first day, the Brylcreemed rockabilly roadie with the DTs bitching at me for leaving my drums in the wrong place. Instead, the opposite: day after day after day, and nary a major mistake made. A sense of professionalism, of bourgeois "going to work" pervaded, which was comforting.

All of the places we played, called "sheds," looked more or less the same: sheet metal-roofed amphitheaters with brightly colored plastic seats encircled by a grassy ring, all guarded by muscular, mustachioed men. The larger area around the grass ring circling the shed was paved to oblivion. All of the sheds were well outside even the most distant suburbs of the closest city, all were antiseptically clean, and all were often staffed by rosy high schoolers in matching tennis outfits. In addition to looking the same, all of the Lollapalooza sites also had the same creosote/diesel exhaust/cigarette/hot dog smell in the air, supplemented by a *soupçon* of french fries and, if you whiffed carefully enough, the ever present scent of funnel cakes. Thus, Maryland Heights, Missouri, looked and smelled an awful lot like Noblesville, Indiana, which reminded us all of Clarkston, Michigan, which really, when you got right down to it, wasn't all that different from Burgettstown, Pennsylvania, which, perhaps not surprisingly, bore a striking resemblance to Barrie, Ontario. Etc.

One afternoon, I realized while in the van that I'd left my case of cymbals at the previous show in Maryland Heights, a suburb of St Louis. Cymbals are expensive, and I spent nearly twenty-four tortured hours cursing my absentmindedness, being stuck in a gut-wrenching loop of anxiety, and thinking that some scum-sucking dirtbag like the wasted stagehand in Chicago had already traded my thousand bucks worth of Sabian and Zildjian for a few crack rocks. How in the world might I afford a new set of cymbals? How in the world might I play a decent set without being able to hide behind the din of my cymbals, those flattened discs of bronze whose clattering, deafening wash of noise were able to hide any number of drummer's mistakes? Arriving in Columbus the following day, however, there was my cymbal safe, sitting on the side of the stage, lit by an errant sun's ray, waiting for me.

Everything about the backstage area at Lollapalooza ran counter to my fantasy of the touring musician's life, which I assumed would be, well, a fantasy. Instead, Nick Cave, Mick

Harvey, and the rest of the Seeds; Adam Yauch, Adam Horowitz, and Mike Diamond; the Lips' frazzled road crew; the Luscious Jackson ladies; it seemed like everyone worked their butts off every day in the interest of putting on as good a show as they possibly could. I can't speak for George Clinton, for Q-Tip, for Phife, or Billy Corgan because I rarely saw them, or if I did it was a fleeting glance as they strode from their trailers to the stage, but we watched the Beasties and the Bad Seeds bring a superhuman effort to every show every single day. Being outside and engaging with the crowds appeared to be part of their shared performer's ethos. There was an old-fashioned show business element in everything they did. Their work ethic moved me, allowed me to know that I was not doing myself much honor by continuing to worship the slacker ethos, the laissez-faire "whatever happens happens" attitude I'd had since college. I became determined to work harder at my craft, once I figured out what my craft actually was.

IN ADDITION TO THE daily Lollapalooza shows, we frequently played local clubs at night, which was a direct breach of the contract we'd signed with the Lollapalooza folks. It's called a radius clause. I hope the statute of limitations has passed so we are not fined for our illegal transgressions. The Lolla-legal team's thinking was that a fan would be less likely to shell out the cabbage for a full-on Lollapalooza ticket if said fan's favorite band was also playing a show at a local club nearby without all the other bands, and for a far cheaper ticket price. This may well have been true for the big names, Smashing Pumpkins or whomever, but not for us—no one was coming to Lollapalooza for just the Palace Songs experience, I don't think—so we supplemented our Lollapalooza income by playing a few extra shows along the way, contract be damned. We were rebels, punk-rockers, who paid no heed to contracts, to lawyers in their sharkskin suits and ridiculous demands, we would do it all ourselves, by any means necessary...actually this is not true. We did in fact consider the implications of our breach of contract with Lollapalooza, and nervously agreed among ourselves to keep the news that we were playing shows along the way a secret from the other bands.

So, after a certain number of Lolla shows we'd pack up our gear and pretend to head out to the next stop on the Lolla-tour, only to mosey the few miles into the nearest burg where we'd play one of our illegal shows.

At each of these shows, we supplied the soundman with a TDK ninety-minute tape from a pack that Will had bought in Charleston, and picked up the tapes after each show. (I'd love to know where these tapes are now.) We'd listen to them in the van as we drove. Not once—never—did I think anything other than this was some of the best music I'd ever heard.

WE HAD TO SOUND-CHECK before each and every show we played, at both Lollapalooza and the clubs, and I suppose it's time to try and describe what happens to one's sense of hearing when one is the drummer onstage with a loud rock band.

First, I'm sure that every musician reading the words "sound check" felt their ovaries twinge, or, alternately, their testicles drawing up into their lower pelvic region as they imagined, against their will, the steady *whomp whomp whomp whomp crack crack crack crack smash smash smash thud thud thud thud whomp whomp whomp whomp* of a drummer sound checking. If Dante were alive today and writing an addendum to the *Inferno*, I think he might add a tenth circle to Hell, wherein the poor doomed bastards and bitches would be subjected to listening to an eternity of drummers' sound checks. There is nothing worse. The sound of a drummer sound checking remains to me a perfect auditory example of the fundamentally *stoopid* nature of rock and roll.

I'll make it short, but the grinding nature of the process is actually essential to understanding a number of things, including why so many drummers are often surly sons of bitches and why they're often the first to quit bands. First, drum sets themselves are heavy and cumbersome; a kick drum, one or two mounted toms, a floor tom, and a snare. The snare sits on a sturdy, solid stand, which is supposed to conveniently fold up, but which often does not, and frequently one's fingers get pinched in the various folding joints of the stands. Those two cymbals smashed together to the drummer's left, the high-hat, is also an evil thing. Like the high-hat stand, cymbal stands are similarly filled with the evil intent of harming fingers. There's the bass drum pedal that needs to be fastened to the rim of the drum, requiring the drummer to crouch on the ground and try to wrestle with a tiny set screw...I'll stop there. But understand that these things needed to be set up as quickly as possible before the set, then broken down as quickly as possible after the set, so while Ned and Will and Aram and Jason were frequently enjoying their first Corona of the afternoon, having been able to walk off the stage with their amps and guitars, I was getting my thumb smashed by the legs of another cymbal stand.

Speaking of the guitarists, each has his own unique desires as far as the volume of their amps, and for pretty much every single guitarist I've ever played with, that desire is to be as loud as humanly possible and, at the very least, to be louder than the guy standing next to him.

Here's what often happens: During sound check guitarists are very modest and well-behaved and play at a normal volume, which allows the soundman to set the house levels properly. A war begins, however, as soon as the band takes the stage and the show starts. As one guitarist leans over to pretend to tie his shoe, he'll quickly turn his master volume up. The next guitarist will drop a pick on the ground or reach for a water bottle or beer sitting on top of his amp, and if one wasn't trained to spot the movement one might miss that the second guitarist has, instead of grabbing the beer bottle, turned his volume up as well. The first guitarist, having noted that he's been outdone, might wait patiently until the first song begins, at which point, perhaps during the second guitarists' solo, he might wander over to his amp, again reaching for a beer or water bottle, and turn up his own amp. And so on.

The drummer, having noticed that both guitarists have cranked up their volumes, recognizes that, if he's going to enact his God-given right to be the loudest person onstage, he's going to have to pound that pedal to his bass drum all the more forcefully and hit the crash cymbals more often, and also more forcefully.

One can often see the soundman standing behind the audience at the soundboard shaking his head or otherwise being grumpy as this volume war rages.

Besides the onstage amps, each musician has a monitor, which is just a speaker aimed straight at his head. Such an arrangement seems counterintuitive: on a stage full of blaring speakers why on earth would someone need one more speaker just to hear what the other speakers are already blaring out into the crowd? The answer is that on many stages the sound from multiple instruments is so loud that one loses the ability to hear one's own playing, even, in my case, with an instrument as obnoxiously loud as the drums.

Most soundmen are able to mix each musician's monitor specifically to what that musician wants to hear. I keyed in most-ly on Will and Ned's vocals and guitars rather than the bass, what many drummers listen for, and I also liked hearing my snare and kick drum in the monitor mix. Remember that I am sitting more or less at amp level while the guitarists and keyboard players are standing above the speakers in the amps. They can also move out of the way if something is too loud. What most people don't realize is that the backs of some amps are open, and speakers project noise out of the backs as well, and when I'm sitting behind my kit, I'm pretty much staring at the backs of every amp on the stage. So, the drums are often in the one spot on stage where as many as five amps, plus my own monitor, are all spewing their noise in an out-of-control sound fountain.

I'm not going to apologize for mixing my metaphors—explosions, sound fountain, it all works to describe the ear-bleedingly loud chaos I often heard on the stage.

It was whispered among a few of the second stage bands that well-known major label talent scouts were prowling the second stage at Lollapalooza looking for the next Nirvana, and every so often a coterie of well-dressed young men and women whose heads glistened with hair product would swoop in with a kind of nervous, coky energy and fling business cards onto the ground. Some bands would dive into the fracas, fighting over the cards as if they were starving and the cards were bacon-flavored potato chips.

It's important to remember that at the time record companies were making money hand over fist and events such as Lollapalooza still played an essential role in the dissemination of popular music. The "music festival" as a marketing concept has been diluted since then, with the rise of Bonnaroo, Firefly, SXSW, Coachella, Stagecoach, and Warped, and it's easy to forget how events such as Lollapalooza were once used to focus the attention of the great pubescent unwashed on an organized array of bands for the purposes of selling more product. Even though the previous years' Lollapaloozas had been a fundamental part of what was then being called "alternative" culture, which was little more than an updating of the "college rock" and "indie" movements of the eighties, 1994 was the year that Lollapalooza was supposed to cement itself as a mainstream event aimed less at breaking bands and more at presenting bands at the tops of their commercial strengths. Nirvana, Tribe Called Quest, the Beastie Boys, and Smashing Pumpkins all sat at or near the top of the charts in '93, while bands like the Breeders, Pavement, and Flaming Lips waited in the wings.

Interestingly, the week before we began our Lollapalooza experience in 1994, Aerosmith released the first song available for purchase on the internet, a 4 MB file for CompuServe members called "Head First" that took over an hour to download using dial-up. An hour to listen to a single song, and by Aerosmith!

Perhaps some of the backstage uptightness mentioned above was the result of some of the other bands' anxieties about claiming windfalls of industry cash, which I hope I've made clear was still more than plentiful. The internet was years away and the bottom hadn't fallen out of the music biz yet. One could still get rich by being blessed, anointed, as it were, by the hand of a recently-graduated-from-Northwestern twenty-something "talent scout" from Geffen, Virgin, or Warner Brothers, so it's safe to say that many bands were thinking to themselves, "Hell, if Urge Overkill can score a major label deal, and the Flaming Lips and Royal Trux for Pete's sake, then *why not us?*"

Even though the Lips had signed a major deal with Warner Brothers in '91, the seeds of their commercial success had been planted in 1993 with their hit single "She Don't Use Jelly" and there's no doubt that the summer's tour and their high energy DIY stagecraft acted as potent fertilizers for their later popularity. Guided By Voices wouldn't sign with Capitol Records until 1998, but I'm sure one of those young scouts cruising the Lollapalooza second stage watched as innumerable fratty bruhs wearing backward baseball caps and cargo shorts bellowed along with Robert Pollard as he sang, "I am a scientist, I seek to understand...," and knew that GBV might one day sell records.

AT THE POLARIS AMPHITHEATER in Columbus, Ohio, I glanced up from my paper plate of beef stroganoff just in time to see three of the Lips lads gallivanting on a grassy hillock just above the backstage area. They appeared to be having a smashing time, engaging in some archetypally male fellowship.

Upon closer inspection, I noted that drummer Stephen and singer Wayne appeared to be forcing bassist Michael Ivins to ride down the steep grassy hill on a large piece of cardboard box. Michael didn't appear particularly comfortable with his bandmates' attempts to force him down the hill on the cardboard; he sat stiff-backed as it slid and bumped down the hill. As I watched, shameful memories burbled up of me forcing the guitar player in my middle school band to sit on a banana-colored (and shaped) skateboard at the top of our bass player's absurdly steep driveway. Time and again, we'd shove him down the black asphalt ribbon, hoping for a dramatic and painful crash into the three foot-deep concrete culvert at the bottom of the drive. It was like a very early version of *Jackass*. It's a wonder he was never killed.

In Philadelphia the backstage area was an open field filled with backed-up raw sewage. Tampons and toilet paper floated in oily pools of waste, along with cigar-shaped turds. Picking from the trays of baked chicken and rice and mayonnaisey salads and shredded pork wraps were pneumatic young Eastern European girls in bikinis with too much foundation caking their faces. Mafiosi in cheap sharkskin suits and oversized sunglasses smoked cigars and leered at the girls' fake breasts as they glistened like raw chicken in the summer sun. I watched the ladies tiptoeing through the sewage-rank area in their high heels, and noted that Beastie Boy Mike Diamond was also bouncing through the area, having donned his white mullet wig, a disguise he wore regularly that made him look no different than any other loaded teen stumbling through the crowd.

After our show in Philly, we went back to our hospitality space to grab a beer, only to find that the case of Corona was gone. We were bummed, having worked up a good thirst onstage, and wondered if the five middle-aged farmer-tanned white people who happened to be standing over a full case of Corona as if guarding it might know something about where our particular case of Corona went. A few of the mens' hair looked remarkably like Mike Diamond's mullet wig, all business up front, all party in the back.

"Hey, fellas," I said, "y'all didn't happen to grab that case of Corona from our space—"

"Hell naw," said the red-faced man with the bleached mullet. He sucked on his cigarette and, with a rather simian-appearing paw, adjusted his balls, which appeared to be tucked uncomfortably into a tight seam of his ill-fitting cut-off jean shorts. He pulled deeply from a bottle of Corona that, quite apparently, was not his first. "These ain't your beers. They're mine. End of story."

"Okay!" I said, clapping my hands together once. "Just thought I'd check."

At that moment, who should appear to quell any negativity but the lighthearted and likable comedienne Kerri Kenney, one of the Girls Against Boys' lady friends. Kerri was finding some success on MTV with her comedy troupe The State, and her quips and comic presence served to counterbalance some of the more intense backstage vibes.

I actually really liked the GBV dudes. Drummer Kevin, like most drummers, was an openly friendly guy who appeared to mostly just want to bang his drums and have a good time. GBV bassist Greg, who wore smashing candy-striped bell bottoms every day onstage, told us he was quitting the band and would enter law school at the end of the tour, which he did. He's now a practicing attorney in Ohio.

It wasn't difficult to notice that Girls Against Boys might be on the short list for "next big things," something that happened when they signed a deal with Geffen in '97, and the resultant record deal and appearance on numerous nineties teen movie soundtracks allowed bassist Johnny Temple to start the publishing company Akashic, who would one day publish our friend Bobby Arellano's books.

One afternoon at a water park next to the Riverbend Music Amphitheater in Cincinnati, we saw Beastie Boy Ad-Rock running up the wooden steps next to us as we all ascended to the departure point for one of the slides—"This is the bomb!" he yelled to us, and it was the first time I'd ever heard that saying. Later we all watched as the Buddhist monks invited by Ad-Rock's bandmate Adam Yauch careened down the swooping fiberglass slide gleefully, still wearing their long saffron robes, into the pool below. Beautiful, gorgeous, moving, strange. Much later, Will recalled that underneath the saffron robes, the monks wore matching Speedo-style briefs. At that afternoon's Beasties show Ad-Rock was still in the bathing suit and Seattle Supersonics jersey we'd seen him wearing earlier at the slide.

Another afternoon Nick Cave stood at the door of his trailer beckoning us, waving his long, thin arm dramatically as a thunderstorm broke over the commons and inviting us all into his trailer during the storm. I was wearing a rain slicker, and as I rushed breathlessly into the trailer as the deluge began, Bad Seeds guitarist Mick Harvey asked me sarcastically if I'd been fishing.

"I wish!" I chirped.

Harvey's face dropped.

The conversation died a quick death.

At some point that summer, during some money exchange, Will invented the phrase "niggardly, with malice" and we repeated it ad infinitum throughout the remainder of the summer.

"Geez, when that girl selling me the energy smoothie was handing me my change," Jason might've said, "she was really niggardly about it, and with malice. It was like she expected a tip."

One day, listening to the radio in the van, Ned announced that he was tired of *yarl*.

"Tired of what?" I asked.

"Yarl," Ned said. "Yarl music. The kind of rock music where it sounds like the singer is *yarling* rather than singing."

We discussed the matter for a time and recognized that Ned had identified an entire strain of rock vocalizing, one whose first modern practitioner might've been Joan Armatrading. Singers like Eddie Vedder, Layne Staley from Alice in Chains, Scott Weiland from Stone Temple Pilots, they were all yarlers; even Dave Matthews wasn't untouched by the finger of yarl. Yarling has only grown more popular. For whatever reasons, lots of female singers who also play the ukulele are practitioners of yarl. It is a kind of weird, back-of-throat, tonguey singing that frequently accompanies tampon commercials. Listen for it. You'll know it when you hear it.

Thank Ned for that one.

Every afternoon after our show we'd wander over to a stand run by a cute dreadlocked raver who reminded me of the female singer from Haysi Fantayzee or Hope Nichols from Fetchin Bones and buy one of her special energy smoothies filled with bee pollen and God knows what else. We'd then wander around enjoying the weird body buzz from the unknown natural ingredients in the energy shake while we took in all that Lolla had to offer, while in the background Phife and Q-Tip rapped about leaving their wallets in El Segundo. And what did it offer us? An awful lot from an era that is now dead to time, the final gasp of a living, breathing human culture unsullied by the community-fracturing technologies that were on the horizon: cell phones and the internet and downloads. People had no objects in their hands to stare at, no internet where they could double-check L7's latest Instagram post; there were no selfies, no one holding phones up to film bands as they played. Audiences paid attention to what was going on.

All for One,
and One for All

LIKE OUR OWN NEAL Cassady, Will would sit in the driver's seat, his hands locked to the wheel, his eyes scanning the horizon for cops as he flaunted every posted speed limit on each and every highway. He would weave in and out of traffic like Mario Andretti at Le Mans as he sang along with the Wipers. Will drove twenty, thirty miles over the speed limit as if he knew, felt to his very bones, that he'd never get pulled over. And he never did. Not then during Lollapallooza, not ever.

The band, me, Ned, Aram, and Jason, weren't a whole lot of help with the running of the tour, and I began to wonder if this wasn't weighing Will down. Only Numbers, who sat in the passenger seat next to Will, a ballpoint pen frequently held to her red lips as Will flew down the highways and byways of the Midwest, really helped. The cashbox rattled at her feet, an open window tossed her thick black hair around her face as she tried to look at a road map, offering Will directions, while we sat in the van and read our books.

An old friend of mine from high school had formed a friendship with a heavy hitter in the music biz and later told me that a celebrity dealmaker with a massive record company had made various offers to Will over the course of the summer. In retrospect I understand that the summer's tour may have served as a watershed moment for Will's understanding of his own career, and perhaps his reckoning of how he might navigate a noble path through this dauntingly powerful and corrupt industry. The devil, put simply, was asking him to dance, not Jason, Aram, Ned, or me.

We had no idea, of course, that Will was being tempted by Virgin, or other corporate satanic overlords. "Why would he share these stories with us?" you might well ask, and the Jack Carneal of today would agree wholeheartedly. But back then, well, *that* Jack Carneal would've argued that we should've been told about these prospective deals because *we were a band.* Did I want to stick my hand in the Palace honeypot? Why the hell not? We were a band! All for one and one for all.

In any case, Will shunned all of the deals.

ONE OF THE WIVES back home was convinced that we were attending orgies every night, that girls were following us after every show waiting to rip our clothes off, which, sadly, could not have been further from the truth.

The majority of our fans appeared to be skinny, unsmiling, almost translucent boys in dark clothing with dark circles under their eyes carrying small notebooks, who would approach Will warily, like shy baby opossums. Girls at Lollapalooza were far more interested in the Breeders, in Luscious Jackson, in cute Wayne Coyne from Flaming Lips than they were in us, what with our bland Teva and cargo-shorted fashions, our short hair, our utter inability to pose, and our failed experiments with organic crystal deodorant. The wives didn't believe us.

Somewhere in my imagination floated the specter of what would happen after Lollapalooza and the European tours ended, but the specter was distant, unthreatening, little more than a thinly chattering voice. Sure, Chris and I were on the path to what I assumed was marriage, but we hadn't mentioned the word a single time to one another, and I suppose at some level I still considered myself a man whose free will might allow him to venture into any experiential realm of the twenty-something year-old male, excluding having sex with a woman who was not Chris. I assumed she was in the same state of unknowing. We had not yet performed the marriage mind meld and were still, perhaps barely, in the late-honeymoon phase of our relationship, where the possibility of breaking up without causing serious damage still existed.

Still, as someone who faced the real but distant prospect of marriage and the forty-hour work week with nothing short of panic, I don't mind admitting now that beneath that calm and ambitionless exterior I fostered a burning fantasy: I would spend the rest of my days as a touring rock musician playing drums for a band called the Palace Brothers.

The second to last Lollapalooza show we played was in Providence, where Will and Numbers were reunited with many of their old crew from Brown University, including Bobby Arellano, who was working in Brown's English Department with Robert Coover on what was then called "literary hypertext." I asked Bob exactly what that meant, and his answer to my question only muddied the waters further. If literary hypertext was somewhat experimental, let's assume that the following dialogue is equally so:

"You're reading along, okay?" said this simulacrum of Bob that exists in my memory. "And you're reading this thing that's been written. By someone, right. By some dude, or dudette, as the case could very well be. Or someone in the middle. It's a narrative, a story. But then you, the reader, the participant, get to choose to jump out of the line of action and join another one, at your whim. It's not binary, like, two stories, but poly-nary, multi-nary, many lines of plot, of action, of setting, of narrative, and you get to choose—"

"But Bob, how do you *jump out* of a book?"

"Hyperlinks, dude. Freaking hyperlinks."

"What in the world is a *hyperlink*?"

"You know how on a computer, sometimes there are words that are a different color or something, yellow or red, maybe, and you can click on them and…"

"No," I answered. "I'm actually unaware of that."

"Yeah, well, sounds like somebody needs to get with the program. Pun intended."

As I understood it, hyperlinks were found in computer-based instead of print-based fiction, and during the course of reading the story the reader could click on certain words or phrases, which would take them to another story thread. It was partici-patory fiction, that much I understood, but I wondered why any writer would want to cede control of the narrative to the reader.

"You're not really ceding anything," Bob may have argued, face bright with his usual madman's smile. "Just giving the reader options."

"But," I muttered, "isn't that the point of being a writer, to convince the reader that the decisions you've made are the best ones? That you've already thought through the options and chosen the best *option*, singular?"

"Maybe," Bob said. "And maybe not! Who knows? Who cares? That's what we're trying to figure out!"

My inability to understand literary hypertext was yet another opportunity for me to sense that there were an awful lot of people in the world who were a lot smarter than I was, and a bunch of them were Will's friends from Louisville and Brown.

Colin Gagon was also there, one of Will's early collaborators, who I'd get to know much better later on, as was his girlfriend, now wife, Liz. Rich Shuler was there, a man who had the distinction of being the first drummer ever to play in one of Will's Palace-named projects. The vibe was heavy. The books that lie on coffee tables were unfamiliar, as was the music being played. I was feeling like the bumpkin I was, educated at a bland suburban private school in Richmond and at an isolated southern college, completely at sea among these northeastern liberals. In one of those completely unsurprising turnarounds, I soon found out that Colin was, pretty much like everyone else in this crew, utterly hilarious and warm and friendly, as was Liz, and my early impressions of all of these intimidating intellectual-seeming folks were way off.

Both Bob and Colin became two of Will's go-to sidemen in later incarnations of Palace and Bonnie Prince Billy bands.

More on them anon.

It's painful to admit now that the same naive ambition that allowed me to think I'd be a bestselling author the month after finishing my MFA also allowed me to assume that all of the bands on Lollapalooza would become fast friends that I'd shoot hoops with King Ad-Rock and George Clinton, that Nick Cave and I would exchange our own short fiction, that Q-Tip might sample one of my Palace drum beats for some new Tribe tune. But the final show at Providence proved to be the last time I ever saw these fellow traveling troubadours with whom we spent such a memorable few weeks.

The Lollapalooza show in Providence was at a giant sunbaked, disused military airport complete with Quonset huts. A pale late summer sun tried to burn through the haze, casting a thin, shadowless light over the broken concrete whose plentiful cracks were painted with paisley swirls of tar.

In a phone call made from a landline, I'd promised my sister Ann Barron, who lived in Providence, and her friends free passes into the festival but had neglected to make any definite meeting plans. Ann Barron had finished grad school up the road in Cambridge the year before and gotten a job at a school in Providence. I was looking forward to catching up and was upset with myself that I hadn't worked harder to make a plan to meet. But walking away from the backstage area into the crowds of thousands of kids streaming from the parking lot toward the chain-link fence serving as the gates, I realized that there was zero chance of finding a single woman in the stream of thousands of teenage revelers surging toward me. It would be sheer luck to stumble across her in this mass of humanity. If they really wanted to see the show that badly, sis and her pals could buy some tickets in the lot, I thought, I wasn't going to allow myself to feel guilty for something that was unavoidable…

After convincing myself to turn around, I looked up and standing not ten feet away was my sis and her friends, among the thousands and thousands.

We hugged, I greeted her friends, and we turned and, flashing my badge, a badge that hangs in my room to this day, we all walked through the gates and into the penultimate Lollapalooza show Palace Music would play.

THAT NIGHT, WE PLAYED one of our illegal shows at the Last Call club in Providence. It wasn't a great show. I'd be haunted by the false homecoming in the coming years, the sense that shows we played in places we'd lived—Providence, Richmond, Charlottesville, and later DC, Baltimore, and Louisville—were never as good as I wanted them to be.

After the show, beginning our night's drive to New York, where we'd play our final Lolla show, followed by a set at the legendary Maxwell's club in Hoboken, we listened to the soundboard tape in the van, as was our habit. It was only then in the van, as Will careened down I-95 toward New York, that I was reminded of what had gotten the show started on such a bad note.

We'd played our late set after a blues band had finished, and it so happened that the drummer of the blues band was also the lead singer. So, my vocal mic, during which I'd usually moan one or two frog-like notes during maybe three of Palace's songs, was not mixed into the main board as a backup mic but instead as the lead vocal mic onstage. And for whatever reason that night was the night I decided I'd actually sing. A lot. No one ever heard me, anyway, so why not lift up my voice and sing along with Will? During our first song or two I belted out my accompaniment to Will, trying to sing harmonies, doubling his lead vocals, basically just yelling as loud as I could into my usually silent mic. And, of course, my mic was twice as loud as anyone else's because the drummer of the previous band had been the lead singer. And, of course, I didn't know this until we all were listening to the tape in the van. Imagine our surprise when instead of Will's interesting and in-key voice was replaced instead by an adenoidal and embarrassingly off-key moaning by yours truly.

AFTER THE NEXT AND final Lollapalooza show at Downing Stadium on Randall's Island in New York we went to Kramer's studio in leafy suburban Cloisters, New Jersey, to record two songs, "Gulf Shores" and "West Palm Beach." Neil and Jennifer of the Royal Trux had recorded a couple of songs with Kramer and reports about the experience had been good enough to pique Will's interest in working with the legendary musician/producer.

Interestingly, a *New York Times* article about the Lollapalooza show at Randall's published on August 8, 1994, doesn't mention us, even though we were one of three bands that played before an enormous thunderstorm rolled in, which resulted in the show being canceled. The same article states that Green Day was part of the main stage line-up, which I don't recall. I do recall having driven all night from Providence after the club show and arriving on Randall's Island as the sun rose. We all slept in the van for a few hours that morning before our 1:00 p.m. show, and before the intense storms rolled in.

The following day we headed out to Kramer's. The previous day's storms had blown away the summer's miasmal fug, and in its place was one of those glorious East Coast days of brilliantly sparkling sun and fresh, cool breezes blowing in from the North Atlantic. It was warm in the sun but cool in the shade. Jason and Aram had no idea who Kramer was, had never heard of Bongwater, Shockabilly, Butthole Surfers, or Ween, whereas I was pretty nervous to meet a man who'd been at the center of so much music I'd listened to in the previous few years. If I wasn't crazy about most of the music Kramer had made, I appreciated his time with the Surfers, and I was a big fan of Ween. We arrived at his home to find Kramer embroiled in some domestic squabble and a little frayed at the edges. He was happy to see us, or happy to see our resident genius Will, and happy to be pulled out of some kind of argument with his partner and to get to work.

At the studio, Kramer already had a four-piece drum kit set up for me and asked me to adjust things to my liking. This was easy for me. Some drummers are rather picky about drum setup, whereas I could pretty much sit at any kit and figure it out without futzing around too much. That said, I liked having my throne high, the high-hat a bit lower than most, and I've always preferred looking down at the drums rather than looking up at them. I approached kit setup less like a typical rock drummer and more like a jazz player, although the early British drummers like Ringo and Keith Moon also had sets where the toms were lower. A lot of tom-tom height had to do with the size of the kick drum...the bigger the kick drum, the louder, and since most rock drummers wanted to be loud, they usually used kick drums that were oversized. Led Zep's John Bonham's final kick drum was 26" for example, while a jazz drummer like Art Blakey's was 20" and actually I'd come to prefer an 18" kick. The bigger the bass drum, the higher from the ground the mounted toms had to be...and I've lost you.

Moving on.

At Kramer's, it was nice not having to set anything up. I'd grown quite tired of the grind of dragging my heavy drums to and from our van and spending far too much time setting up my drums as my bandmates milled about and drank Coronas.

None of us had ever heard the songs we were recording until Kramer pressed record on our first tracking session, played live in the studio. This would've been probably August 5 or 6. I think we played each song once. Yes, "West Palm Beach" and "Gulf Shores" were both not only one-take wonders, but songs we'd never heard or played before, both recorded live to tape with minimal overdubbing.

During mixdown we watched a Shimmy Disc promo video of Kramer and Ween in Jamaica smoking a bunch of weed from a chillum pipe, and then *The Greatest Sinner in the World* with the mind-blowing Timothy Carey, also on VHS. Kramer showed us a photograph of Dean Martin that a friend of his had taken of Martin at a bar in LA, clearly drunk, his fly gaping open, shirt unbuttoned, hair disheveled, clothes a mess. It's fascinating to think that there was a distant period of time when one man could harbor such secrets as a Timothy Carey movie on tape and a depressing photo of a trashed Dean Martin and disburse them only at special times to special guests. These things still had value as talismans from a secret world.

Now, Timothy Carey is all over YouTube. I just Googled "Dean Martin drunk photo" and the first hit featured a blog entry about the exact photo I saw back in '94. It even included the detail that Kramer had been given a print by the original photographer.

(The photo on the web page is different than my recollection, and I think my memory of it is actually more interesting. Take everything you read on these pages with a grain of salt, dear reader.)

It was a gorgeous and cool August afternoon as Ned and I drove Kramer to a local bagel shop to pick up some lunch.

"That's Stevie Wonder's house," he said, pointing at a large mansion fronted by a pristine Japanese garden, complete with an ornate pagoda. It was wild laying down my first recording a few houses away from Stevie's house; his song "You Are the Sunshine of My Life" had been a favorite of mine since I was a kid, and much of Wonder's music had served as the FM radio soundtrack to my youth in Richmond.

After our late-afternoon lunch of bagels and coffee and after *World's Greatest Sinner* ended, we were invited into the mixing room to listen to the songs. He cued up the first song, "West Palm Beach," on the console, twiddled a few knobs, and sat back.

It's a hard thing to describe the feeling you have when you hear something you've been a part of that you're pretty sure will last forever.

As soon as Will sings the line "when her son lost his lights," there's a pause, followed in time by a snare and cymbal hit, the slow hissing of the sizzler I'd hung onto the cymbal sounding like a small wave disappearing into the glittering white sand. You can hear me pause as I'm watching my bandmates, trying to figure out what's next, having never heard the song before, Jason sliding his finger up the neck of the bass, plucking a rising note just as Will sings the line "she ain't yet risen from bed," accompanied by Ned and Aram's faultless, patient guitar interplay. Kramer played the mellotron part as an overdub, during which I play a heavily reverbed shaker and tambourine. The way Kramer engineered the songs, the wet snare, all instruments bathed in this shimmering, narcotic haze, perfectly evoked an afternoon at the beach, the glorious summer sunlight, that cool layer of sand beneath the blazing surface.

Amazingly, for never having played the song before, we nailed the ending.

Then, in "Gulf Shores," there are the playful snare triplets on the fourth beat of every third bar, and Ned's mirroring vocals to Will's lead…you can hear the tempo lag at the line "have you thought that you could waste away?" And again, during the line "there are circles deep beneath your eyes." I have a vague recollection of hearing myself slowing down while playing and thinking, *Well, no worries, I'll nail it on the second take*, which, of course, never happened. Jason's piano bit during the second solo verse is somewhat hesitant; he admitted to being nervous, having never really played the keyboards, maybe only having taken some lessons in elementary school. Then Will's wonderfully sweet and evocative lead vocals sing through the final verse, the back-up vocals in that moment reminded me even then of Murmur's "Pilgrimage," and then there's my horrific, flubbed ending, which, if I'm feeling charitable to myself, still works, mirroring the confused, slow retreat from the central narrative of the song as Will sings the final line, "So let's disappear from sight…"

> *A cold and fruity drink awaits us both.*
> *Watch me frolic in the sand.*
> *Oh, did you see me in the surf?*
> *With a starfish in my hand.*
> *Soon the restaurants will open up.*
> *Soon the bars will light their lights.*
> *You have aged, you must start looking up.*
> *Ugly things will come tonight.*

Numbers drew the cover.

Much later, I would pick up a *Rolling Stone* and see that the single was number one on the college charts.

ON THE WAY BACK south we stopped in Richmond, where we played a show at the Chronos Café with a Richmond band called LaBradford. If I remember correctly, Britt Walford and David Pajo, who'd been in Slint together, came to the show. I'd met Britt once when he and Will were visiting Ned in Charlottesville, but had never met Pajo. Come to think it, it may have been Todd Brashear who'd made the drive with Britt from Louisville, I can't be sure. I could email one of them of course, but that'd be a waste of time because it doesn't matter which one of them was there, really, and this is my recollection of things, not a historical record. In any case, this bit of name-dropping is important to bring back the question of my own insecurity about our band identity. These were, of course, a few of the Slint guys, including the drummer Britt, whose name I'd been called more than once in the previous month, coming to see what Will was up to. Naturally, I wanted them to like us.

Before opener LaBradford's set I'd turned off my snares so they wouldn't buzz during the group's atmospheric and intense music, then forgot to turn them back on when we took the stage. Therefore, my first snare hit during "Gulf Shores" was a hollow, tom-tom-like wallop instead of the sharp crack I'd expected, and, stunned by the crack-free sound, meant to signal the beginning groove of the song, I fumbled for an awkwardly long time to snap the snares into place. Will, Ned, Aram, and Jason all turned around and looked at me as if I was an idiot. The whole set proceeded from this initial boner. A few of my old friends from Richmond were there, and I was disappointed that we'd given them such a soft show, having been quite excited to play in my hometown and, of course, conquer it. Did not happen.

THE RICHMOND SHOW, AND the tour, ended on a down note. Later, I'd learn more about the odd, melancholic atmosphere that often surrounded the ends of tours. On one hand, I obviously wanted to get back to Chris, to some semblance of a stable domestic life, but on the other, well, what could be better than playing music to appreciative crowds with incredibly skilled musicians who were also my friends? In a particularly self-lacerating way, I was obsessed with the possibility that I hadn't been good enough, and that Will would announce, after the tour's end, that I was being uninvited from the European tour. Just like Ringo, one of my heroes, who'd once thought he wasn't good enough to be in the Beatles, I doubted my skills.

That's not what happened, and after a much-needed rest, Will, Jason, Aram, Aram's wife Mclean, and I found ourselves in the Detroit airport, ready to board our flight to Amsterdam.

Where's the Bridge?

NED'S TEACHING JOB BEGAN in the fall semester, so he would not be joining us on our post-Lollapalooza thirty-show jaunt through Belgium, Germany, France, the Netherlands, Switzerland, and Austria. Even though I felt bad that Ned was being pulled into the straight world—married to a med student, full-time teacher at a Baptist university, the owner of a gold Ford Escort station wagon—he did not appear at all upset about taking a break from the rigors of touring.

On my twenty-seventh birthday, we landed at Amsterdam's Schiphol airport where we were greeted by Tonny, our tour manager, a bald sparkplug of a Dutchman with Lennon glasses, Doc Marten boots, and rolled-up jeans. After quick introductions and grabbing our luggage, which consisted mostly of guitars, the no-nonsense Ton led us out into the thin Dutch morning light to the Mercedes Sprint van where we'd be living for the next month. Tonny would serve as the director–producer– banker–henchman–soundman–cultural liaison of the tour. He held our passports and presented them to uniformed soldiers guarding the old pre-EU European borders. Ton was fluent in English, Dutch, German, French, and Italian. He knew the labyrinthine directions to clubs frequently located in the center of feudal European towns, he was in charge of collecting checks from club owners, he handled all of the cash. Ton would also handle soundman duties at the clubs that didn't have one on staff. He also had to act as the contract specialist and payout negotiator at each and every club we played, so he was a pseudo lawyer/henchman as well.

Having a stubborn, capable tour manager was essential, but not as essential as having a responsible and sober one. We were all relieved when the diminutive Tonny stated while sitting in our van in the Schiphol lot that he'd quit drinking long ago, and couldn't handle alcohol anymore—"You really should have seen me, I'd pick a fight with a telephone pole," he told us. Meanwhile, he spoke these encouraging words in his thick Dutch accent while rolling a tobacco and hash joint the size of a seedless cucumber.

WE SPENT THE NIGHT in a mosquito-infested hotel in northern Belgium, then woke up and drove to Kontich just outside of Antwerp where we picked up our rented amps and drum kit and played our first European show at the Lintfabriek. Rocked with jet lag, I have almost no specific recollections of the show itself but instead a vague, David Lynchian dream vision of a darkened club with two or three couples swaying on the floor clutching one another. No one was smiling as they swayed and clutched. Outside it was still light, and just before we began, walking in from having grabbed a bite somewhere, I remember the way the club was painted in the evening's golden Flemish light: ivy-covered brick, the sign for the club hanging from a scrolled iron post, the door partly hidden behind the growth of ivy, as if we'd stumbled upon an ancient toll road inn.

Onstage, we missed Ned's guitar, the natural interplay between him and Aram, but mostly we missed his natural tenor, the Everlyesque harmonies of the brothers Oldham. You learn over time that a million people can play guitar, there are millions of drummers and bassists playing in innumerable bands, all of them perfectly skilled, but the true singers are rare, great harmony singers even more so. Ned and Will were gorgeous singing together, and without Ned I felt our sound was thinner and not as focused.

There were fewer layers without Ned, which ended up allowing us to become more of a straight-ahead rock band, almost a power quartet.

The following day, back in the Netherlands, en route to our second show in Enger, Germany, Ton mentioned he had to stop at his squat somewhere in the Dutch countryside, and naturally, hearing the noun "squat," I imagined we'd soon arrive at some decrepit fleabag stinkhole full of lanky Dutch junkies. I was surprised when we pulled up to a large and nice-looking post-war stucco house in a tidy suburban neighborhood. Attractive people, freshly showered, were making tea in the kitchen. We stepped out onto the roof of the tidy house to find ourselves lost in a thick jungle of enormous marijuana plants. There was some political explanation, said Ton, about why such a nice home was being inhabited by five or six people who were not paying a penny for the home itself and growing pounds and pounds of primo weed on its roof, but I didn't understand.

Something to do with Socialism, I gathered.

ONE DAY WHILE CAREENING at maximum speed down the autobahn in Germany I heard a bang along our left flank, felt the van shudder, watched the driver's hands clutch the wild wheel as, outside, the world spun around us. Jason, who'd just stood up to stretch, assuming a surfer's pose between the two front seats, fell to the ground as the van fought to stay on four wheels. None of us were wearing seatbelts and there was an awful suspended moment where I waited for the van to flip, or for someone to go flying out of the front windshield.

Instead, within a few horrible seconds we'd come to rest quite peacefully against the guardrail in the middle of the roadway. Only feet away on the other side of the guardrail cars sped past at over a hundred miles per hour. Our tire had blown. The van emptied and in our tire track along the soft sandy shoulder of the median I spied a single dead mouse, lying on its back, paws curled in the air. I reached down and rubbed its soft belly. It was still warm. It had chosen a terrible time to be hanging out on the median.

Within minutes, a sporty and butch-looking sedan with ringing sirens pulled up behind us and four men leaped out of the car, each dressed in bodysuits that made them look like a Formula 1 pit crew. One placed blinking cones behind the crumpled van, another checked in with us and the driver, a third dropped to his knees and peered under the van, trying to deduce whether or not it'd need to be towed. "It would," he said formally, offering us a slight bow of the head. There was a tiny break in the traffic, so one of the men directed us across the highway to the shoulder, informing Ton that the tow truck would be here presently.

While we waited for the tow, we left Tonny and wandered off the highway through some shrubs and tall grasses, following a walking path that led toward a strange and foreboding tower in the distance. After a few-minute walk, we found ourselves in a former East German ghost town (the Berlin Wall had only come down five years earlier) called Ziesar. A cold fall wind was blowing, the skies were dim and gray. As we entered the empty and lifeless town, we spotted people peeking at us from behind closed shop doors and window curtains as if we were aliens. After walking down the town's single street, we found ourselves standing and looking up at what I remember as an ancient greenhouse, so huge that it took up an entire block. Perhaps I dreamt this, or perhaps it was an enormous abandoned building and not necessarily a greenhouse. But in this vision, not a single pane of glass among the thousands in the greenhouse was broken but the structure was nevertheless abandoned, empty and rusting. Inside the greenhouse grew only a scattering of indigenous weeds.

We walked past more closed storefronts and stucco buildings toward the tower we'd spotted from the autobahn. It sat atop an old church at the end of the street past the greenhouse. Finally, signs of life: Jason said hello to some teenagers sitting at tables in front of a bodega, also closed, and they tittered and giggled in response. Other than these teenagers the town was empty of human life, and enveloped in a near total stillness, a disorienting suspension of time and movement.

Once we'd arrived at the church, we found that it was abandoned too.

BACK AT THE AUTOBAHN, we were told to get in the van even though it now sat on the bed of the tow truck. We climbed onto the flatbed then into the van and rode to the next show in Berlin seated in the carcass of our vehicle while it rested on the bed of a tow truck, high above the teeming autobahn.

Before that night's show in Berlin, alone in the bedroom with Jason and me, having heard about our brush with death earlier, the female promoter told us that she'd once slept with an entire band, one after the other. It's what rock chicks do, she said with a wink, the cold sore on her lip bursting out from its flaking layer of concealer. I slapped Jason, our sole bachelor, on the back. He looked at me and tried to laugh.

The promoter told us the name of the band she'd slept with. We'd heard of them. Frankly, they didn't strike me as the kind of band you'd brag about sleeping with. There've been others, she said, tugging on her ear lobe and looking at us out of the sides of her eyes.

"Really?" Jason said. "Golly. That's wild."

"I kind of, er," I began. "I'm sort of am feeling the need to, uh, I have to use the bathroom, so…"

During this pause, we both rose from the bed at the same time, each rubbing our faces and claiming exhaustion, then fled through the bedroom door and crashed into one another in the hallway like chastened schoolboys racing to the bathroom to wash off cooties.

In Munich at the Kulturstation, the stage was crammed into the corner of the room, surrounded on all sides by teetering speakers and unbalanced monitors. Everything was atilt, the leering faces of the crowd crammed up against the front of the stage, swaying from drink, a medieval display of hair, teeth, and wild eyes, backlit by blood-red lights, everything suspended in a cotton-thick cloud of cigarette smoke, my eyes burning, lungs wailing from pain, Aram's guitar neck clunking up against my cymbal stands, Jason lurching back and forth like a drunk on a boat being tossed by a stormy sea, Will up front, head thrown back, yowling…

In Berlin, at Huxley's, the hall was wide and shadowed but well lit, with streams of pure fresh air blowing across the stage at odd moments. Will, Aram, and Jason appeared to be miles away from me, connected only by our monitors. In Haarlem there were more bikes than cars and we ate both Surinamese and Indonesian food for the first time, and I recall marvelously clean sheets at our hostel room. We had an open day in Paris but it rained torrentially as Jason and I walked through the Place d'Italie. We'd both forgotten our raincoats, so we got soaked during a downpour and ran into an open door and down a dark flight of steps. We found ourselves in a strange underground mall, where I tried to find Gainsbourg CDs and Jason purchased a pair of corduroy slippers for fifteen francs. He wore them on stage that night. During our walk Will was at L'Arapaho club being interviewed by *Les Inrockuptibles*, a magazine title I didn't understand, and later we met the writer, a shaggy-haired journo sucking on Gauloises. I recall that the stage sound in Paris was fantastic, and even though I'd forgotten my earplugs (we were all a little drunk) the sound was so good, the show so good, that I didn't care, even though the ringing in my ears grew worse.

After the show at Heidelberg's Schwimmbad, a gymnasium/youth club complete with swimming pool, a grizzled hippie with no front teeth asked me if I'd sign a drumstick and give it to him, and I realized it was the first autograph I'd ever been asked to sign. He told me he had 500 signed sticks in his collection. He asked us if we wanted to smoke some hash. We said, "But of course!" He mentioned that he'd been in jail for five years after hijacking a passenger plane from Czechoslovakia with the rest of his bandmates in 1968. He'd threatened the pilot with a pistol.

"One pistol?" Ton asked.

"Nein," the guy answered. "Zwei pistollen."

"Two pistols!" Ton said. "You were quite the tough guy!"

Needless to say, there is no record of this hijacking.

Somewhere in Austria, Graz perhaps, we ate horse (I remembered that the Lippinzaners were from Austria) and the soundwoman at the Theatro was a gorgeous analogue of young Ali McGraw, all crewneck sweater and pegged olive-colored corduroys, bending over as she uncoiled cables and positioned our mics. The landscape around Graz was the most beautiful I'd ever seen, sheer rock mountainsides sharp as arrowheads, crags with fantastic castles clinging to them as if they'd grown out of the rock. In Hamburg we went to the Reeperbahn, walking past the shit-eater video stores, past bums with punch-swollen eyebrows and skinned knees, through clouds of piss-stink and the tallowy scent of kebab meat, to find ourselves in a zoo-like whorehouse along with the rest of the gawkers. In one room a dark-skinned, naked dwarf held a pale, veiny dildo that she could barely wrap her hands around, as thick as the business end of a baseball bat. We didn't stick around to find out where she might hide the dildo.

In Ulm there was a basketball hoop behind the club, a nearby wall covered in faux-NYC graffiti circa 1980, while in Regensburg or Somethingburg we ate our pre-show meal in a catacomb beneath the venue, and after the show in Fulda packed the van under the vulgar, morose faces of gargoyles affixed to tall battlement walls. Also, in Austria an attractive and friendly young woman named Dominique introduced herself to us, and joined our van for a few shows, displacing me from my usual bunk with Jason and forcing me to share Will's room and, at least once, his bed.

Before the show at Cooky's in Frankfurt we learned the Specials' "You're Wondering Now," with which we either opened the show or ended it.

BY THIS POINT IN my life as a touring musician, the bloom was not quite off the rose, but the petals on the bud were getting bruised, so to speak.

There were obvious upsides to touring, number one of which, as has been mentioned, was the opportunity to play music nightly with good musicians who were also your friends. Number two was that we met uncountable numbers of stimulating people whose interests and knowledge of the world often made mine look shallow and ill-informed. I was learning that it's always a good idea to meet people smarter and more interesting than you are. But by this point I'd realized that touring wasn't all upside.

First, on a lighter note—but one that suggests your humble narrator, like Dickens' Pip, had some learning to do as he traveled the wider world—it took me awhile to figure out that the Belgian, Dutch, and German hotel maids folded the duvets sideways across the bed, and you were supposed to unfold them and spread them out lengthwise before climbing into the rack. I spent the first few nights in Europe with my feet sticking out from underneath the covers, wondering if Europeans liked it that way, and thinking, "They don't appear that much shorter generally."

Second, it was exciting to think about visiting the great capitals, towns, and villages of Europe but less exciting in practice. Over the course of thirty days we played twenty-eight shows in twenty-eight different European cities, some of them well-known, others I'd never heard of: Enger, Dornbirn, Hilversum. By the end of the entire tour in September, we'd played a total of forty-six shows in the previous sixty days. These numbers are nothing compared to other touring bands, but for us, touring rookies, that's an awful lot of time spent in a van or onstage with the same group of people. There were jarring, Spinal Tap-esque moments where I'd look at our itinerary and wonder where in the world were the towns called Wien and München, not sure if we were in Graz or Linz, Tubingen or Ravensburg until I asked.

Only now, writing these words, did I recall that we played a few shows with the American band Scrawl and the Canadian band Jale, both of whom I remember liking. We'd see them loading into the clubs, watch their gigs, then load our own stuff onstage as they were breaking theirs down… It was like we were in separate subway cars going in opposite directions across central Europe. A couple of the girls in Jale were single and attractive and killer musicians and being a young healthy heterosexual male I often wondered what might happen if I broke my unspoken bond with Chris and tried to use my wiles to seduce one of the lovely Canadians... What happens on the road stays on the road, and I'm sure Chris would never find out...but no. I was learning, if I hadn't already known, that I was not much of a predatory rock star. To make matters even more embarrassing, from that rock star perspective, I missed Chris terribly and envied Aram and Mclean their sharing of this fantastic European travel experience.

Third, I'd grabbed a paperback of Styron's *Sophie's Choice* before leaving for the tour, so as we were passing signs for Bergen-Belsen, Dachau, and Buchenwald—the days rainy and cool with an eerie mist rising from the fields alongside the highway—I was reading an overstuffed melodrama about Nazi atrocities, trains leading to death camps, Sophie and her doomed family, and Stingo's guilt about his family's slave-owning past. In a used bookstore in Providence during Lollapalooza I'd bought a slim, handsome volume of John Hersey's *Hiroshima*, which originally appeared in *The New Yorker* during the magazine's glory days, also in my duffel bag, which I leafed through when not reading about Stingo and schizophrenic Nathan and Sophie's having to choose to sacrifice her daughter rather than her son. I could feel both of those subjects—nuclear war and the holocaust for Pete's sake!—dragging me deeper into an existential morass. These trauma-inducing books were not exactly a balm, what with being surrounded by so many anxious questions about my continued failure as a fiction writer and my life's special purpose.

Fourth, my ears had been ringing for weeks. During Lollapalooza I began the struggle with tinnitus that I have to this day. Even though I frequently plugged my ears with toilet paper, cigarette butts (from fresh cigs, not smoked ones) in addition to normal foam earplugs, my ears rang all the time and had been ringing that way since June. The more I'd stuff my ears, the more distant I felt from my band. I began to experience oddly panicked moments onstage where the song I'd played fifty times would suddenly feel unfamiliar, as if I'd never heard it before.

When did it end? After the next chorus, or is this the one that ends with the solo verse? Where's the bridge?

THERE WERE STILL MOMENTS of joy, the pure and transformative joy of playing music with friends. I'll never forget that. Never. I really do not want to sound like I am complaining because I'm not.

But night after night, day after day, we'd hump our gear to the next town, set up, meet a few interesting people with whom we'd share a meal, drink a bunch of wine and beer, play a blistering show, pack up, talk to a few fans, drink a few more beers, grab a smoke and a few winks, wake up and start all over again. Lots and lots of hours in the van arguing about what tape to listen to, where to eat lunch, hearing Tonny screeching at people who'd cut in front of him on the roadways of Europe: "Who do you think you are, the mayor?" he'd yell at a passing Opel. He was full of non sequiturs.

Museums? Forget about it.

Tempers grew shorter. A lapsed Catholic, Tonny hated the pope and treated us to his anti-pope diatribes often. Aram and Mclean appeared to be struggling to continue to define their own space in the hotels, the van, the restaurants.

After a few shows, I continued to empathize with the particular burden Will bore as the bandleader, the alpha. I couldn't have done it, this much I knew. I was reminded yet again that the crowds lining up at the doors of clubs, the journalists with their Sprockets glasses and tight black turtlenecks, the submissive club employees who bowed and scraped were there to see Will Oldham, and Will Oldham only. No one cared about the band. It was all about the guy who occupied that space in the front middle of the stage.

If anyone missed the ending of a song—see above paragraph about my weird musical vertigo—a peculiar pressure inside the band would build, and I was guilty more often than not of these flubs. This grew tiresome, and like an athlete who finds himself in a slump, and the more he thinks about the slump the worse the slump gets, I could sense my abilities as a drummer regressing. The more I worried about it, the more stressful it got.

WE WERE SLATED TO play a couple of live sets at the studios of VPRO, the Dutch national radio station. The first session went off beautifully and perfectly—we recorded maybe four songs, including "Come In," "Pushkin," "Meaulnes," and "Whither Thou Goest," all of which sounded to me like definitive versions of the songs, definitely releasable. Where are the masters to these songs? They've never been bootlegged, I don't think. At least they are unavailable on YouTube. The first session went so well that I was truly excited for the second session at VPRO, thinking we'd have five or so more songs recorded for posterity's sake, perhaps enough for an LP. En route to the station in our van, Will, who was, I assumed, generally tired of and annoyed by my drumming, mentioned offhandedly that he'd like me to bring a snare and high-hat and nothing else into the studio. He wasn't being rude, there was no reason for me to react as I did; I didn't have the spirit, the gumption, to view it as a creative challenge, or even a joke, but instead was angered, a clear sign of my own insecurity about my skills.

"Why don't you ask Aram to remove five of his guitar strings, see how that sounds?" I said brattily.

No wonder Will was tired of me.

The show that night at Vera in Groningen wasn't particularly bad, I didn't think, just a little flat, but afterward as we began to pack up our leader unloaded on us. He hated the audience, the stage sound, the sound man, our performances, the fact that we had to share a dressing room with employees of the club. When I caught up to him on his way back to our nearby hotel and asked what we might do to make sure any hurt feelings were smoothed over, Will told me that he'd often rather stew than speak because "most things that come out of our mouths don't help anyway."

"Yes, well, I see your point, but as human animals I think we rely on speech pretty heavily to communicate our ideas to one another…"

"And that's the problem," Will said.

Aram and Mclean hunkered down in their room, huddled together in the van, whispering.

So, Jason and I spent a lot of time together, lying in adjacent beds, talking about farmland on the Eastern Shore, which I thought might be ruined by being between two bodies of saltwater, the Chesapeake and the Atlantic, but which Jason claimed was among the best farmland in the world.

"They grow some special sweet potatoes there," he'd mumble from the darkness. "Haymans. They're white."

"White sweet potatoes?" I'd murmur back, barely awake, my voice a whisper. "That's the craziest thing I've ever heard."

As the European tour continued and we met that many more obsequious fans and journalists whom Will had very little trouble ignoring as they leapt at him like puppies, he began to remind me of that young, fiery, smart-ass version of Dylan in Pennebaker's *Don't Look Back*.

In Vienna (the mysterious Wien, of course) we'd walked past a boutique featuring a male mannequin wearing a pair of black leather pants with silver medallions down the sides, much like Jim Morrison's, and I can't say I was too surprised when Will showed up onstage at that night's show wearing the pants. Over the next few days he transformed himself into our own version of the Lizard King. He'd bought some kind of guitar effect whose buttons would turn his Fender into a screeching tool of Satan, and many was the show that saw all of us drunk on red wine, Aram flailing away on his left-handed Telecaster, Selma thumping away on his bass, me bashing my cymbals in an attempt to be heard over the carnal din, and Will on his knees, head thrown back, a monstrous howl ringing from his amplifier through the club.

Many fans were pissed that Will wasn't a mystical hillbilly bard. The angrier they got and the louder they yelled at us, the more noise we made, another thing that reminded me of Dylan: Palace goes electric! At more than one show I watched as some fans glowered at us, fingers in their ears, thinking they were coming to an acoustical folk show instead of what was, by that point, a very tight rock and roll show played very loudly. In Hanover, one woman chased us down after the show yelling, "NO! You can't! Please. Why?"

"If you wanted it to be just like the record," Will spat, not slowing his pace toward the waiting van, "you should've just stayed home and listened to the record."

There were plenty of shows that were smashing successes. Plenty of nights we left the stage laughing, buoyed by the indescribable floating sensation caused by being onstage during a good show that is all too often compared to being high or otherwise intoxicated. Instead it's a far more satisfying, holistic, whole-body and mind feeling, a combination of the physical—the indescribable floating sense of having been chemically altered by giving the performance in front of a responsive group of people—and the more earthly or mundane—the fulfilling sense that you and your friends and bandmates possessed skills that had tangible worth or commercial value, like being a surgeon, a good plumber, or an HVAC tech.

Perhaps it was an illusion, but I always felt that my life wasn't being wasted when I played the drums, unlike when I wrote. The contrast between writing and performing engendered an oppositional set of psychological responses: playing live music allowed for an immediate and often transformative response from a crowd, while writing was a task performed for an audience who remained silent, unknowable. The audience for my writing might've been gelatinous cryptids on some distant star cluster for all I knew, while the audience for live music was right there in front of you, their emotions in plain sight. They liked you or they didn't.

In just about every case, barring a few exceptions, the European crowds liked us.

THE PROMOTER IN GRAZ included a six-pack of small, narrow cans in our backstage rider. We each drank one just before our show began: sweet and sour, not at all unpleasant, and within minutes the hair was standing up on the back of my neck and my jaw was tingling. We were told it was an underground energy drink made in Austria by a man who'd tried a similar drink in Thailand in the eighties. Red Bull wouldn't make it to the States until '97. I could be wrong, but I've always thought that the drink we drank that night in Graz was far more powerful than any I've had since…

"Hey, you guys ready to play? Yeah? Ready? Let's go play a show! Now! Right now? Yeah! Hell yeah! NOW. Now? NOW!"

We speedwalked onto the stage as Will did a somersault, landing hard on his back. But then he jumped up and waved at the crowd triumphantly, his face split by a giant, manic smile. Jason was shivering, Aram bouncing on his toes. I counted off the first song like I was DeeDee Ramone. Even while playing, I was reminded of those coke-addled versions of live Waylon Jennings shows from the seventies, where every musician sounds as if they're playing at their limit, barely able to keep up, to hang on. Does a tape exist of this show? Was the music as powerful and crackling and rip-roaring as it seemed at the time?

THE LAST SHOW OF the tour took place on September 23, in Krefeld, at a club called Kulturfabrik. Since we were flying out of Schiphol in Amsterdam, we arrived in Amsterdam on the twenty-fourth and spent a final night in the city before flying out the following day. In Amsterdam we stayed up late listening to the brand new album *Voodoo Lounge* by the Stones. Conveniently, our hostel had a pot bar on the first floor, so we smoked ourselves blind on some kind of weed with orange in the name, then later stood like stoned zombies feeding guilders into the candy machine, inhaling delicious and exotic Dutch chocolate bars until we had no more guilders. The night featured laughter, most of it generated by Will and Jason, that grew from silly to tearful then past hysterical and into territory that was dangerous, frightening. I was convinced I might not be able to stop. We all woke up the next morning with sore abs, as if we'd spent all night doing crunches and not smoking weed and eating chocolate while listening to the Stones.

It's almost impossible for me to reckon with the telescoping of time as I remember that callow pothead eating all that chocolate: in two years I'd be married to Chris and within three we'd have our first son.

One of our last nights in Europe, Hannover perhaps, or Oldenburg, we were treated by the promoter to stay in a nice hotel where we each had our own room. After showering the morning following the show, I noted the thick terrycloth bathrobe folded on the towel rack, so I slid into its luxurious folds and headed out into the hallway with my duffel bag, where I watched each of my bandmates, Will, Jason, and Aram, exiting their rooms at the same time, all wearing the same robes.

We all laughed and began to run down the hallway.

While I'd been in Europe Chris had begun graduate school in DC, found an apartment, and she wondered what kind of job I might get when I got to DC...

Job? I thought. Jesus Christ. *A fricking job.*

That sounded awful. I was sure I could milk this Palace experience for another year, continuing to travel, continuing to avoid the call of domestic order, blasted ears notwithstanding. Even though I'd once fantasized about being a part of whatever big-label deal may have risen out of our Lollapalooza experience, I was less interested in money than in sustaining my sense of achievement, of playing music, of basking in the reflected glory of the Palace experience. Even if I didn't like touring all that much, I still gained a great deal of personal satisfaction from our miniscule taste not so much of fame but of the glimmer of a hint of my life's purpose, a *raison d'etre.*

There was also the attraction of aligning myself with someone whom I was convinced would be around for a long time, forever perhaps, and I knew it then: Will, and Palace, was going to be the way I achieved immortality.

The World
and Elsewhere

A MONTH AFTER RETURNING from the European tour I was sitting on the back stoop of our new apartment in northwest DC in my stolen bathrobe drinking a can of beer. The stoop was a small square of concrete that looked out on an alley. I'd already met Mr. Peabody, the basset hound puppy who lived in the yard across from us. He now peered at me through picket slats, sucking his floppy chops as if he'd like to come share the beer with me.

It was a mild, late fall evening, the sky slate blue, stars pricking and glinting. Planes flew overhead en route to National (not yet Reagan International) Airport. The air was cooling and each gust of wind was accompanied by the fluttering down of hardwood leaves and the small sound they made as they skidded across the alley. Chris was attending a night class just a few blocks away and would be arriving on her bike any minute to join me for a beer and some soup I'd made out of the Halloween pumpkins we'd taken from our neighbor's stoops. Our one-room English basement efficiency was near a series of trails cutting through the woods of northwest DC, on the edge of which was a series of garden plots available for residents. Come spring, we'd have our own plot where we'd grow tomatoes, habañeros, jalapeños, lettuces, eggplant.

Supposedly Henry Rollins had gone to the neighborhood elementary school at the end of our alley.

AN OLDER COUSIN OF mine was building a house in rural northern Virginia near Middleburg not far from DC and he'd already told the construction crew that I'd help carry plywood, pick up trash, be the lowest-on-the-totem pole gofer. Part of the property needed to be cleared of some dead trees. My cousin was a writer/teacher himself and respected my desire to be a struggling artist, so he paid me ten bucks an hour to help clear the smaller trees out, and to have a go at some of the bigger ones.

I was pulling in to the worksite an hour away for the first time when I realized that I'd left my boots in DC next to the back door. Having driven out to the site in my stocking feet, I realized that the only footwear in my car was a pair of road biking shoes. So, I wore plastic-soled biking shoes on my first day of working construction with a crew of rounders and roughnecks from West Virginia.

"Them's some fancy work shoes you got there," said Larry between pulls on his ever present Winston.

"Yeah, I forgot my boots. These are bike shoes."

"Really? Why, I had no idea. I didn't know they made shoes specially for bikes! Mostly I just wore my go-fasters when I used to ride a bike."

"Me, too," said Rex. "My tenny runners worked fine for bike-pedaling."

That morning I was asked to wheelbarrow a few tons of rock into the foundation, and by lunch was surprised, and rather proud, especially with my bike shoes, to have made it through an eighth of the pile, which I figured was about three or so tons. Slope-shouldered Rex, whose shaggy hair reminded me of the type worn by the fellows in Def Leppard, was polite in his praise for the hard-working, bike-shoe wearing city slicker, but underneath his praise I detected, what? Was it envy that the new kid could wheelbarrow crush and run with the best of them, and had some innate shoveling and wheelbarrow skills? He looked at Larry, who tugged on his smoke and took a pull from his Mountain Dew.

"We's hoping you'd be finished by lunch," he said.

"Finished?" I said. "The whole pile? This must be three tons I've moved."

"Not bad, not bad," Larry said accommodatingly. "Rex, show the man how to move rock."

Within an hour the entire pile, at least ten tons if not more, had been moved and raked into place.

AT A MEKONS SHOW at the old 9:30 Club, when they played "Horses," I drunkenly shouted something about Palace's version being better or some such nonsense, which Timms and Langford acknowledged from the stage, and for annoyingly good measure, I announced from the crowd that I'd been the drummer for Palace Brothers. Langford and Timms cared not a whit. Later I awoke in the middle of the night to pee, already hungover and suffering from paroxysms of shame at my outburst. In the morning I could feel my face flushing every time I recalled the way Langford and Timms had looked out into the audience trying to spy the idiot who would yell such a thing, and how the people standing next to me, including Chris, had given me space as I yelled.

Most days it was a great comfort to be out in the woods by myself.

DURING THE SNOWY WINTER after the European tour, Ned, Jason, Aram, and I, along with our old friend Willie MacLean of Louisville's King Kong, formalized our band as the Anomoanon, a name meant to riff on the idea of being what we'd been, more or less, during our time with Will: the anonymous backing band. It was meant to reference the bland, anonymous name The Band, because, speaking for me, I viewed Will through the same lens I viewed Bob Dylan, as a guy who wasn't going to do what people expected of him and whose path through a career would probably be unpredictable, full of surprises. And if we could align ourselves with The Band, even cryptically, who went on to fame and fortune after leaving Dylan, why, all the better. Coincidentally, the made-up word rhymes with "phenomonon," and is comprised of the word "anomo," meaning unusual; and "anon," meaning soon or later. Jason agreed to play mostly keyboards, while Willie took over on bass.

So for the remainder of this book, whenever you see the word "Anomoanon," just think "phenomenon." Do not trouble yourself with questions about whether or not it's a good or bad band name. Given the chance, my hunch is that we'd probably have spent a bit more time on it. Or less, perhaps.

Paul Oldham, Ned and Will's youngest brother (whose band Pale Horse Riders had played the show with us at Lounge Ax in Chicago), had spent the previous few months at Indiana University in Bloomington's sound engineering school and had offered to record us whenever we wanted to make the trek to Bloomington. We decided to take advantage of his skills and the free studio and record a few songs. All we had to do was to get there and to pay for the tape.

A lightheartedness pervaded the freezing winter weekend in Bloomington, and the songs Ned wrote were fun to play. The resultant Anomoanon songs echoed this angst-free milieu, especially "Hello My" with its burbling farfisa, played by Jason, and double-time hi-hat, and its tumbling and intricate melody sung by Ned.

One morning we were joined by Joe Oldham, who'd driven up from Louisville to visit with us for the day and to document this historic recording session with his ever-present camera. As usual, Joe's presence was welcome. He seemed to enjoy our company, and we certainly enjoyed his, even though he was Will, Ned, and Paul's dad, which, if it sounds like damning with faint praise, it's not. Like a lot of great photographers, Joe disappeared into the scenery when he was taking pictures, an ability aided by his natural quietude and mellow nature. A photo that he took of us all gathered around a microphone singing a back-up track looks not unlike a staged performance of a Python skit, each of us cutting up, our faces twisted into goofy smiles, eyebrows arched, fingers held up affectedly, even though, as I recall, we were not cutting up for the camera, and instead were struggling, each in our own way, to hit a particular note. Our faces, our body language, is that of five men in a state of collective grace, of pure happiness, as they engage in the joy of making music.

The Anomoanon (remember: phenomenon) was a band born in the realm of positive face. We would retain that positive face for the remainder of our bandness.

Will, always generous, helped us put out a single we recorded with Paul through Palace Records and Drag City. Ned ran the design show, as was his right, and the cover featured a photo of a piece of coiled rope set on the Xerox machine's glass, and on the back a photo of a field of sunflowers. A few months later, back in DC, I opened a padded manila envelope and held the Anomoanon's debut record in my hand—the dream of every rocker since the dawn of time. I wondered how this black vinyl disc might improve me, make me a different person than I was.

The single, "Free Web"/"Hello My," Palace Records #14, sold a few copies, may have been reviewed in a zine or two, but didn't exactly crush it in sales. Any dreams I'd had about the Anomoanon allowing me to quit chopping down trees or pretending to learn carpentry didn't so much as disappear, but perhaps grew slightly foggier. The timeline shifted. I think this was the first moment I realized that our path forward was not going to be as easy as I may have once thought. It was our first project that had not been tied to Will, and the initial reaction from the record-buying public was that us minus Will might not be as powerful a commercial entity as, well, just plain old Will.

Still, I loved the record. Still do. We'd done everything short of melting the vinyl and pressing it ourselves, and this holistic engagement with our own product felt good.

To paraphrase Ray Bradbury, I was on my way to accepting rejection and rejecting acceptance.

THE FIRST TIME I saw Will after the end of the European tour was during a weekend in the Spring of '95, a few months after we'd gotten home from Europe. Chris and I had driven down to Birmingham from DC to spend a weekend with Ned and Jennie, and Will and Numbers lived nearby. In fact, they'd recently hosted a fish fry and their kitchen still reeked of fish grease. The weekend wasn't supposed to be freighted with anything, just a mellow few days with old friends, but I was still smarting from Will's rejection of my skills as a skin man after Europe. Admittedly, I brought baggage to the weekend. My *feewins* had been hurt. I'm not sure I was particularly friendly to Will and Numbers, but I could be misremembering and maybe was instead just anxious, my perception being that I'd been fired.

That night, May 12, we bought tickets to go see a concert at a local joint. The performer was Tiny Tim. Yes, that Tiny Tim, doing a solo set, just him and his uke. I found the show strangely moving. These were songs my grandparents would've listened to and enjoyed, simple and corny songs about love and soldiers and heartbreak. Vaudevillian, a twisted early American songbook, but with the patina of Anglophone Victoriana. In the songs, men were protectors of women and country, while women were stolid as they kept the home fires burning, but also equally prone to vapors. "Yankee Doodle Dandy"; "What Kind of American Are You?"; "Stay Home, Little Girl, Stay Home."

Tiny Tim whaled through what seemed to be a hundred and fifty songs at a punk rock pace, barely pausing to take a breath, or to open his eyes. There was something touched, otherworldly, freakish about him, but also familiar. I'd seen Tiny Tim perform on countless seventies TV programs, often watching with my parents or grandparents, Merv Griffin or Sonny and Cher or the Johnny Cash show, thinking that there was something off, perhaps unpleasant about Tim's eccentricity, about the strange dark circles around his eyes and the patronizing way he spoke to his barely pubescent wife, whom he called Miss Vicki.

That night in Birmingham I was surprised at Tim's vocal range, the power of his voice, even with the bizarre vibrato lifted straight out of the vocal stylings of the teens and twenties. Will and Ned were nonplussed. I wrote something about the show and sent it to Ned, who was surprised at my mostly nostalgic take. His was a lot more pointed, more critical.

Later we found out the concert was recorded and released as *Tiny Tim: Unplugged*, and if I'm not mistaken the inner jacket features a photo of an attractive couple, the male turning away from the camera just as the photo is taken, but the raven-haired beauty he is with is visible. It's clearly Dianne; the male is Will.

A FULL YEAR AFTER the European tour ended, I got a cryptic postcard. Another version of Palace was coming through DC, Will wrote, and would be playing at the Black Cat. He'd sent Chris and I a few postcards from the road after the weekend in Birmingham, and I always appreciated hearing from him even though I was still envious of his freedom and the critical adulation he continued to enjoy.

Will's latest record *Viva Last Blues* had been released to huge critical acclaim, and I loved the record. *Viva* was Will's first straight rock record and I always thought it was influenced in some ways by his time with what had become the Anomoanon. Engineered by Steve Albini in Birmingham, with Ned providing bass, some guitar, and vocals. Ned told me that during recording they'd frequently eat at a local barbecue spot, where one day Britt Walford ordered the pig's ear sandwich. Albini, one of my favorite current food writers, took a bite, as did Will, as did Ned, and they'd all agreed it was pretty awful. I'd love to read Albini's review of the sandwich.

Being in a band was easier for me than trying to be a writer, its demands more concrete, more fulfilling, and I wondered if I should be working toward being a professional musician rather than struggling to write. I knew how to play the drums. I knew how to pack a van. I was comfortable meeting new people and eating new foods and sleeping on floors. Sure, my bandmates hadn't gotten along perfectly all the time, but we knew one another well enough to know how far to push a joke, and if we weren't all alike, we were different in a way that fit together.

But I also knew I'd learned something about myself from watching Will's hard work, and the news wasn't good. I lacked Will's steel spine, that almost sociopathic conviction to be good at something. The qualities that made him a real artist stood in contrast to those I desired in my own life. Deep down, I knew I wanted my own version of happiness, and that happiness would sit on a foundation of safety, stability, and not the ruthless pursuit of an ideal founded on trying to destroy everything I'd worked to build. In the year since our tour had ended, Will had been on the road with four different incarnations of his band; played almost forty new shows; had recorded and released two or three records, each of them different from the other; and had lived in Birmingham, Iowa, and Louisville.

And here I was living in the same basement apartment having worked the same construction job for a year, eating Halloween pumpkins and otherwise sharing my life with a woman I'd soon marry, a woman whose professional goals were ambitious and clear-cut. A few years at a Master's program then, most likely, a PhD program followed by a stint overseas. It was easy to envision a job with a PhD's salary, a steady income, a house, a dog, a cat, some kids. At worst I knew this conservative desire stood in opposition to wanting to be the kind of artist that Will was, with his constant and tireless searching, his desire to destroy and start again.

Still, deep down, I remained convinced I could have it both ways: a stable domestic life and an enriching, successful, artistic one.

ON THE NIGHT OF October 29, 1995, barely three weeks after I'd stood around the open door of a pickup truck with my workmates and listened to the verdict of the O. J. Simpson trial, Chris and I drove across town to the Black Cat to see Will and his new band. The West Virginians and I had stood in stunned silence when the OJ verdict was announced, and I was surprised that nary a negative word about OJ was uttered by this rascally collection of country boys, most of whom, I would've guessed, might've had stronger opinions on the matter. Still, the world shuddered when the verdict came out, not unlike when Cobain had killed himself. There was a national imbalance of humors as Yeats's great beast continued to draw his body from the sand, stretched his thighs, arched his gigantic back, and yawned.

At the Black Cat, Chris and I greeted Will and met his new band, and then got a couple of beers and headed out into the crowd to watch. Did the Geraldine Fibbers open the show? Whoever it was, I recall not liking them. The beer was going down my gullet wrong, it tasted sour. I had heartburn because I'd eaten too much, or too little, for supper. Everything was wrong.

Before Will and his band started, I told Chris that I was going to hate the show.

"Would you just take a deep breath," she said. "Relax."

"You relax," I snapped. "Don't tell me to relax. I *am* relaxed."

Will and his band took the stage to uproarious applause. The first song began sloppily, awkwardly so. The song ended. Silence from the crowd, a few confused whoops. After another song or two, nothing had changed: the musicians, billed as Will's "jazz band," were lopsided, out of sync, and genuinely strange—I felt some degree of satisfaction bordering on schadenfreude. Had these guys even practiced once? People standing nearby rubbed their chins and muttered to themselves: "I thought this would be a lot better," they said to one another.

Where's the banjo player?

Which one is the guy in Slint?

This doesn't sound anything like his records.

"Told you," I said to Chris.

I watched Will trying to coach the band through the changes onstage. Every so often they'd come together and play a few bars in sync, and I noted that when the gap between utter failure and competence closed, the music sounded interesting, strange, hilarious. The musicians were clearly experienced players but it really did sound like they'd never heard the songs before, like they were engaging in some kind of weird experiment, as if Will, like Werner Herzog did to the actors in *Heart of Glass*, had hypnotized them before taking the stage and was guiding them through an attempt at telepathy.

Every so often I'd laugh out loud, amazed that they'd locked in for a few bars. Then they'd fall apart again. I found myself becoming more patient during the rough spots, anticipating the next moment of order. Every time I thought I was watching a train wreck, something interesting would happen.

Before long, it was as if a strange spell had been cast. My heartburn was gone. Onstage, the band appeared to be having fun. The audience was cheering wildly. Will, of course, had willed the performance into being, had won them over, had convinced us all that he was right—again—and that whatever he did would be draped in a charmed faerie cloak, wherein that within it would be immune to sabotage, immune to sucking. What had appeared earlier to be sure disaster had become an entertaining perversion of showmanship. It was obvious that Will couldn't have cared less what the audience thought. We were watching something that had nothing to do with entertaining; instead we were watching a band entertain itself, performing solely for its own communal edification. Whether or not the audience liked it didn't matter.

At the end of the show Will stood onstage, peering out at the audience with what I may have mistaken as a sly grin playing on his lips. The room was packed, fans crammed shoulder to shoulder, nodding to one another in mutual and communal happiness, clapping and screaming by now, and from the stage I saw that Will was scanning the audience. Finally, he spotted Chris and me from the stage, held up a hand, and smiled.

He Not Busy
Being Born

THE LONGER I SPENT working construction the more I realized that the blue-collar experiment of helping build my cousin's house had run its course. I had no intention of it being a permanent condition; I had a limited amount of humility.

The physical demands of the job had come close to crushing my body and brain. I tweaked my neck carrying a load of plywood one afternoon and would often collapse into bed at the end of a workday, asleep before my head hit the pillow. My hands were like giant mitts made of calluses. I spent the entirety of one day pulling old vines off of a few felled hickory trees my cousin had sold, only to later watch as my hands ballooned to twice their normal size. The vines were poison ivy. My blistered hands didn't operate properly for weeks.

I'd read somewhere that Dylan claimed the dockworkers, the laborers, the clerks at all-night drugstores, the stevedores (I'm paraphrasing here) were the real heroes, the real saints, not the artists and performers who turned these working-class experiences into song. With Dylan's words in my imagination, I'd begun the construction job assuming it would make me a better artist. But like famed agrarian writer Andrew Lytle—author of essay collection *The Hind Tit* and whom I'd been able to get to know when I was at Sewanee—who became a farmer thinking it would be the perfect way to make a living while pursuing becoming a published writer, I had not accounted for the fact that physical work was exhausting.

And that an exhausted brain does not function well, and writing is hard.

My final few months in DC were spent working a temp job at NPR's national studios, and though the job had started as a rather awful grind answering telephones, responding to listener complaints, and taking orders for cassette copies of particular shows, I'd grown to enjoy it. The money was good, the work was often interesting, and my ego was being reinflated by a sense of engagement in professional society after my year spent among the laborers of Loudon County.

Walking into the NPR cafe for a cup of joe, I'd see dumpy men with bad haircuts who'd say hello to me in a deep, euphonic voice, and I'd recognize that I was being addressed by on-air talent, like Bob Edwards, Noah Adams, or Scott Simon. Being able to tell my family and friends I was working full-time at NPR was, in fact, more gratifying than telling them I was ripping sheets of plywood and gathering cigarette butts for Larry and Rex.

The NPR job also introduced me to this new thing called the internet, and predictably, I stayed after work one day and typed the single word "porn" into the Netscape browser window at my desk and spent a solid hour waiting for photos of nude women to appear, line by pixeled line. My description to Ned of this newfound discovery, that online porn was really "just a bunch of nude women kickin' back," was purportedly the kernel that allowed him, a number of years later, to write the closest thing the Anomoanon ever got to a hit. One day in the distant future this discovery of the online nudes kickin' back on my NPR computer would loop back to NPR when our song "Kickin' Back" would serve as the bumper music for a segment of Kai Ryssdal's Marketplace.

I also searched for online reviews or fan reports of the shows we'd played with Will, now two years in the past. While there was plenty of mention of Will on the nascent internet, there was no mention of us, or, more specifically, of me at all, which bummed me out.

LATER, LOOKING THROUGH THE journal I kept in Europe, I was reminded of an afternoon when we stopped for a late lunch at a roadside café somewhere in France. Will and I both ordered the andouillette. The waitress saw that we were foreigners and motioned to her belly. She explained to Ton and Will, both of whom spoke French, that the sausage was made from offal. We didn't care about eating innards (even though this was all the way back in 1994; now everyone eats innards!), but when I cut into the sausage my second or third bite featured a large chewy morsel of unidentifiable cartilaginous connective tissue. I put my fork down in disgust and sighed. Will watched me through half-closed eyes, grabbed his sausage with his fingers, dipped its tip into a pile of brown mustard and ate the entire pale tube in four or five bites, leaving his mouth open for me to see the masticated tripes and chitlins and lungs and heart as he chewed. He enjoyed it more as the result of my disgust.

After sound checking the drums that night, I found Will asleep on the vinyl banquette in our backstage area. A garish light cast down by the bank of fluorescents overhead bathed the room in a sickly blue-white glow. The banquette was small and it was difficult for me to imagine how Will had curled himself onto the seat and willed himself to sleep. In the next room Jason's bass thumped annoyingly as the soundman tried to find the levels, but there Will was, eyes closed, his hand folded under his chin, blissful, unperturbed.

I was reminded of a scene from any number of sci-fi movies where the crew has been suspended in a chemical coma for their multiple-year journey through space. The air in the room was clammy, the scent of something antiseptic, toilet pucks, disinfectant, adding to the strange illusion that we were on the Sulaco careening through multiple dimensions, Will in deep slumber.

There were only a few shows left of the tour, and beyond them was the yawning black hole of the unknown realm of domesticity, of work, of the hard landing, and I found myself suddenly in need of the information that was held beneath that dreaming countenance in some unimaginably private and protected place. I was upset, acutely, that Will held all knowledge. I was angry that nothing was being shared. I was not the captain of my fate. He was leading us farther away from earth, into an uncharted realm. I had to know the answer to a secret. I reached down and shook his shoulder. He opened his eyes.

"What's our future hold?" I asked him.

Those were my exact words. Was I trying to imbue this moment with the dramatic? Disoriented, in shock from having been woken up, he peered up at me, head tilted slightly, a creature of vast and complicated intelligence studying a mortal whose concepts of existence were opaque, childlike. It was as if the word *future* did not exist in his vocabulary, nor his comprehension.

"I've got some plans," I lied. "And was wondering what we might be up to come winter…"

"We will not be up to anything," he said, immediately awake. It was if he had never been asleep. His eyes were clear and focused. "Do whatever you need to do."

"We won't be playing any more shows, won't be recording—"

"No. Do whatever you want."

He stretched back out on the banquette, closed his eyes, and within seconds was asleep again.

Will took no obvious pleasure in deflating me or making me look like a fool for asking a stupid question. At the same time there was no attempt to be conciliatory or careful about the possibility of allaying my potential disappointment.

Perhaps it was a direct challenge: Go do something interesting for yourself, quit being a loser sideman, go make something, write something. Take something seriously. Devote your life to a pursuit that might allow you to burn like a blue flame. Stop worrying about deals being made or making a living playing the drums or making a living at all. Figure out a way to keep making art, to keep making records, to keep writing, to keep breathing, to keep moving.

Destroy your safe and happy lives, before it is too late!

Because soon you're going to have to start from scratch.

Part Two

In the beginner's mind there are many possibilities, but in the expert's mind there are few.

—Shunryu Suzuki, *Zen Mind, Beginner's Mind*

Around the Road...

ON MAY 29, 1996, Chris and I locked our English basement door in DC for the last time, said goodbye to Mr. Peabody, crammed an old futon and a few other pieces of furniture into our 1987 Jeep Cherokee, dropped them off at a Goodwill in DC, and drove north through snow showers to Rochester where, on June 1, we were married. The weekend turned out to be the first time Aram, Jason, Ned, Will, Numbers Bellino and I had all been together since the Lollapalooza shows in the summer and the European shows in the fall of '94; naturally, Jennie and Mclean were there as well, and Jason brought his future wife Kollette, so the wedding served as a gathering of the entire Ano-Palace tribe. Willie MacLean, our new Anomoanon bandmate, came up from Louisville. This was the big reunion you've been waiting for, dear reader, and I was waiting for it as well. I missed these people, Chris knew that I missed these people, and having us all together, along with our families and friends from far and wide, during this celebration of marriage was nothing short of joyous.

At our wedding, a few rounds deep into rehearsal dinner toasts, I looked around at all who'd gathered in Rochester to celebrate with me and Chris and had a vision that would inform my dreams for what our musical family might become, if certain factors worked in our favor. The vision was influenced by the photograph in the gatefold of the Allman Brothers' *Brothers and Sisters* LP, where each Allman band or crew member poses with a significant other; a few men and women are holding babies; toddlers stand with hands in mouths. Jaimoe and Lamar's families are there, too, so there's a multiracial element to this utopian vision. The photo represented a perfect distillation of what I wanted the future to look like: an extended and diverse family built on the making of music. We already had multiple members of multiple families in our circle. That this hippie dream might've been fundamentally naive never crossed my mind. The photograph suggested that the domestic life and the traveling rock life were not mutually exclusive. I found this notion comforting. It combined many themes that were important to me: music, friendship, strength in numbers, facial hair, cooperation, family, and, yes, making money.

One of my last cogent memories the night before we were married, after consuming an entire handle of Knob Creek bourbon my sister Ann Barron had procured, was Aram's tall and Nico-esque wife Mclean cradling the still waifish Will in her arms like a giant infant, Will's head tucked against her breasts. The image of a fully relaxed Will submitting himself to the cradling of the tall woman, white-haired, white-skinned, dressed in white, an elf princess, would somehow serve as a symbol to me in the coming years of the rebirth of the temperamental punk bandleader from the Palace era into the jolly troubadour Bonnie "Prince" Billy.

AFTER OUR WEDDING, a few weeks before we moved to Tallahassee, Florida, where Chris would begin a PhD program, we were passing through Charlottesville when Will and David Berman of the Silver Jews were first meeting to plan out the collaborative Silver Palace record.

David was a poet. He'd gone to UVA with Steve and Bob from Pavement, and they'd been in the first incarnation of the Silver Jews, David's band. David wrote great poems and smart but funny essays that appeared in intellectual publications like *The Minus Times* and *The Baffler* and his band the Silver Jews had released a couple of enigmatic records on Drag City, including an early experimental project called *The Arizona Record* and the slightly more straightforward and super great *Starlite Walker*.

Will and David were both a part of the Drag City mafia (which also included Bill Callahan of Smog and Jennifer and Neil of the Royal Trux), and the potential collaboration between Will and Berman was an exciting prospect for the denizens of the underground who were aware of the potential greatness of the Silver Palace project. Suffice to say, this was a meeting between two legendary voices.

Paul Oldham was there to help twiddle the knobs, there were guitars and mics, a DAT recorder, a mixing board, a couple of stools on an oriental rug, so contrary to Berman/Oldham lore, every indication was that they were prepared to record. Tea bags, lots and lots of stained tea bags, were lying around. It certainly looked like a place where work would soon commence, but as deep Palace and Jews fans know, nothing ever came of the session.

It was summertime in Charlottesville. Insects screeched from the swollen greenery. Chris and I were newlyweds and suspended in that lovers' glow. The future was wide open, and blessedly so. There was a big bottle of jug wine, some beers. We watched a VHS tape of the Heidi Fleiss *Hollywood Madam* documentary on a small television while we ate a baked rice dish.

Afterward, Berman was arguing with Paul, challenging him to defend the Krautrock band Can, whom Berman loathed. Paul was using the Henry Jamesian mechanism of "I like Can, that is enough," but Berman was having none of it. Hectoring (where does that word come from? Wasn't the *Iliad*'s Hector the only honorable guy in the whole war?), anyway, hectoring comes to mind. Paul, having grown up with Ned and Will, had long ago learned to defend himself, but at the same time I could tell that having someone yelling at him about Can, forcing him into the position of explaining why he liked Can, was jarring. He was used perhaps to more intensely quiet lines of questioning.

"Defend them, Paul!" Berman yelled. "Why on earth would you like such a shitty, pointless band? I'm still waiting for someone to explain to me why this band is so great, and you're not doing a very good job of it, either."

"Why should I? I like Can, what's the big deal?"

"Because they're terrible," Berman bellowed.

I kept my mouth shut. Jaki Liebezeit was a drummer I thought about a lot when playing our songs. Later, I'd listen to Can and wonder if Berman was right. They had a lot of great songs but…maybe not that many? Were Damo Suzuki's vocalizations sometimes a bit comical? Silly, maybe?

After a few half-hearted attempts to explain Can to Berman, Paul finally gave up.

Paul has always exhibited remarkably good sense. He, too, will play an important role in our adventure as it continues.

Even though I never got to know David that well, I was able, for the years following this initial meeting in Charlottesville, to view him through the lens of friendship. I still have a manila envelope filled with letters he sent me over the years, and a folder of emails we traded after the letter writing ended. Each one, each letter, each email, is constructed like a fine jewel made of words. Nothing wasted, a pure expression of the person writing the words. A few of them rank among the funniest things I've ever read. Equally, there was a warmth in the way he chose to share his time and ideas with me through our correspondence. I'd hear stories that reminded me that David could be prickly, that some people considered him difficult, but I never saw that. Even when he was hectoring Paul, I noted that David really did want Paul to change his, David's, mind about Can, and appeared frustrated that Paul might not succeed. It wasn't bullying instead David was seeking knowledge, knowledge that was being denied, and that's what made him angry. Not that I doubted the stories about David were true, far from it, as I could see that David was intensely engaged with the world around him, perhaps too intensely, weighing everything in the world against an ideal and finding most of the world inferior. It didn't surprise me that he made some people angry. David was a fundamental part of my understanding of why this time period, the end of one century and the beginning of a new one, was so vibrant, alive with possibility but also, in some ways, doomed. The best parts of the old way of doing things were being replaced. David fit in better with the old way.

David Berman will appear again in this book; sadly, he died in the summer of 2019.

CHRIS AND I MOVED to Tallahassee in August and Chris began her PhD program in International Education Development at Florida State. It was a big leap to leave DC for the Big Bend of Florida. We moved into a small, cheap apartment. It was half of a duplex that had once been a shotgun shack until some enterprising developer split the house down the middle with cheap framing and drywall and added a second front door. The back of the house sloped precipitously downward toward the fence separating our wooded yard from the outfield of Leon High School's baseball diamond. The living room walls would often come alive with five-inch-long cockroaches, euphemized as palmetto bugs, and only one room, the bedroom, had an air conditioning unit, even though the first hundred-degree days in that crook of North Florida often arrived in April.

Outside: elephant ear plants, dangling shocks of gray moss, sprawling live oaks, strange shadows, golden silk orb weaver spiders as wide as your hand, unfamiliar night noises, and pummeling heat.

Next door lived a single woman in her forties, potbellied, stick-legged, who'd sit for hours on our shared porch smoking cigarettes and drinking from an ever present half gallon of iced sweet tea served in a giant plastic cup that resembled a bucket. We shared the same floorboards that ran under the flimsy wall separating our apartments, so Chris and I could feel her insomniac footfalls at night as she wandered around her half of the house like some nocturnal mammal. Her Florida twang and cigarette-ruined voice sounded like a rusty screen door. She had dentures and a homemade tattoo on the knuckles of her left hand: L-O-V-E, just like Robert Mitchum in *The Night of the Hunter*.

Many was the afternoon that late summer and fall that I spent sitting on the porch with a notebook and listening to the Leon High School marching band practice Chicago's "25 or 6 to 4." It was great hearing them go from incompetence to competence over the course of a couple of months. I'd spend hours on our back porch writing and reading and listening to the band practice daily, noting their improvements, then hop on the bike and head out to the trails south of town while Chris went to class. Hard work was all that mattered. Or at least it mattered a lot more than sitting and waiting for inspiration. Will had taught me that. So did the high school band.

ONCE SETTLED, I HAD to find a job. I thought my experience at NPR those final months in DC would be résumé gold down there in the sticks of north Florida among the simple crackers, but I was wrong. Overexcited expectations of my own employability had been a pattern since our time in DC. I recalled complaining bitterly to Ned soon after Chris and I moved to DC about how

Georgetown University hadn't even responded to my cover letter asking to teach a creative writing course. Ned didn't even laugh.

"Jesus, Jack, Georgetown is one of the best universities in the US, do you really think they're dying to hire unpublished guys with MFAs?"

"But it's from UVA," I answered.

Frustrated silence.

Orpheus-like, having not gotten a job at the local NPR affiliate, I was pulled back into the underworld of working as a clerk at a record store called Vinyl Fever. I'd visited the Feve one or two times and had been able to conclude within minutes that it was actually a better record store than Plan 9 in Charlottesville, whose conservative managers stocked the store with titles that would appeal to the mostly conservative students at UVA (like the Dave Matthews Band). At Plan 9 we'd get yelled at for playing Sonic Youth or even Palace over the store system, our mortified manager hustling over to cut the volume before anyone in the store became too upset by noises that might offend. Meanwhile, I'd heard Merzbow and Wu Tang Clan and Sonny Sharrock blaring over the Feve's house system on one of my first visits.

When I was being interviewed at Vinyl Fever, I told the owner of the store about Plan 9's rules and asked him if any music was off limits for the house system. He laughed.

"No way, man," he said. "I tell my employees the weirder the better!"

MANY OF THE EMPLOYEES at Vinyl Fever were musicians, artists, DJs, tattoo artists and piercers, or otherwise denizens of the artistic or bohemian demimonde.

A welcome difference between Plan 9 in Charlottesville and the Feve was that among the Feve's many customers were the students at nearby Florida A&M University, a Historically Black College, so the staff at the Feve was not made up solely of white indie kids, and if we weren't Jesse Jackson's Rainbow Coalition it was still the most diverse place I'd ever worked. The staff included a portly African-American song-identifying machine named Will Spraggins (may he rest in peace), whose knowledge of R&B and gospel was vast and impressive, but who could also answer just about any question about rock and roll. Like a lot of first gen hip-hop freaks, the guy listened to everything, an honest-to-God crate digger from birth. I learned a lot from Spraggins. If you've worked in a record store, you've been approached by a customer and asked some variation of the question, "Hey, man, what's that song that goes *boppity boppity doo dah*, lady's singing it, she says something about love or somethin', jeepers creepers and whatnot?" Will would rub his goateed chin, adjust his eyeglasses and say, "Oh, yeah man, butcept it's not a girl, sounds to me like Jodeci, "Forever My Lady," or, "Yeah, man, that's Procul Harum." One day I asked Spraggins if we had any more copies of Prince's Constipation, a scatological reference to his latest release *Emancipation*. Spraggins skipped no beats: "Jack, lemme tell you somethin'. The idea of emancipation is very important to Black people. When white people say ignorant stuff like that, constipation instead of emancipation, it gets me a little steamed up, know what I'm saying? Makes you sound like a dumbass cracker. Show some respect."

WHILE I WAS BACK to my record store clerking ways, my old Palace-Anomoanon bandmates had continued to be engaged in functional, focused lives. Ned had quit after four years of being an adjunct college professor in Birmingham and was now building an impressive portfolio as a staff writer for the local weekly, called *Black & White*. He was also writing Ano-songs and had helped brother Will make his records, *Viva Last Blues* and *Arise, Therefore*. Aram was about to start a physical therapy program and was working at a local hospital with elderly patients, while Jason was working on an organic farm outside of Blacksburg, Virginia. Willie was still in Louisville, running his own house-painting business in addition to playing bass with King Kong (another post-Slint band led by Ethan Buckler) and Satchel's Pawn Shop.

My point of view of the cutting edge of culture at Vinyl Fever allowed me to observe how the true movers and shakers were reacting to Will's output, mainly by buying his products. More interesting, however, was Will's effect on what I'd identified as an emerging, well-defined cultural force. It appeared to me that Will's fans, and by this point there were many of them, weren't cultural lemmings following the next trend, as often happened in pop music, but instead, for the most part, were people who appeared to be more disciplined about what they liked, what they read, what they said. There was a holistic nature to Will's fandom. They liked music, sure, but were also well-read and watched classic movies and made their own beer and knew who their congresspeople were. They were almost exclusively liberal or progressive, both politically and socially, and I was surprised one afternoon when one of my gay friends told me that Will was beloved in the gay community. Will's burgeoning fanbase appeared to be remarkably intelligent and aware. If there wasn't anything cultish about those who chose to follow Will's career, there was still a sense that Will's fans were part of a semi-secret club whose members shared traits with their hero. If you played *Arise, Therefore* to ten people, nine might dislike it, but that one person who enjoyed it would be the most interesting person of the bunch.

What was happening with Will reminded me on a smaller scale of what I'd seen years before at Plan 9, when Dave Matthews' fame began to blossom pretty much the minute he brought the box of recently burned CDs into the store. Unlike Matthews, Will appeared to be carving out a place within the realm of independent music and culture that was utterly unique, and my position at the Feve was a great place to watch his growth.

Will's headlong and stubborn movement through his career was heroic in his utter disdain for doing what was expected. It was as if he could make no wrong decisions. By rewriting the script of how to pursue a career in music, Will was continuing to gain the sort of praise reserved not for mere musicians but genuine *artistes*.

ON NOVEMBER 24, 1996, two days before Chris's twenty-ninth birthday, Will came to play a show in Tallahassee with tour manager Howard Greynolds, plus musicians Colin Gagon and Rick Rizzo. I'd met Colin at the first Lollapalooza show in Providence; he was one of those dark, moody guys on the perimeter smoking cigs before the gig, intimidatingly silent until he wasn't, when I found out he was instead a warm, funny person, another reminder of the vast gulf between subjective perception and objective reality. Howard ran a record label called All City. Rick was in Chicago-based rock band Eleventh Dream Day with then-wife Janet Bean of Freakwater, another Louisvillian whom I ended up meeting when the Anomoanon played a show with her years later.

The small band was touring to support *Arise, Therefore* and were in Tallahassee to play a show at the Cow Haus. Before the show we ate Cuban sandwiches and drank a couple of pitchers of cold beer at Gordo's and caught up. I enjoyed meeting Rick and Howard, and seeing Colin again was great. At the show, I was reminded of how difficult it must be to have people grabbing at you, wanting something from you.

The show in Tallahassee was great. It was the second time I'd seen Will play with a band that was not us, and the second time I'd seen him do something completely different, completely unexpected, and completely perfect.

10

Follow the Flow

IN WINTER OF 1997, Will invited the Anomoanon to be his backing band on a short spring tour of the US. The news arrived during another period when I was struggling to try to *find my purpose* and was therefore another welcome gift. I was still spending my days behind a counter at the Feve, working daily on stories but spending equal amounts of time not working on stories, and I knew it was time to fish or cut bait. About to turn thirty, generally unhappy with my continued struggles to publish (or even write), a long-term goal had snapped into focus: I'd have to make living, and why not make it as a musician? I wasn't a writer, I wasn't a record store clerk, I was a musician chosen by the pagan gods of yore to pound the drums as the shaman danced around the fire. I was reborn. Hope bloomed. The light shone down on me. All that stuff.

In many ways, some of them sad and pathetic, others noble and true, I'd been waiting for this call since the final show of the summer tour of Europe in '94. But you'd probably figured that out already.

ON A GORGEOUS MAY afternoon, we all met in Charleston again, where the tour would begin, set up our gear in Aram and Mclean's living room, and practiced for a few days. It was wonderful being back with the band. I was behind the kit, of course, while Will, Ned, and Aram handled guitar duties. Willie played bass while Jason took his spot at the keyboards. Will decided to just have us play *Lost Blues and Other Songs*, his latest singles collection, all the way through. Instead of trying to copy the songs as recorded, we played around with form and tempo, even arranging a reggae version of our hit "West Palm Beach" and a Jimmy Buffettesque "Gulf Shores" complete with cheesy keyboard percussion played by Jason.

Invited to join us as tour manager was Justin Vogt, a Brown University undergrad we nicknamed the Wrangler, which during the course of the short tour mutated into the entirely ironic Mangler. We'd been trading a paperback copy of Phil Kaufman's memoir *Road Mangler Deluxe*, and though Justin was about as un-Kaufmanesque as one could possibly be, he became Mangler for the rest of the tour, rarely called by his given name. (One of Charlie Manson's pals, Kaufman worked for the Stones for a few years but was most infamously the guy who stole musician and songwriter Gram Parson's dead body, drove it out to Joshua Tree, and burned it.)

Not sure how we convinced the young Mangler to join us. He was a bright-eyed and bushy-tailed youth from Sea Cliff, Long Island, who did not drink too much, did not smoke at all, and whose upright sense of responsibility resulted in his being an excellent tour manager. He showed up at Aram's house with shirt tucked in, hair freshly cut, and toting an enormous suitcase.

Justin is now a successful journalist and the managing editor at *Foreign Affairs* magazine, so obviously whatever damage we wrought on his young mind healed many years ago, and no permanent impairment was done.

The soundtrack to our summer's journey was the triple CD Hits Collection by Prince.

As the tour was being planned, Ned told us that we would stop in Providence to record a few songs that would comprise our first Anomoanon release since the single "Hello My" / "Free Web." It would be a CD-only EP and Will would put it out under his Palace Records umbrella at Drag City, the same arm of DC that had put out our single. This was great news. Will's generosity, his willingness to support the Anomoanon, to help us get jump-started, was huge for us.

Both Ned and I had rediscovered the Mother Goose rhymes but noted as adult readers that they were far darker and more twisted than we'd remembered. Perhaps when we were kids our parents and teachers were just hiding the more disturbing ones from us, the ones about premature death, pet murder, equine torture, and those portraying a generally threatening, unstable, and violent world, which meant most of them, some of which are genuinely disturbing. Ned had put a couple of them to music and the results were unique, strange, and good. It was the first in a long line of musical adaptations of literary sources that Ned would become increasingly interested in over the coming decades, and the first signs were promising.

During practice at Aram's we ran through a few of the Mother Goose songs Ned had arranged, and they sounded great, they really swung. Up-tempo, great chord changes, melodies... the tits! With Will, we also worked up covers of two Everly Brothers' songs, "I'm on My Way Home Again" and "Green River," which both indicated a development in Will's persona, one of sentiment, of looking back, of nostalgia. That we had two brothers, also from Kentucky, whose voices melded in ways not unlike the Everlys, was not lost on any of us.

THE TOUR STARTED IN Charleston in late May, where we played a wobbly first show at a large and impersonal music venue. There's at least one of these places in every city, the kind where the night before us might've been a goateed ska band wearing pork pie hats, the night afterward a country cover band, karaoke the night after that, then David Allan Coe or Eddie Money or Southern Culture on the Skids to bring in the weekend. Budweiser or Corona products on tap, enormous posters of Spuds Mackenzie draped over the walls, huge advertisements for margarita night featuring women with balloony and oil-slick fake breasts barely strapped in by their tiny bikini tops, a boomy and bassy sound system. That sort of place. I have a memory of the house lights remaining on for the show, not many people in the audience. Entirely forgettable.

The next night's show in Savannah took place in a small skeezy club that smelled like a revolting mixture of sour beer and bleach, with an underlying note of rot that hinted at any number of sub-smells: backed-up sewage, vomit, old food.

Our straightforward contract rider asked either for "a hot meal for each musician" or a buyout. This is a common contractual agreement between band and promoter or club owner: the promoter is responsible for either feeding the band members a "hot meal" at the club, or giving the band thirty or forty bucks in cash to go get something to eat before the show. This is called a buyout. At Savannah the promoter said he had some great grub for us, a hot meal, indeed, no buyout necessary.

"You guys hungry?" he asked.

"Sure are," we said.

He snapped his fingers, and a tubby white dude with bad tats, wearing a basketball jersey and a fake gold chain, leaning to one side not unlike Igor in *Young Frankenstein*, appeared from the shadows at the back of the club. He plunked down a tinfoil steam table pan in front of us, and with a strange leer twisting his face, peeled back the lid. Beneath the lid lay a scattering of round nacho chips covered with a cold layer of mucilaginous pump cheese, and besmirched with rubbery discs of canned black olives. It had been in the refrigerator for a while so the pump cheese had a skin on it, slightly darker than the cheese itself.

"We can't eat this," Will said, interrupting Jason and I as we each held a handful of the crap, about to stuff it into our mouths.

"What do you mean?"

Will told the guy that this was a breach of our rider. We required a warm meal. This wasn't warm and was not a meal.

"I'd stick it in the oven," the helper said, "but we ain't got no oven."

The promoter refused our request for a buyout, pointing at the steam tray. Rather than continue to fight, we ended up grabbing sandwiches at a shop around the corner. At the show, I remember lots of blinding white thigh skin and perhaps a few Goth kids, one dressed in garters and a rubber skirt. I wish they'd brought more of their freaky friends. Where were all the southern wackadoos and pleasant eccentrics featured in John Berendt's *Midnight in the Garden of Good and Evil*? Where were the art students at SCAD? Not at our show, that's for sure.

There was some late-night arguing with the owner, who not only had fed us a tray of repugnant chemical cheese and chips but was trying to stiff us out of our guarantee. Poor Mangler had bitten off more than he could chew. Thankfully Ned and Will stepped in to help him with the negotiations, and after a lot of arguing we were able to secure our contracted guarantee. (A guarantee is an amount of money negotiated by a booking agent, in our case Boche Billions, and agreed upon before the band even sets foot on the stage.) Ned said that the club owner's subterranean office stank of piss, and during the argument about money the owner had yelled at the tubby, Igor-esque assistant for using the office as his pissoir. The assistant had shrugged, as if to say, *Yeah, well, the bathroom is all the way up the stairs...*

The next night in Columbia, South Carolina, we played at a brewpub called Hunter-Gatherer. Good name for a brewpub, that. We ate in the dining room of the bar and during supper were served many, too many, perhaps, of the brewery's thick and high-alcohol beers. Before we'd even begun to play, Aram, Will, and I were arguing across the table about what a mentor was.

"Why would you even admit that you have a mentor?" I slurred. "That's pathetic."

"A mentor doesn't even have to know he's a mentor," Aram said. Will agreed.

"But isn't a mentor," I said, angry they were ganging up on me, "by definition, someone who is aware that you're kissing their ass, and who probably enjoys it?"

Aram and Will's point was that Merle Haggard could be your mentor, or Oprah Winfrey or Frederick Douglass, Steve Jobs, Kareem Abdul-Jabbar, or the Dalai Lama.

I didn't agree, and that night I gave no quarter, and we were yelling at one another like high school debaters even as we took the stage.

Onstage, loopy and fired up from our argument, Will held up a mug of the thick, unfiltered beer and announced to the audience, "Thanks for the *soup!*"

OUR FRIEND BOBBY ARELLANO joined us onstage in Cambridge, Massachusetts. This information comes from Leo Meijer's encyclopedic Royal Stable web page, the go-to source for all things Palace and which has helped tremendously during the course of writing this narrative. I wonder why Bob didn't join us the following night in Providence where he lived? Maybe he did. Bob was one of Will's oldest friends from his days at Brown, a recurring and fundamental part of the Palace/Oldham/

Bonnie Billy continuum, who has already appeared, and who will appear again, on these pages. You might recall that it was Bob with the madman's smile who once studied with Coover at Brown, establishing hypertext as a new literary genre, and who'd since published an online novel called *Sunshine '69*. Nowadays, Bob's an English prof and a writer with a few great books under his belt, all of which are available for purchase, living out in Oregon with his better half Jodie Jean and two strapping lads. I remember he sang three songs in Spanish that night, but it's Leo's page that reminds me those songs were "West Palm Beach," "Valle de Vinales," and "Rancho Grande."

After the show we drove back to Providence where we were staying with Bob, who was house-sitting for a Brown professor at a nice if slightly dishabille house outside of town. After arriving home from Cambridge at four in the morning, I was crawling onto a couch to collapse in sleep when I was prodded by a cold nose. I opened my eyes to find that Bob's rescue greyhound Argo was staring at me intently about four inches away from my face. The dog's default mode was a neurotic skittishness and it was weird to find him so focused and calm and intense.

"What's up, Argo?" I muttered.

His response might as well have been, "What's up is that you're lying on my couch."

He didn't even wait for me to scoot over before leaping up onto the couch and settling his bony shanks against mine. I tried to make space for Argo, but at some point during the night just gave up and rolled down onto the floor, where I slept fitfully until morning.

THE FOLLOWING DAY, WE played badminton in the sunny front yard of the professor's house, and after a few heated matches we boarded the van and headed into town, where we went to a classroom on Brown's campus that had been fitted out as a casual studio. We'd been practicing and playing the Mother Goose songs all tour so after setting up our instruments in a single room and allowing the engineer to place a few mics, we began to record. The session was very efficient, and I'm not sure we did more than two takes of any song.

Another pattern was established that stuck with the Anomoanon for the remainder of our "career": every record the Anomoanon ever made was done under tight time constraints, so every song we ever recorded became a document not of our expertise in making records but instead aural snapshots of particular times in our lives when we could not stop moving to overthink. It was "first thought, best thought" all the way, not because that's what we wanted, exactly, but because that's how it had to be.

In any case, after two hours at most, we'd completed tracking the songs that would comprise what I thought would be our first EP.

THE RECORDING, PRODUCTION, AND release of the EP would turn into a very early indication of a fundamental challenge facing every cooperative project. The Anomoanon prided ourselves on being a working band without a central leader, but a band without a central leader is not, by nature, a very efficient body. Things are too loosy-goosy, too hippy-dippy, without someone stepping up and taking control of the direction a group is headed. Obviously, if the Anomoanon had a leader, it would be Ned.

And over the course of the development of the *Mother Goose* release, it became clear that the EP was in fact going to be an LP with the vast majority of songs being stuff Ned had already recorded by himself in Birmingham, often accompanied by Jennie. The other songs Ned had written and arranged were great, and Jennie's contributions were essential to the record's greatness. If our contributions as a band would be a smaller part of the release than I'd originally imagined, it didn't matter much. This short recording session in Providence and the ensuing record served as an early lesson to us that adaptation and change were part of life, and if we wanted our band to last, we'd all have to get used to almost constant change.

AFTER PROVIDENCE, WE WENT to New York City to play a show at Tramp's, where we met musicians Alan Licht and Loren MazzaCane Connors, who were opening the show. At the time I had no idea how important Alan was, or would become, in the world in which I would soon find myself increasingly interested, that of experimental noise and improvised music, most of it coming out of downtown New York. In the early aughts, I'd appreciate his subjective take on the music of the eighties in his great book *An Emotional Memoir of Martha Quinn*, published by Drag City, and I always enjoyed reading the pieces he'd get published in *The Wire* and other magazines. Much later Will would choose Alan as the sole interviewer in charge of constructing the book *Will Oldham on Bonnie Prince Billy*.

Before the set, Alan invited us to go grab a drink with him and Loren, guitarist and soundscapist extraordinaire. I'd been a fan of Loren's for a few years and if I wasn't starstruck, I was still interested to meet the man. I'd also become a fan of Alan's bands Run-On and Love Child, as Will had brought along CD copies of each and we'd been listening to them in the van. I was impressed that Alan had played with a recent version of Love, the legendary LA rock band, but was too intimidated to ask how he'd gotten along with Arthur Lee, Love's unstable genius.

Alan and Loren were two intense New York intellectuals, hip deep in the fascinating world of improvised music, brainy, unforgiving, terrifyingly intelligent, and very much smarter than I was, or so I thought as we waited for Connors. Maybe we'd go to a coffee shop to a poetry reading, or an art gallery, or an underground bar specializing in absinthe.

Then Alan mentioned that Loren wanted to go to a strip club.

I saw a flash of panic blaze across Mangler's innocent and stubble-free face.

"Really? A strip club?" Mangler said. "There aren't other places we could go to hang out?"

"It's okay," Alan said. "We can walk to it. It's right around the corner."

"So, it's a strip club we're going to, is it?" Mangler said. "Fine." Shrug. "Okay by me. First time for everything, as they say. Are they going to be totally naked, or just...?"

Presently Connors showed up, looking not unlike Leonard Cohen's younger brother, dressed in rumpled tweed and dress pants, and within minutes, after a short walk, we were seated in a club and bathed in blue light as pneumatic young women prowled around us in the nearly nude. Will bought Mangler a lap dance, which Connors, a connoisseur, later pronounced "a good one."

AFTER A BLISTERINGLY GREAT Tramps show we were supposed to stay at Mangler's aunt's empty Midtown apartment. She'd already moved but the apartment hadn't been sold, so it would be ours for the night. Will decided to head down to Philly a night early, so he bought himself a train ticket to Philadelphia. We'd meet him at the club the following day for load-in.

The rest of us arrived at Mangler's aunt's apartment to find that it was truly empty: there was no furniture in the entire place, no rugs, no art on the walls, nothing except for two spindly houseplants positioned near the windows. We were hungry and it was late, and we were able to find an all-night burger joint right around the corner, which was packed even though it was after 2:00 a.m. We each ordered absurdly large burgers and fries, probably ordered beers, then wolfed down our salty burgers and limped back to the apartment, where we all proceeded to collapse on her parquet floors, no blankets, no pillows, no nothing.

I awoke early in the morning. The sun was beating in through the drapeless windows like a fist, right in to my greasy and sleep- and burger-swollen face. The air conditioning in the apartment had been turned off so we were enveloped in a moldy, wet fug. I did not feel too well, and knew that if I did not drink water immediately I might die. There, not far from my hand, as if placed there by a benign spirit, was a gallon jug filled with water, so I flicked off the cap and drank deeply, three, four, five enormous glugs, then six and seven for good measure. It was only after I'd drunk the water, replaced the cap, and put the jug back on the ground that I noted the liquid in the jug was bluish, not Kool-Aid blue but close. I wondered what might've caused the water's sickly hue. I peered around the barren room. Not far from me on the floor sat a container of Miracle-Gro, also blue, and not far from that the dreary-looking houseplants. I'd just consumed their breakfast.

On the night of June 7, 1997, we met up with Will at Nick's in Old City Philly, set up our gear and played a fine set. Afterward, we packed the van and began a walk around the neighborhood looking for some late-night chow. The vibe on the streets was murderous. Men strode past us with hate in their eyes. Drunks stumbled sullenly in the shadows. A few fistfights broke out, cars peeled out and screeched past, raised voices could be heard echoing down streets and alleyways. The sound of bottles breaking punctuated the warm night. We finally ended up in a late-night cheese-steakery and consumed our sandwiches in silence.

Brotherly love? Nope. Medieval-seeming spite and murderousness? Yes. Any Philadelphian reading this might already know what's coming, having seen the date above. Or not, depending on whether or not said Philadelphian follows sports. Specifically, ice hockey.

At the cheesesteak place a young black guy eating across from us finally mentioned what was up. The Philadelphia Flyers had been down three games to nothing in the Stanley Cup finals to the Detroit Red Wings, and that night, probably not long before our show ended, they'd lost the final deciding game.

THE DAY AFTER NICK'S we pulled into tiny Rehoboth Beach, Delaware, and I wondered why on earth Boche Billions had booked us a show in a quaint little boardwalk beach town complete with french fry stands and saltwater taffy emporiums. There was a large gazebo next to the boardwalk where a German brass band played oompa loompa music as a crowd full of geezers watched from their electric scooters and huffed from their oxygen tanks. Will parked the van and we went down to the beach for an afternoon swim in the Atlantic, arriving afterward at the club still wet with sand in our bathing suits.

Dogfish Head was a modest little gastro-pub, and soon after arriving for load-in we were served plates of deliciously fresh, nearly raw, tuna, and the beer, especially as compared to the soup we drank in Columbia, was fantastic. Were we drinking a Belgian-style Saison, perhaps the first one I'd tasted, in the proper tulip glass? The staff was smart, well-trained, and I seem to recall an attractive young female barkeep offering to keep our beers full. Finally, there was owner Sam Calagione, the man who was responsible for our welcome and who was shuttling out more plates of fresh tuna from the kitchen.

While we were eating our tuna and enjoying our beers, Boston's first record came on the house system. Every one of us began smiling as the music filled the room. I'd seen a Boston concert in sixth grade at the Richmond Coliseum. Pre-Van

Halen Sammy Hagar had opened the show. His hits "Bad Motor Scooter" and "Three Lock Box" were on the radio at the time, neither of which I liked, and I spent at least a portion of Hagar's set watching him scamper around hyperactively in his yoga tights and squealing like a stuck pig while plugging my ears with my fingers. He was terrible.

Boston? Magical.

In the upstairs room at Dogfish, afternoon light filtered in through the windows, beers and plates of tuna on the table in front of us, Tom Scholz's swelling, multi-tracked solos floated above his crunchy but smooth riffs, taking me back to that distant day in sixth grade, where I may well have smelled pot for the first time. Mr. Leedes, a law professor at, a law professor at the University of Richmond's T. C. Williams School of Law, and the father of my friend and elementary school bandmate John, had taken us. Mr. Leedes smoked a pipe and spent much of the show turning away people who assumed he had the bowl crammed with Maui Wowie instead of Borkum Riff.

THE FINAL SHOW OF the tour took place at the Route 1 South Festival in Richmond, which was held at the Biograph Theater. In the seventies and eighties, the Biograph was Richmond's sole art movie house, and legendary in my development as a fan of movies. My straight-laced attorney father had taken attendees of my thirteenth birthday party to the Biograph for a midnight showing of the *Rocky Horror Picture Show* in 1980, and in high school my attempts to seduce my then-girlfriend were set back by making her sit through *Liquid Sky*, whose psychosexual overtones really freaked her out and offended her chaste Virginia lass's sensibilities.

"I'm never going to have sex in my life," she cried in the car on the way home.

My heart sank.

Mom and Dad were there at the show at the Biograph, Aram and Jason's parents as well. If it hasn't yet been made clear, every parent of every member of the band had been supportive of our dreams since we were kids. It was my parents' record collection that first turned me on to rock and roll in the first place, and my mom would love cooking huge spreads for the band members whenever we'd roll through Richmond in the coming years. If my folks hated my being a professional musician (they didn't), they had no one to blame but themselves.

The final show of our first tour with Will since 1994 should've been triumphant, but the show was flat, uninteresting, uninspired. The tour had been great, I thought, and it was more than a little disappointing that this final show, with Stith and Carneal parents in attendance, was so dull. I never figured out why some nights were better than others.

WE WENT WEST, TO visit Joe and Joanne in Louisville. We were sitting in the Oldhams' living room visiting with Joe's mother, the boys' grandmother, whom the family called Bep. Will had just received a copy of the split 7" he was about to release with Rising Shotgun, which featured vocals from Brett Ralph, the former singer of Louisville legends Malignant Growth and Fading Out. The music on the split 7" was played by legendary former Slinters David Pajo and Todd Brashear, who were sitting there with us. We'd met these guys a few times over the years, and Todd had just founded his movie rental place Wild and Wooly Video in Louisville. Pajo's solo project Papa M was definitely gaining traction.

Will asked Bep if she'd like to hear the new record.

"Of course," she said in her cultured southern accent. "Whyever not?"

Bep sat on the couch in a neat sweater and skirt, her back straight and knees together, hands on knees, as Will put the record on the Oldham family stereo.

As we sat there with Bep, Brett's version of David Allan Coe's "Spotlight" began. Bep bent her ear toward the speaker, a thoughtful look on her face. The tempo of the song through the first verse was slow and plodding, reminiscent of the first Palace Brothers record. Then Brett began singing Coe's hokey lyrics in a deep, adenoidal voice, which would every so often skew out of key. *"Somebody shoot out that spotlight / Spotlights ain't nothin' but jive…"* Bep began to smile a little bit, but then I noted that it may not have been a smile, but instead a somewhat confused frown. After the verse, the tempo doubled, then quadrupled as the musicians carried Brett on their shoulders into the rousing chorus, accompanied by Will and Todd Brashear's high harmonies:

"Roll me a smoke, Give me some coke…"

Mrs. Oldham sat stock still, a patient smile on her face.

"How did you like it, Bep?" Will asked when the record was finished.

"Well," she said. "It's interesting. I don't think it's very good. It sounds more like a comedy piece. Like he's trying to be funny."

"Then you do like it," Will prodded.

"Hmmm. I didn't say that."

"You just said it was funny," Will said, "and if it makes you laugh, then you're enjoying it and that means it's good!"

"Well…"

"Come on, Bep! You just told me you laughed. Everyone loves to laugh, right?"

Bep smiled.

"And if it makes you laugh," Will continued, "then it's good!"

"I suppose you're right," she said.

It clearly wasn't the first time Bep had had one of her grandsons giving her a good-humored hard time. I found it quite sweet. Bep could be in our Allmans family, too, if she wanted.

11

Hello, What's This?

ONE AFTERNOON IN THE summer of 1997 soon after returning from the tour, Chris and I went to the local cineplex to watch John Woo's *Face/Off*, starring Nic Cage and John Travolta. My ego had been reinflated by the success of the tour and our bank account was flush with a thousand or so bucks from the tour's receipts. All was well with the world. Not just well, but damn near close to perfect, and, as Jerry once croaked, "When life looks like easy street…"

During the movie we felt the subaudible tremors of a thunderstorm moving above us, and soon the movie flickered and went out. We sat in the darkened theater for a few minutes eating our popcorn, and soon the movie resumed. It wasn't the first time we'd sat in a theater in Tallahassee darkened by a subtropical thunderstorm and it wouldn't be the last (the same thing happened when we watched *Titanic*, which we both hated). After the movie, which included lots of disturbing graphic surgical shots of Cage and Travolta having one another's faces removed and then sewn back onto one another's skulls, we exited the theater into a psychedelically gorgeous post-storm sky, the breeze fresh, deep pools of water spreading across the parking lot where the pink and purple phantasms spinning in the sky above were reflected.

The world felt different, somehow.

There was a Publix grocery nearby so we stopped to get some grub for the evening, giant tiger prawns, I remember. As we were walking down one aisle after having chosen our prawns Chris said, "Yeah, I know I'm not pregnant, it's allergies, but I'm going to get this pregnancy test. I haven't been feeling right lately, I'm 100 percent sure I'm not pregnant, but, well..."

At the checkout counter with our prawns and pregnancy test I slapped my pockets and realized my wallet was gone. Panicked, I fled back to the movie theater. I asked to be let into the theater where the next showing of *Face/Off* was playing, went directly to where Chris and I were sitting, now occupied by an older man and a very young woman, who I took to be his granddaughter. I explained what I was doing and got on my knees at the girl's lap, reached under her where I found my wallet on the floor.

It was a good sign: all was fine. No need to panic. Of course my wife wasn't pregnant!

Back at the Publix, Chris stood there waiting for me with our prawns and pregnancy test.

Once at home, she took the test in the bathroom, then handed the thing to me.

"I can't look," she said.

"Okay, well, what do I do?"

"If you see a plus sign, well, I think that means I'm pregnant."

A plus sign appeared.

"According to this thing, you're pregnant."

We cooked then put our mouths on the prawns, masticated them and swallowed, but it was not eating. Immediately afterward, it may have been 8:00 p.m., we lay down in our bed and curled up, backs to one another. I was not sleeping but instead passed into a natural protective state akin to shock.

I was making six dollars an hour at a record store, we were struggling to pay our $450-per-month rent, my wife was in the second year of a PhD program, we'd been married barely over a year, and she was pregnant.

Was I worried? Nope. After getting through the initial shock, having a kid seemed to Chris and me like another adventure, another means of keeping our lives exciting and not static. There, in my consciousness, were those healthy-looking hippies on the gatefold of the Allmans' record, with the babies and little kids playing nearby. That dream, that vision, of an extended family built on fellowship and art, on the making of music together, had to include kids, and Chris and me were the first to take the plunge.

Two months later, good news from Birmingham: Jennie was pregnant as well.

BACK IN TALLY-TOWN AFTER the tour, with a freshly pregnant wife, life took a rather pointed turn. The juvenile homosocial camaraderie of the road was rudely replaced by the jolting realization that I was supposedly a functioning adult who would soon be a father. I'd just turned thirty. I picked up a second job teaching English at Tallahassee Community College. I taught two sections of freshman composition and found that I was pretty good at connecting with the students in my attempt to illuminate some fundamental principles about the written word. What those fundamental principles were is still a bit confusing to me, but the students didn't know that, and I learned a fundamental lesson of teaching: projecting confidence and speaking with a loud voice covers many intellectual weaknesses. As Steve Martin wrote much later in his memoir *Born Standing Up*, teaching was just another form of show business. If I wasn't a natural performer onstage—I wasn't—then perhaps I felt more comfortable performing for a bunch of bored undergrads.

Also, with a baby on the way and still living on top of Ms. Screen Door Voice with the knuckle tats, invaded every fifteen minutes by the steady stream of cigarette smoke leaking under our doors directly from her nostrils, not to mention the regular bolting of giant roaches across our ceilings and walls or the family of opossums that had taken up residence in our attic, Chris and I decided to leave the shotgun shack for a larger shack across town. It was a house with one more bedroom and a nice yard. It was also a hundred dollars more expensive per month.

In an attempt to make up that extra hundred dollars we'd need, I picked up yet another job as an editor/proofreader at a local company that published municipal legal codes. The CEO was a former Marine who demanded his staff clock in at 6:30 every morning, and clock in is what we did: each employee had a card that we'd have to put into a machine not unlike the one on the beginning montage of the Flintstones, press a button on the machine from which came an annoying buzz and loud clack as the time that signaled the start of our work day was stamped onto the card. If you clocked in at 6:32, your desk would be visited later by the manager, who'd remind you that the day started at 6:30 and not 6:32. The entire work day, minus a single half hour for lunch, was spent reading through legal codes and searching for typographical errors. Forty hours of my week were therefore spent reading things like this:

Sec. 2-50—Decorum-Required. (a) While the council is in session, the members shall preserve order and decorum, and a member shall neither, by conversation or otherwise, delay or disrupt the proceedings or the peace of the council nor interrupt any member while speaking or refuse to obey the orders of the council or its presiding officer, except as otherwise herein provided. (b) Members of the public shall not

willfully disrupt the meeting or act in a manner that actually impairs
the orderly conduct of the meeting. For the purposes of this code,
"willfully disrupt" includes, but is not limited to, continuing to do any
of the following after being warned by the Mayor that continuing to
do so will be a violation of law: a. Addressing the Mayor and City
Council without first being recognized. b. Persisting in addressing a
subject or subjects, other than that before the Mayor and City Council.
c. Repetitiously addressing the same subject.

EXACTLY. MY HUNCH IS that most readers made it through a sentence or two before skipping to these words. If the above dissuades you from attending law school, then perhaps I've done you a favor.

We all sat at desks in a loose circle. My coworkers, all of them nearly translucent white people with whitish hair, light-colored eyeballs, doughy, strange-looking bodies, and poor posture, would, in the utter silence of the office, suddenly put their pencils down and say things like, "Wow. I was just thinking. I started this job because I thought it would be a great job to have while I wrote novels. That was thirty-two years ago." The others would nod their heads and mutter, "Yeah, I wanted to be a poet. And here I am, twenty-three years later..." The speaker would pick her pencil up and go back to proofreading codes. I lasted maybe two months.

So, I hustled for yet another job: writing copy for an ad agency whose biggest client made gigantic sewage processing machines. My boss at the agency looked like Ricky Gervais as David Brent, but unlike Brent, my boss wore a seventies moustache and had puffy, blow-dried hair.

The sewage processing machines were called "belt filter presses" and one of the company's selling points was that their BFPs created lighter "cake," which was nothing more than de-watered "floc," short for flocculant. Flocculant was the word they used to describe the millions of gallons of waste that would, by design, flow across the porous belts of the abovementioned BFPs, and would then be squeezed together, thereby removing the liquid portion of the waste and leaving the "solids" lying there on the belt. The solids, a.k.a. the cake, would then have to be trucked elsewhere. So, our company wanted us to emphasize the angle that our client's particular BFPs squeezed more liquid out of the floc, thereby making lighter cake, thereby reducing trucking costs.

One morning we had a conference call with the manufacturers of the BFPs. Since I was helping write the copy, my boss let me sit in on the call. Imagine a disembodied voice coming from a speakerphone, a straight-faced David Brent lookalike staring at said speakerphone, and me, sitting there next to him, barely able to contain my glee:

"Well, we've done some tests and we get maximum throughput for the floc, better than our competitors," the company rep begins.

"So your floc, so you can not only get the lightest cake, but your floc moves more quickly through the press…" my boss responds.

"Exactly. Exactly. We've designed them for maximum throughput, even including an enzyme bath…"

"An enzyme bath?"

"Yeah, yeah, really exciting stuff. A tank full of enzyme polymers that not only make the floc *softer* but actually chemically separates water molecules from the more solid flocculant, so—"

"Great. Great stuff. Enzymes. Soft floc. Got a lot to work with here."

"And the enzyme polymer is reusable."

"Reusable? Well, slam dunk. Awesome. So there's that, the environmental angle…"

"Right, definitely, and with the light cake, because we've pressed so much liquid out of the floc, with that light cake your muni trucks use less gas, less pollution, reduced carbon footprint, all that good stuff."

Me, so far silent:

"So what exactly does the cake look like, smell like? Can you still, you know, sense that it was not too long in the past, you know…"

My boss looks at me, his mouth underneath his ridiculous 'stache creased in annoyance. Speaker phone says:

"Ummm. Good question. Actually, I see your point. It's really not unlike, well, cake, in fact. A dryish brick of very dark brown sugar, say, a chunk of chocolate…let's just say the word cake is apt…"

IN MARCH, OUR BOY was born. We named him Tabb after the farmer who ran my grandparents' farm from the early 1940s until the late seventies, when the farm was sold. The first time in my life I was ever truly frightened, genuinely scared down to my very core, was placing the tiny little bundle into the baby seat in the back of our ramshackle Jeep with completely bald tires, buckling him in and pulling out of the parking lot into the mean streets of Tallahassee. It was as if I'd never driven before.

Chris had a short break from school, our parents all came down to visit, so really the first month was gravy. Having a baby, I thought, couldn't be more natural! It was no more difficult than having a goldfish. For one, he couldn't escape the confines of his Snugli or his bouncy chair, and also like a goldfish, he offered us hours of entertainment, when we'd just sit and watch his bright eyes flash as he gummed his tiny fingers and learned to take in the world surrounding him. Sure, he cried some. And yes, the first week he was home we each averaged about an hour's sleep per night and spent our days stumbling through that strange, amphetamine blur of the perpetually sleep-deprived. Changing a diaper that appeared to have been sprayed by a pint of yellow mustard, and which smelled like nothing I'd ever smelled before? It took some getting used to. But we did get used to it, and easily. We loved being parents.

For me, being married and having a baby were both expansive and awesome experiences. Having a steady, hard-working rock like Chris holding down the fort allowed me to pursue being a writer and a musician with more confidence. It's no exaggeration to say that having Tabb made life much more interesting and livable. My goals were no longer entirely selfish, and I was forced to think in broader terms. Thinking outside of myself forced me to act on someone else's needs and not just my own.

There was also the far more daunting recognition that Chris and I were now responsible for the life of another creature who was capable of communicating its needs with us, unlike a goldfish. Also unlike a goldfish, it sort of looked like me. It looked sort of like Chris. My son's birth was the first time I recognized I was dying as fast as he was growing. A clock began ticking. Every time I left the house, I recognized that I was leaving something precious behind me, something unprotected, and overnight the home, that domestic structure, became a very powerful metaphor, when in the past it had just been a house. No longer a structure designed to store my records and books and my nuptial bed, it was now representative, a symbol of my desire for something long-term, namely a safe and happy life.

By summer, Ned and Jennie's daughter had also been born. They named her Adela. Jennie was still in the thick of medical school, while Ned was writing stories interesting and mundane for *Black & White*.

12

Love Them All

AROUND THE SAME TIME the lad was born, in the spring of 1998, Will came up with the idea to establish Palace Records as independent from Drag City, at least temporarily, and to put out a Will Oldham 7" without Drag City's support. We decided to establish a Palace Records satellite operation at our new house in Tallahassee. I would run it, more or less, under Will's guidance.

It was also agreed that Palace Records would be the home of another Anomoanon release, so Ned organized a recording session at Paul Oldham's new Rove Studio in Shelbyville, Kentucky. Paul had all but finished his degree at Indiana and set up shop at the Oldham family farm; with Will's help he'd purchased some gear, some mics and computers and mixers and such.

I was thrilled to be asked to lead this Palace Records project. My excitement wasn't about money, though anything would've helped our state of relative poverty, but instead a continuation of my utopian, DIY vision represented by the photo from the Allman's LP. As far as jobs went, I'd rather be doing something cooperative, creative, and constructive than writing about sewage processing machines, for example, and running Palace Records fit the bill. (I kept my writing and teaching jobs, FYI, just in case, but quit the record store.) That I didn't know what I was doing didn't matter much, suffused as I was with beginner's mind. Will's friend Howard Greynolds, who'd been with him during Will's most recent stop in Tallahassee, and who ran the label called All City, was an enormous help. With the establishment of a standalone Palace Records, our artistic family was growing more enclosed. Not only would we would write the music, play it, and record it, but we'd also make the cover art ourselves or choose cover art made by other members of the family, like Dianne, Joe, and Joanne. Finally, we'd get the records pressed and the CDs burned ourselves, we'd get the covers printed and then we'd sell them to distributors, and share the profits, all within this closed circle.

In May of '98, I left Chris in charge of the two-month-old lad and headed up to Shelbyville, where the Anomoanon tracked a few songs. It was hard leaving Chris and Tabb behind in our tidy and welcoming domestic nest and to reenter the hard, male world of the band. I was a newly sensitive dad who could squat in the fields surrounding Paul's farm and watch a honey bee clumsily bouncing against a clover flower and feel the sudden tearing up of my eyeballs while behind me hooted Willie and Paul because Ned had just farted on Aram as he napped.

Paul's studio at the farm in Shelbyville was a special place. The farmhouse itself was well over a hundred years old, a simple, modest frame structure with original panes of slightly imperfect glass with a wide front porch. It had been in the family since the 1970s, and sat on a hundred plus acres in Shelbyville, about forty-five minutes outside of Louisville. Surrounding the house were fields of soybeans and tobacco. While taking a break from recording, one might find themselves riding the farm's four-wheeler ATV through lush crops of enormous green tobacco plants. Later, depending on the season, you might see the same tobacco you'd ridden through last summer hanging in the ancient drying shed just steps from the back door of the farmhouse. There were two man-made ponds that had supposedly been swimmable at some point, but they were never usable when we were there, and instead both were filled with electric orange-green muck.

Paul would move the mixing board of the studio around, but the recording rooms always occupied the front rooms in the house. The ceilings were tall. The hallway and stairwell were sometimes used for natural reverb. Outside at night we'd sit on the front porch and drink beer between takes while inside Paul moved mics. Crickets were loud, and the night was filled with calls of night birds, night frogs, unidentifiable night cries floating over from the invisible fields like the voices of ghosts. In the summer heat lightning flashed in the distance. In the winter the stars in the sky sparkled brightly in the clear black night. The house was big enough that everyone had their own bed.

The house was certainly haunted by benign spirits, and that we were recording in a farmhouse among family and friends and not some antiseptic studio with someone we'd never met gave the proceedings the noble air of a familial ritual. We were ruralists, in many ways, comfortable sitting around campfires, unshowered, wearing moth-eaten flannels and flip-flops, tens of miles away from clubs or music halls or restaurants. It was a family, and because Ned and I were now fathers of young children, our efforts to remain enclosed gave those early dreams of mine about the fusion of domestic and artistic life a new and fresh poignance. Ned had written a song for *Summer Never Ends* called "The Wanderer," and though it was written before Tabb and Addie were born, my assumption is that Ned had written it after Chris and Jennie had both become pregnant, in the mind of the soon-to-be father. I listened to the lyrics and imagined the poor soul Ned had created, doomed to wander outside the warmth of a familial circle, one who'd been cast out of his family but damned by the acute self-awareness of what he'd lost, like the narrator of Samuel Taylor Coleridge's *Rime of the Ancient Mariner*, a "grey beard loon" who is scarred but smarter:

I'm a wanderer
So I may not be fit to advise you
In the summertime
I go north and in winter go south
I have no family nor any friends
So well may you wonder
How I can say what I'm about to
Honor your father
Listen to your mother
Help your brother
Care for your sister
And your grandma, grandpa, uncles, aunts, and cousins
Love them all;
Husband, wife, daughter, and son.

WILL HAD RECORDED A couple of songs with Eric Bates at Bates Brothers Studio in Hueytown, Alabama, and soon sent me the DAT tapes along with a neat folder of art. The songs were called "One with the Birds" and "Southside of the World." This was the first real project we'd tackle as a fledgling record company, and naturally I was ready to begin learning.

Upon receiving the DAT and the art I called Will to confirm I'd gotten it. On the title card of the art was written Bonnie "Princ" [sic] Billy, the first time I'd seen or heard of that new moniker.

"And, Will, I'm sure you know, but there's a misspelling."

"Numbers typed it up and forgot to put the 'e' on the end," Will said. "Then we decided we liked it."

Later in the summer, the Anomoanon met again at Ned's house in Birmingham, where we set up a makeshift recording studio in his living room and recorded a few more songs. We listened to a lot of Miles Davis's *On the Corner* and ate a lot of bun and pho from the local Vietnamese place. The songs we recorded in Birmingham had a wonderful room sound, and to this day the song "Summer Never Ends" sounds as good as anything we ever recorded. Even though we'd borrowed some expensive mics and miced each of my drums carefully, one microphone per drum, we ended up scrapping most of those drum tracks and instead used the tracks we got from the two simple mics we'd hung over the drum kit, good old Shure SM57s.

By the end of the two recording sessions, one at Rove, the other at Ned's place in Birmingham, the Anomoanon had ten or eleven songs in the can, seven of which would end up comprising our EP release *Summer Never Ends*.

I loved every song we recorded and enjoyed playing them. These were rock songs the likes of which were just not being written that much at the time: straight ahead, melody-oriented, traditionally structured rock songs with thoughtful lyrics recorded without studio artifice. Our fundamental skill base of traditional folk and rock served Ned's songs well. Listening to the record, I realized we had more in common with Tom Petty and the Heartbreakers than we did with Pavement, and that suited us just fine.

Paul had learned well at Indiana U and was a confident engineer. He followed Steve Albini's example, which meant he preferred to be the technician whose expertise allowed the recording process to run smoothly rather than being the overlord producer imprinting his tastes on every sound the band produced. It was rare to see Paul befuddled by anything and equally rare to hear him express anything remotely like a subjective opinion. If pressed, Paul might make a suggestion or two, and they were always good ones. Paul earned our trust, but if there were any mistakes on the record, they were ours, and not Paul's. The studio at Rove was not a place for endless experiments but instead a relatively sober (haha!) place wherein much work was done.

There were hiccups. The vocals on an early DAT copy of our Rove session sounded "harsh" and "cyber" according to Ned and would have to be remixed. The email he sent to me in Tallahassee to relay this news was entitled URGENT URGENT, which indicated, if nothing else, how seriously we were taking our next foray into the marketplace.

Aram agreed to learn how to do the art for the album and CD covers and booklets, and after hours of teaching himself how to use Photoshop, he became a skilled graphic artist. Ned chose the front and back cover photos of Paul and Ned from a trip to Greece that Jennie had taken at some point (that's a naked Ned underwater on the back of *SNE*, for anyone who's interested, his extraordinarily white butt shining from beneath the water's surface like a submerged moon), and Aram said he'd ask an artist friend of his in Charleston to do some drawings for the lyric sheet inside the record, which would also appear in the CD booklet.

Alas, when we saw the proofs a few weeks later we realized that Aram's friend's drawings were hilariously bad, looking like something made by an elementary schooler, but by that point it was too late. And I remain disappointed that we totally forgot to credit Jason for playing a mournful and out-of-tune trumpet during the solo verse of the song "Summer Never Ends."

These early lessons were essential. We were becoming more efficient as we learned what worked best. The only way to do this is to make mistakes, to have beginner's mind.

I WAS RESPONSIBLE FOR getting these two releases made, Will's "Birds" 7" and the Anomoanon's (remember: phenomenon) *Summer Never Ends*. The local computer tech I found to make the film transfers that we'd send to the printer who'd make the covers, an older dude with a perfectly round gut and dandruffy beard, asked me if we could make the covers for the "Princ" single four color instead of six, which would mean knocking out a color or two on the original art. We'd save some money, he said, maybe even a lot. I called Will, Will said fine, so the guy made his films. They looked good to me, I cut him a check, sent the films off to California and a few weeks later the proofs came back from the printer. Again, they looked good to me so I okayed the printing of 4,000 jackets.

I listened to the test pressing from Erika Records, the pressing plant, and heard that there were no pops or ticks or screwups in the pressing, so I okayed that as well.

Another few weeks later and huge boxes were plopped down on my porch by the FedEx man, whom I'd get to know quite well in the coming months. I peeled the first one open and pulled out a copy of Will's brand-new record. The red on Will's face in the picture was super-saturated. I overnighted Will a few copies and the next afternoon my home phone rang. The conversation may have gone something like this:

"So I got the records," Will may have said.

"Great! Hey, that's, this is exciting, isn't it?"

"Numbers and I think the cover looks odd. My face is… really red."

"Yes. I noticed that. Well."

"You approved the covers, right? I mean, you had to sign off on these?"

"Yeah, I did. But they looked way different, you weren't quite so sunburnt. This is a printing error. I mean, the original art looked totally different—"

"I wonder if we should ask for our money back and scrap the release."

I braced myself for a hellstorm of fury. Bonnie Billy was about to disappear, and instead the Palace King would return.

The old Will sure as shit would want his money back. The old Will would never accept anything but his version of perfection.

"It's alright," Will sighed. "I kind of like it."

And that was that. We sold out the records in no time and put in another order for a few more thousand vinyl records. We sold out of those as well.

ALSO, IN THE SUMMER of '98, Will sent me another DAT and folder of art for what would be his next full length. He'd recorded these new songs in Shelbyville with Paul, his old Brown University friends Bob Arellano and Colin Gagon, and the drummer in Paul's great band Speed to Roam, Peter Townsend. The great news was that the art was all black and white so the production of the sleeves would presumably be easier and cheaper than for the single done by the Bonnie Prince. I opened the envelope to see a gorgeous drawing by Joanne Oldham of an Inuit-style skull that evoked the Misfits' logo, a color photograph of a smiling and mustachioed Will taken by Joe, and another drawing by Will's friend, artist Sammy Harkham, of a larger figure holding the hand of a smaller figure, presumably a child. Additionally, there were a bunch of great drawings also by Sammy already printed on sheets containing Will's typed lyrics, which would comprise the booklet included in the CD.

Across the top of Joanne's leering skull was printed in simple lowercase font the title of the record:

i see a darkness.

No longer "Princ," the record was credited, also in lowercase, to bonnie "prince" billy.

I followed much the same procedure as before, having learned my lesson from the misprinted "One with the Birds" single jackets, so I was extra-cautious this go 'round.

This time however the first run of LP and CD covers were too dark, especially on Sammy's drawing for the back cover, so if you bought a CD or LP of *I See a Darkness* early on, well, chances are 1) that it once sat in my living room in Tallahassee and may have been slobbered on by my toddler, and 2) if you compare it to another newer copy and see that your cover is substantially darker than the newer, well, you, my friend, own an original first-run of *ISAD*.

Put it up on eBay as a priceless first edition!

One afternoon a gigantic eighteen-wheeler pulled up in front of my house and with a small hydraulic lift the driver unloaded box after enormous box of *ISAD*s, and fewer boxes of *Summer Never Ends*. None of us, not Will nor Ned nor Chris nor I, had ever considered that dozens of boxes filled with hundreds of CDs and LPs per box, thousands and thousands of them in total, would take up so much room. After a full day of moving boxes, double-checking them against shipping lists, and general unpacking, the boxes were stacked in my living room, dining room, and kitchen. There were boxes next to the boy's crib, boxes in the hallway, in the kitchen, in the bathroom. The entire house smelled of cardboard. Our life was taken over by boxes of *ISAD* LPs and CDs.

Everywhere you turned: *I See a Darkness*.

13

Joyful and Triumphant

On January 19, 1999, we were able to officially release *I See a Darkness*. I knew that something strange was happening in the marketplace. The invisible hand was pushing and prodding Will's fans, directing them to their neighborhood record stores in huge numbers where they were purchasing copies of *ISAD* by the thousands. I was again reminded of that distant day when I'd taken the box of CDs from Dave Matthews' hands, having no clue that I'd be part of the literal founding of one of the most lucrative music careers of the nineties and aughts. Our numbers were obviously not the same as Matthews', but the upswelling of demand for Will's record was not linear but exponential.

As the faxes scrolled in on by one, I'd read them, then place the boy on the floor as I tried to organize the product to be packed, and as Chris continued to take her graduate courses at FSU. Tabb started walking early, so he'd stagger around using the boxes as stabilizers, moving and cooing and gurgling and chewing on everything he could get his hands on as he wobbled from one box to the next, boxes, records, invoices, the rug. I'd often chase him around the room, looking similar to Nic Cage's H. I. "Hi" McDunnough hoofing after one of the Arizona Quints in *Raising Arizona*, as I unpacked boxes of CDs and LPs, printed invoices and repacked boxes to send to distributors and stores. In some cases I'd open a box, make sure the box was actually filled with *ISAD*s and not something else, slap a pre-printed bar code label onto each of the hundreds of CDs, print out an invoice and slap it inside the box, then write a new address on the front—Revolver Distribution, Touch and Go, Carrot Top, Forced Exposure—and tape the box back up and forward it to them. I'd compiled a list of every record store in the US, so I'd spend hours calling them on the phone and giving my pitch, or faxing them our one sheet, and wait for the orders to roll in. And roll in they did.

I'd hit the grocery store on the way home from UPS, get something fun to cook, and would greet Chris at night, coming in from class, with a home-cooked meal and a bottle of wine. We'd sit at our dining room table and eat as the boy mashed peas and blueberries and pasta into his face, trying to ignore the mountains of boxes surrounding us and the ever-present stench of damp cardboard. It was fun being parents. It was fun running a thus-far successful record company.

Times were good.

JOE OLDHAM WAS HIGHLY suspect of my ability to keep an eye on every penny that came and went. This was his lawyerly cautiousness kicking in, and he had good reason to be suspect. Joe wanted to make sure his son was spending his money wisely and wanted to know that the man Will had asked to run the show, a fiction-writing drummer of all things, was sharp and honest enough to stay on top of his duties.

We had no credit card. Will didn't like interest charges. He said that Palace Records would follow the Muslim rule: no interest would be ever be charged to customers, and we'd never pay interest. Everything was cash and carry, and everything we paid for—everything—came out of Will's pocket, including my salary. I was never upset when Joe would call and demand in his lawyerly way that I send every receipt for every purchase I'd made, from mailing tape to shipping fees to reams of paper and cartridges for my printer, plus my home phone bill, to his home address in Louisville so he could check it out. It meant that we were successful.

A few days later he'd call. He was always relieved. "Things look pretty good. You guys are making a little bit of money," he'd say, a hint of incredulity mixed with pride in his voice. Then he'd chuckle. "And you're not ripping off Palace Records."

Never even crossed my mind.

I wasn't totally selfless, and at one point asked Will if the company would buy me a laptop and a cell phone.

"No," Will said.

AMONG THESE ENORMOUS PILES of *ISAD* LPs and CDs was a much smaller selection of the Anomoanon product, *Summer Never Ends*, which distros and stores were also buying but in smaller numbers. My inner salesman understood why a distro would place more faith in selling Will's stuff than the Anomoanon's but I was still disappointed that our record often appeared to be an afterthought.

Many of the people to whom I tried to pitch *Summer Never Ends* asked if Will was on it, whether or not he sang any songs, as if that was a more important indicator of its quality than anything else. Most often I'd answer that yes, he sang backup on a few songs, but really this was a record made by a band, the Anomoanon, who were playing songs written not by Will but by his older brother Ned. "Are the Anomoanon the Palace Brothers?" many would ask.

I wanted to sell as many copies of the record as I could, so if I thought I could move a few more copies of our record by mentioning Will's involvement, well, I did. If a customer purchased our record because she thought Will was on it, well, that was fine too. A rising tide lifts all boats. After a bunch of people had bought our record, I figured, they'd recognize that Ned wrote great songs and that we were a great band that made great records. That's how we'd build our own fanbase.

BY THIS POINT THE Anomoanon had recorded a few more songs in Shelbyville. Continuing a trend that would carry on for decades, these were yet more musical adaptations of literary sources, in this case songs Ned had written using Robert Louis Stevenson's *Child's Garden of Verses* as source material.

Ned and I were parents of youngsters, and we talked about how there was a marked dearth of good music for kids, so we strove to fill a void by making intelligent music that could be appreciated by a youngster and that youngsters' parents. We'd been able to rediscover many of the things we'd read when we were kids, like Mother Goose rhymes and these RLS verses, and we tried to introduce our own kids to what we might've considered a canon of great childrens' literature. My grandmother had read the RLS verses to me as a child, and the exploration of these classic works with our own toddlers was a cool way to revisit these epochal moments from our childhoods. So projects like *Mother Goose* and *Robert Louis Stevenson's Child's Garden of Verses* had value to us, even if that value was not shared by the invisible hand of the marketplace.

In October of 1998, Will rented a car and drove from Las Vegas to Los Angeles then up the West Coast doing solo in-stores and radio shows. These were the first shows featuring the songs on *I See a Darkness*. Later in the fall, after he got back from the West Coast, we all met for a long weekend in Tallahassee. Aram, Jason, Willie, Ned, Will, and me went out to Wakulla Springs to swim, and learned a few songs from *ISAD*, playing a few of them at a one-off show at the Cow Haus. It was a great night, great fun, and that show in Tallahassee was the first time a handful of the new *I See a Darkness* and *RLS* songs were played by a band, and that band was the Anomoanon.

The Tallahassee show was a warm-up: in December, Will would invite us out on the road for what would be called the Christmas Tour, where the Anomoanon would become the first band to tour with Will in support of the now legendary *ISAD*. This tour would also be different in that the Anomoanon would begin the show with a set of Ned's original Anomoanon songs, then we'd play a second set of Will's songs, mostly from *I See a Darkness*. So, we had our work cut out for us.

We'd be joined on the Christmas Tour by violist David Michael Curry, a musician from Cambridge, Massachusetts. David had played with some great Boston bands like Willard Grant Conspiracy and a few of musicians in Come, like the Thalia Zedek Band and Chris Brokaw. He was an excellent guy to have onstage and his viola sometimes reminded me of John Cale's, though DMC wasn't wild about that comparison, claiming that if anyone knew any violist it would probably be John Cale.

Back in the nineties there were two primary ways to get paid: either from the door or bar proceeds or, if you had a great booker/promoter, through a guarantee. A guarantee was a set amount of money negotiated between the booking agent and the respective promoter of each show before the tour even began. Will had one of the best in the business booking his shows, Boche Billions, who secured Will guarantees almost from the start of his touring career, including the tour we'd done in '97 with Mangler Vogt. Guarantees always reduced financial risk and increased reward.

By 1997, Bonnie Prince Billy was a powerful enough commercial commodity to command both a guarantee in addition to a cut of the door, in addition to a potential cut of alcohol sales at some clubs. There were many nights, particularly in cities like New York, where we might be handed thousands of dollars in cash, maybe a check for another few grand as well, at the end of the show. This resulted in many tense nights as the promoter tried to hide certain receipts from us in order to save a few bucks, but it rarely worked and we usually got what we were contracted to earn.

There were always daily costs that would subtract from our total take, from gas to band per diems (twenty bucks a day for each musician) to the odd hotel room, but these were somewhat predictable, and in any case staying in a hotel room was, in those early days, considered a failure of gumption. We'd much rather find a floor on which to crash, a few couches, than pony up the cabbage needed for multiple hotel rooms. Nothing drained the budget quicker than hotels.

How much could we make on each tour? I was but a simple drummer, people, and was not privy to many of the agreements between Boche, Will, and the clubs, but I'm going to try to test my memory skills with the stated assumption that I could be dead wrong.

Let's take a quick look at some basic numbers. The capacity of the Bowery Ballroom in Manhattan is 575. If tickets to our shows back in the nineties and early aughts cost twelve dollars, then the total gross at the door might be $6,900. Let's factor in that the vast majority of those customers were buying drinks. If we apply a simple and round number like ten dollars of alcohol purchased per person, we have $5,750 in alcohol sales. Added to the door gross, the Bowery Ballroom had a potential total take of $12,650 in a single night. Obviously, the club had costs, employees, licenses, all that stuff, and obviously not everyone at the show has paid to get in nor is everyone paying to drink, or even drinking at all. But also consider those possible $150 or $200 bar tabs. If we double the potential per-person alcohol costs to $20, then the total take in alcohol alone is almost twelve grand. With the door gross, it's not impossible to imagine a night when the Bowery Ballroom might've grossed close to twenty grand during a Bonnie Prince Billy show, a big chunk of which was ours.

The potential for big payouts at these big city shows was an important part of every tour. They'd often offset the lower gross shows in smaller clubs in smaller cities that might not be able to afford a high guarantee. Therefore, it was always a good idea to play New York as often as possible.

THE CHRISTMAS TOUR WAS a success. It was fun. We made a lot of people happy. We were happy. The air was wintry and biting outside, but inside the clubs things were warm, convivial, and I recall many flushes of love and Christmas spirit flooding my synapses as we traveled from one show to the next. Love for my wife, for my son, for my bandmates, for life generally. These tours were the most life-affirming collective experiences I'd ever had, and I had my friends in the band to thank. We learned Sinatra's "Christmas Waltz" ("Frosted window panes, candles gleaming inside, painted candy canes, on the tree, Santa's on his way…"), a punk rock "Deck the Halls," and a Queen-like instrumental "O Come All Ye Faithful," which brought down the house every time, with Will donning a Santa hat and tossing candy canes to appreciative crowd members. We covered John Cougar Mellencamp's "Jack and Diane," and I recall that whether or not I was able to nail Kenny Aronoff's big drum break before the final triumphant verse always depended on exactly how many beers I'd consumed up to that point. If it was a small number, the mini solo was easy, a snap, simple counting. If I'd had one or two over the line, I always lost count and the natural flow of the song. A few times I really screwed it up, but no one appeared to care too much.

The tour wasn't perfect, no tour is, and, well, with permission from Ned and Birmingham's long defunct *Black & White* weekly magazine, I'll let Ned's more gimlet-eyed POV fill in a few memorable anecdotes:

(At Bard) They buy us pizza and beer and then eat and drink it. Beer seems to be a rare commodity. In the middle of the BPB set, drummer Jack has to piss; he can't play another beat without pissing. We announce that Jack's wife is due to deliver their baby and he has to call and see if anything's happening. The crowd cheers, we cheer, Jack runs off to pee out the window of the scummy band area. He comes back saying everything's fine, no baby yet. We play John C. Mellencamp's "Jack and Diane"; the crowd drinks it thirstily just as they have our beer. After the show, I reach into the barrel of ice and find only one bottle left, broken. A kid descends on Will and forces Will to listen to a couple of his songs, played on an acoustic. Another kid is offended when Will tells him the story about Jack's baby was a lie. "People will believe anything you say onstage," Will observes.

We spend the night at a friend of Jack's, just down the lane from Natalie Merchant's house.

(At Maxwell's in Hoboken) Gummo director Harmony Korine, a fan of Will's, is in the audience. After the show, I ask him about Gummo's "skinhead/mock fight in the kitchen," in which two brothers trade hard punches, kidding and laughing the whole time.

"They weren't supposed to do that," Korine says, "there wasn't a script; they were just supposed to ad-lib for the camera and they started punching each other. They're not really skinheads. They'd just rather fight than talk."

The contract information for our Princeton, New Jersey, gig at the Terrace Club—not a nightclub at all, but one of Princeton's "eating clubs" (coed fraternities in aristocrats' clothing)—says "Dinner will be prepared by chef Christopher Nord." This turns out to be a euphemism for "institutional food." This is the Math Rock house. They have jokes with the punchlines like, "But every accent was on the subdominant."

The clubees take all the tables out of the dining hall of the great gothic house and the soundman shows up. We tell him we've been listening to Thin Lizzy; he says, "I've always had a thing against Thin Lizzy because back in the seventies my band went against them in a battle of the bands and they blew us out of the water." For the relatively small room, the system is monstrous—the stage area in front of the great fireplace now takes up at least a third of the room.

After the first BPB song, "One with the Birds," Will says, "Raise your hand: who can name at least three birds mentioned in that song?"

Someone starts to blurt out an answer

"Raise your hand!" Will insists.

A kid from up front raises his hand; Will calls on him. "Robins, doves, and thrushes," he blurts out. He says it exactly like a student in a classroom.

We have the first hotel reservations of the tour here, but we cancel them and spend the night in the club's plush TV room. As we're laughing in amazement at some porn channel (I had no idea how hard they were pushing the censorship envelope these days!), a female clubee sticks her head in and quickly withdraws. There's a lot of lip service to feminism at Princeton. Yet someone—someone on the inside—had to have ordered and paid for this channel.

The Anomoanon smells like onions and mustard in Providence.
They are filmy because of not washing. They eat near the venue—a
black box student-run theater—at a Thai restaurant that has roaches
in its condiment caddy and too many onions in its beef salad. The
onions make the Anomoanon smell even more like mustard and onions.

The Anomoanon has decided not to drink until the Bonnie Prince
Billy set. The drunk promoter, a Brown University student named
Nick, has brought several cases of beer for the band and put it in the
band room, but somehow there are only a couple of Icehouses left when
we reach into the bucket before Will's set. There are none left after.

We go to a party at a graduate fiction writer's house. Vic
Chestnutt, who played in between the Anomoanon and Bonnie Billy
sets, is there with his wife and C. D. Wright, the poet/professor who
conceived this "writer's night" gig.

It's hard to talk with Vic Chestnutt because there are always those
looking out for him and those who want to bask in his presence—not
too many, but a couple—so every conversation seems to take place on
a stage, as part of a presentation; every word he says seems like part
of a play.

(A quick note: we were reunited with our beloved Mangler,
Brown student Justin Vogt, whose band Year of the... opened
the set for us.) Back to Ned:

A tour highlight: Jack's sister Ann Barron teaches fifth grade at
a small fifth-through-eighth-grade private school just across the river
from Providence. She's been playing the Anomoanon's Mother Goose
album for her students and working up some lessons from it. We'd
agreed before the tour ever started to do an afternoon "acoustic" set for
the school. We have no acoustic instruments and we are sort of bent
because of (the previous night's) Maker's Mark and sleeping on floors

and couches. But we arrive at the agreed-upon time—2:30 p.m., the last period of the day.

We set up in the bottom of a stairwell next to some couches and drink machines. We use a minimum of equipment; Jack plays with brushes. There is no vocal amplification, so we turn way down and everybody sings loud. The students' attention spans are much better than many of the adults of our usual audiences. We each sign a dozen autographs and in the van mutter, "Why not more of these kinds of shows?"

The waitress at The Middle East tells us that the braised lamb shank is delicious. Willie, the bassist, and I order it. It is horrible—a great, ugly, gray flavorless shin, boiled without the slightest seasoning, not even salt, and without sauce.

In the cavernous downstairs, the Mighty Mighty Bosstones are playing one of several completely sold-out shows for their largely collegiate male audience.

Before the show, Will had been wanting to call some Burundians, one of whom he'd met in Burundi a few years before, but he couldn't find a number. After the show, he finds the Burundians by chance, sitting in one of The Middle East's several bars. They want to come with us to Providence. One of them is a journalist; the other, it seems, is the nephew of Mobutu Sese Seko.

As we pull into one of the last I-95 service areas before NYC, I'm sitting in the middle of a bench seat, buffeted by waves of intense nausea. I can't quite blame the horrid lamb shank—the waves aren't hitting Willie—but I can't help envisioning it and a thousand more boiled gray lamb shanks, floating in the ceaseless, sick-making waves. It's my turn to drive—according to the rental agreement, only Jason and I are supposed to drive the van, and he's done his shift for the day. At least driving takes my mind off the rotten sea of lamb shanks. We miss only one exit, and it's an easy turnaround."

During the Anomoanon set the lights feel like sunlamps and I'm drenched with sweat after the first song. It feels like a fever breaking. The others look cool as cucumbers.

(Note: During the Anomoanon set, Alan Licht was suddenly onstage, sort of dancing around, and only then did I realize he was dribbling a basketball. Alan dribbled from one end of the stage to another, then dribbled right into the wings. Seconds later he showed up onstage with a guitar and we blazed into a killer, out of control version of "Know It's Alright" by Alan's former band Love Child. After Will's set we signed the basketball with what I remember as a silver Sharpie marker. Supposedly Alan still has the basketball. Also, the opening band was Actress, from New York, featuring Lizzie Bougatsos, later of Gang Gang Dance, and visual artist Spencer Sweeney. This was the first night we'd meet Spencer's cousin Matt Sweeney, who was our host for the evening. Matt will make many more appearances in this narrative; he is a Zelig-like figure in the past two decades of modern music. I won't see Lizzie again until I meet her in a dusty one-horse town in the high desert of New Mexico…)

In the upstairs band room, Harmony Korine is talking about his Clark Wallabies, the soles of which wrap up in front and back like on running shoes. "I bought them in Japan," he says. "This is just the way Wallabees are over there."

Chavez's Matt Sweeney, our Thin Lizzy connection, is wearing white Birkenstock wallabies.

(We go a few blocks to an after-hours club in the Lower East Side…)

At the club doorway a short, slight, Eastern European-looking man with long dark hair and a dark beard asks us who we know; Will tells him. A larger, Italian-looking man in a tight black vest comes up and repeats the smaller one's question. The larger says it's okay and follows us to the bar. He tells the bartender, a willowy and weathered Native American-looking individual of indeterminate sex, "No drinks for this bunch until so-and-so gets here." For some odd reason, he allows us to order beer, but not drinks to start out. I still feel weak, and order a cranberry and soda.

Two silent films are being projected side-by-side onto a wall. One is an old episode of Kung Fu. The other is bare-bones, hardcore porn, and judging from the stars' hairstyles and the decor of the space in which they act out their roles, of an early seventies vintage. Later we learned it was filmed just a month ago, and the film treated to give it that look.

The DJ plays the Sex Pistols and overdriven digital hardcore—jumping genres always, maintaining the NY edge.

The next day Jack and I are standing out front of Yonah Shimmel's Knishery, blowing steam and eating Shimmel's delicious potato soup and spinach and potato knishes with some hot sauce we bought at a grocery down the street. A woman with a camera approaches us saying she's a journalist from the New York News, doing a piece on ethnic holidays during the Christmas season. "This is so perfect," she says. "You even know to bring your own hot sauce. So you're down here, eating your favorite knishes, getting ready for Hanukkah." But I'm not Jewish and neither is Jack, and this is our first time at Yonah Shimmel's. I hope not the last. We play along with the photojournalist but aren't in town long enough to see if she runs one of the photos.

We get a hotel in Philly. The gig is upstairs at Nick's Roast Beef. They wouldn't give us a buyout either, but our experience of hunting decent cheap food in Philly's Old Town area (we found it impossible) and tight time make us suck it up and eat Nick's decent roast beef and greasy trimmings.

Brother JT opens, sort of like Roky Erikson crossed with a toad. "A promoter told me that sometimes Brother JT looks at you," says Paul, who'd been on tour with him when BJT opened a few shows for the Royal Trux, "and he doesn't see you; he sees some psychedelic mass."

The Irish bartender tries to get ahead of the game by filling several pitchers full of the bargain draft, Yuengling lager. He pours orders for draft from the pitchers. The beers are warmish and flat. I nurse a resentment toward him for this practice.

After the show, Jack and I approach the bar and the bartender says with his brogue, "Was that you up on the stage, then?"

"Yes."

"That was great," he says. "Will you join me for a drink?"

Affirmative.

He lines three drink glasses in front of us and pours a few ounces of cold Jägermeister into each. "Cheers, then," he says.

AFTER SPENDING CHRISTMAS IN Tallahassee post tour, our first with a child, the year 1999 began with Chris beginning her final semester of the PhD program at FSU and with a tempting but preliminary offer on the table for a research fellowship to Mali, West Africa.

In 1999 the Anomoanon had a total of four releases: *Summer Never Ends*, a 7", *"Portland"* / *"Now Is the Season"* on Low Fly Records, based in Portugal, a song on Netherland's national radio VPRO's Christmas compilation and, finally, *Songs from Robert Louis Stevenson's "A Child's Garden of Verses."* It had been a watershed year for us. We were making records and getting them out into the marketplace. Our records were getting good reviews and we were getting good feedback. They were not exactly selling like the proverbial hotcakes, but this didn't bother us particularly. It would happen. We were optimists.

Having established some small degree of momentum with the Christmas shows with Bonnie Prince Billy, it made sense to us that we should try to keep this momentum by playing more shows with Bonnie Prince Billy.

Looking back on the West Coast shows in which we would open for Bonnie Prince Billy in the spring of 1999, a few months after the enormously successful and fulfilling Christmas Tour, I have a vague recollection of insisting that we join him rather than him inviting us. By this point we had a business to run, and the Anomoanon's sales were lagging behind Will's. Ned argued that the Anomoanon had not yet traveled west, and that we thought West Coast audiences might be receptive to our brand of rock.

ISAD was going nuts. I'd liked the record since I first heard the test pressings back in my living room in Tallahassee and knew it was a good record, probably even a great one, but I couldn't predict just how popular the record would become or how quickly it would establish itself in the Will Oldham pantheon. Reviews were laudatory. People were calling it Will's best album yet. *Pitchfork* gave it one of their rare tens and would later name it number nine on the best albums of the nineties. Some were calling it a masterpiece.

WILLIE WAS TOURING WITH King Kong, Jason was taking some summer courses and couldn't take off work from the farm, so rather than finding someone to fill the keys and bass spots, Ned, Aram, and I decided to become a power trio for the West Coast shows. We'd join the BPB band starting in Phoenix, then follow them to San Diego, Los Angeles, then to Irvine for a date at the This Ain't No Picnic festival, to San Francisco and Berkeley, then up to Eugene, then Portland, and finally to Seattle, which was also the last of Will and the band's twenty-seven-show tour.

Will had put together a crack BPB band for this huge tour, which would be managed by Lizzie Bougatsos, whom we'd met at the Bowery Ballroom when her band Actress had opened for us during the Christmas Tour. Later, Lizzie would flourish in New York's electro-psychedelic rock band Gang Gang Dance. Legendary DC stalwart Mike Fellows of Mighty Flashlight (and who'd once been the bass player for DC's Rites of Spring) was playing bass, while Joe Propatier, a drummer who'd played in a Providence band called Scarce, completed the rhythm section. Our old friend Bobby Arellano, still a professor at Brown, would play lead guitar while Colin Gagon would tickle the ivories.

Aram, Ned, and I would open the shows with Ano-music and would have nothing to do with the Bonnie band. Lodging, food, all that stuff, we were on our own. Both Ned and I were still swamped by our roles as domestic generals while our wives worked, we both had jobs, and I was still barely whelmed in keeping Palace Records up and running, so imagining leaving hearth and home for any longer than two weeks would cause domestic and perhaps fiscal chaos for Palace Records, and none of us wanted that.

Ned, Aram, and I had all grown up as fans of Rush, of Hendrix and Cream, while Ned and I had once bonded over a shared love of the Minutemen, of Dino Jr., the Meat Puppets, and Husker Du, so we enjoyed the idea of a stripped-down rock trio. We'd played a one-off at Louisville's Mercury Paw at some point as a trio, and it sounded and felt great. Ned played bass and sang lead, just like Geddy Lee or Thin Lizzy's Phil Lynott, while Aram tackled guitar duties and I held us in the pocket.

Having called a combination of grandparents in for child-watching reinforcements, and while Chris began her final semester of grad school while continuing to try to secure the possible dissertation research grant to rural Mali (in addition to filling duties as head of Palace Records while I was in absentia), and while Jennie made her medical school rounds in Birmingham, Ned, Aram, and I—the Ano Power Trio—practiced for a day or so in Tallahassee, packed up my Ford Taurus wagon, and headed west.

THE FIRST DAY ON the road, in Beaumont, Texas, about ten hours into our trip, we found ourselves approaching a stop light at a crossroads behind a large eighteen-wheeler container truck. Ned was at the wheel, Aram in the passenger seat, me in the back. I noted the light ahead was green and that the eighteen-wheeler was taking a right turn, the same right we were going to take, so we approached the big truck from behind and waited as it navigated the tight turn. Remember, this was pre-smartphone, so one of us, Aram or me, was looking at a map and guiding Ned.

From my back seat, I saw that the truck in front of us wasn't going to make the turn cleanly. Its back wheels were going to hit the curb. No big deal. But when the truck hit the curb, I saw movement atop the truck and realized it was an open container truck with no roof. A mass not quite liquid but not quite solid sloshed out, landing in a gelatinous pile on the corner of the intersection, right on the sidewalk about twenty feet away from us as we waited for the truck. The dark grey pile was about the size of a human being. Before any of us had the chance to wonder what it might be, the car was filled with a stench so overpowering that my diaphragm froze in reflex. At the same time, I heard strange gargling sounds from Ned and Aram and watched as they began to twitch uncontrollably in the front seats, like cartoon spastics.

The truck in front of us had stopped, put its hazards on. Since we'd rolled forward a bit, the human-shaped pile was now about ten feet from us on the sidewalk. It was guts, I could see that through my watering eyes, bovine or porcine I could not tell. We were trapped in the oily miasma. It was comparable to drowning. Gasping and croaking, Ned finally steered us around the truck, around the trooper that had shown up, and pegged the accelerator. We made our way down the road choking the whole way, still unable to breathe. We weren't free of the cloud of stench for a half mile or so, and even then, the ghost stink lingered in the car like, well, a bad smell.

Later that night we stopped at a diner in a dusty town surrounded by cornfields and silos straight out of Bogdonavich's *The Last Picture Show*. Menu items were limited to hamburgers, hamburgers, cheeseburgers, and hamburgers, so we each ordered cheeseburgers. The three waitresses at the diner appeared barely pubescent, and were dressed in uniforms comprised of short crinoline skirts, frilly blouses, and paper hats. They were interested in the three foreign interlopers, a little too interested, perhaps, hanging around our table as we tried to eat, flirting and giggling and batting their eyes.

I'm not sure any of us finished our meal.

It was a dry town where we'd stopped for the night. The late-night motel clerk told us we'd have to drive to the next county to get a six-pack. Back at the motel, we each drank a beer in hopes that it might wash the taste of cow guts out of our mouths. It didn't work. The bedspread, walls, and rug were all shades of mustard, the TV was black and white and the room reeked of stale cigarette smoke. The rug appeared to be made of a synthetic petroleum-based fabric long-outlawed in most developed countries. There was only one queen-sized bed in the room, which Aram and Ned shared. I slept on the floor, my T-shirt balled under my head as a pillow, and awoke with my face covered in welts.

THE NEXT DAY WE made our way into New Mexico. We were headed toward Phoenix where we were supposed to meet up with Will and the gang to play our first show. In the middle of nowhere during a stop for gas we decided to call them from a payphone to see where they were on the highway. Neither Aram nor Ned nor I had a cell phone yet, but Will did. Turns out that they were at another gas station in the same dusty town, not a mile away.

The show in Phoenix was in an arts space, and before we went on the Anomoanon asked where we might grab a good bite. One of the employees of the gallery said there was a great Mexican restaurant about a mile away, but that even though it was easily walkable we should drive. We thought it strange that she would warn us about walking rather than driving to the restaurant.

We'd been in the car all day and told her that a walk would do us good. The Anomoanon was actually always into exercise.

"Yeah, well," she shrugged. "Kind of a rough neighborhood. Be careful."

So, we set out on our walk as the sun was beginning to droop, and almost immediately I noted slight figures skittering past us in the shadows. Like mice, they'd scoot past and I'd only catch them in the corner of my eye before they disappeared. We were soon approached by a young man and woman whose faces appeared more scabbed than most people's faces. They had a strange mouthy way of smoking their cigarettes, as if eating rather than smoking them. They asked us for money. When we told them we didn't have any, they, like the woman at the art gallery, told us we needed to be more careful in this particular neighborhood.

"Not a great place," the woman said with concern, kind of shivering. We looked around. Piles of dog crap were everywhere.

Wait a minute…not dog crap. Human crap.

The Mexican restaurant was fantastic. We speed walked back to the club afterward, and played a good, short set.

THE NEXT NIGHT IN San Diego at the Casbah, we met up with another band that we'd be playing with on our jaunt up the coast, at least to San Francisco. They were called the Supreme Dicks. Matt Sweeney had agreed to be the Dicks' drummer for this tour. Aside from Matt, who'd gone to Northwestern, the Dicks had all gone to Hampshire College at the height of the eighties hippie revival and said they'd come up with the most obnoxious name possible mostly in order to tweak the earnest hippie sensibilities of their liberal Yankee counterparts.

One of the Supreme Dicks looked familiar to us but we couldn't place him, almost as if he'd been on a TV show when we were kids and now, all grown up, he bore only a slight resemblance to the cute child actor he'd once been. Every night he wore an Izod shirt, clean Levi's jeans, and boat shoes. He wore his hair short and did not drink much, if at all, standing mildly off to the side and strumming his guitar. After the show he'd pack his gear neatly.

In San Diego there was a very drunk superfan of the Dicks, which struck me as strange on multiple levels. First, he was clearly trashed, but on closer inspection it became clear that perhaps other forces were at play, either harder drugs or, possibly, a diagnosable mental illness. Second, he could not have chosen a weirder band with which to become obsessed. Dicks' lead singer Dan, as I recall, sat slumped on a stool while the band played their midtempo songs. Sweeney was hesitant in his approach to beat or consistency on the drum kit, and the familiar-appearing guy strummed a simple series of chords, the bassist plunking on the bass, while the superfan danced and gyrated and screeched out lyrics, much to the annoyance of the band. Or so it appeared to me. Maybe the superfan was an extra member of the band, something like one of those rave bands from the early nineties Madchester scene who had a dancer named Baz or Bogs who'd bounce around on stage in X'd-out bliss with a pair of maracas and try to hype up the crowd? The Dicks appeared annoyed with the guy to the point of distraction, but there he was in the crowd, doing his shtick.

I couldn't tell if they hated or loved him.

THE NEXT DAY IN LA, we went swimming at one of Sweeney's friends' dad's places. Matt had been in a band called Chavez with a guy from Los Angeles named Scott Marshall, who happened to be Hollywood legend Garry Marshall's son. It wasn't Marshall's house but someone else's who ran in the same super-producer circles but who now, without naming names, is married to a Dame. So, we drove up into the Hills to a locked gate. Sweeney knew the code and presently we were driving our white van up the driveway at the foot of the famous producer's house. We pulled in and fell out of the van into the hazy Los Angeles sun.

Below us spread the city of angels. It was like something out of a bad TV movie about a young rock band about to sell their souls to an evil music executive.

A starlet was there, pretty but with bad skin, and a semi-famous young actor whom I'd loved in an epochal movie about the seventies. He sat poolside reading a gigantic tome made out of pressed leather with yellowed and crumbling pages. So intent was he to figure out the book he did not look at us as we all stripped down to our bathing suits. He didn't say hello, barely glanced in our direction, and it was easy to sense how annoyed he was with our intrusion.

We all took turns jumping off the diving board into the pool. It transpired that Sweeney didn't know how to jump off a diving board. That is, he couldn't get the pattern of steps right that would enable him to bounce off the end of the board in a way that would allow the board to flex and send him into the air. Instead, he'd run straight off the board like a two-year-old. A six-foot-plus two-year-old, it must be added. I was surprised he'd never learned how to jump off a board, but there it was, time after time after time, Matt just running straight off the board after making lame attempts to bounce. Sweeney just could not do it. We tried to teach him how to do it, with increasingly comic results, until we finally gave up.

In one attempt to show Sweeney how to jump off the board, Ned splashed the actor reading the book in his chaise lounge with the huge eruption from an effective cannonball. The actor glowered at us, returning forthwith to the yellowed and now wet pages of his tome, visibly angered. We swam for a few more hours, and the actor never said a word to us. Later, in a show of good sportsmanship we invited him to join us for some sushi, and Adam Goldberg came along and forgave us for splashing him. We had a good time. I never asked him about being in *Dazed and Confused* even though I really wanted to.

I didn't want to seem uncool.

AFTER AN AFTERNOON SHOW at the This Ain't No Picnic festival in Carlsbad, where Mike Watt's band included Nels Cline and Carla Bozulich, where we were reunited with our Lolla-bros from GBV (we did not speak to them) and Boredoms (them neither), and before which Sonic Youth famously got their gear stolen (which became a national story, actually, as SY had so many customized pedals and guitars that this robbery ground their national tour to a halt), we arrived home to Will's friend D. V. Devincentis's house in Los Angeles with the express request to be careful to make sure that his dog, who was very nervous and had acute anxiety issues, would not run away as we brought our gear into the house. DV was, and still is, a screenwriter in Hollywood. DV was away so we were the dog-sitters, the parties solely responsible for the dog's safety in exchange for staying in the house for a night.

It was essential that we not let his dog get out of the house, DV had said. The dog had been alone in the house all day, and DV was worried how the dog might respond to a bunch of sweaty, stinky band people when we arrived at his home after the show. He was a real rounder, this dog, and would bolt at first chance, and once he was outside he was apparently more or less gone forever. D.V. really liked the dog, loved it perhaps, but hinted that the dog might be borderline special-needy so not only were we to be firm, but also sensitive and empathetic to the dog's needs and eccentricities.

"So *please* be *super wary*," he pleaded.

We pulled up in front of DV's bungalow and all very soberly and seriously reminded one another to be careful about the dog as we approached the house. We could see the dog pacing back and forth through the window, panting as Will pulled the keys from his pocket. As Will put the key into the lock, the dog ran into the back of the house out of our sight; still, we all stood at the ready, prepared to enter the house and to corral the dog so he wouldn't bolt. The key turned, Will began to push the door open, we were still in positions of readiness...

…and as soon as there was a two-inch crack in the door it burst open. We all stood slackmouthed as the dog tore off between our legs and into the neighborhood like a shot. It was out of sight within seconds.

Will took off first, Sweeney second, then the rest of us, heading into the Hollywood Hills after the dog. I wonder how many actresses and actors and writers and producers and denizens of the LA underworld saw a bunch of bearded sweaty freaks in madras shirts and black jeans running through their lemon and avocado trees that afternoon chasing DV's dog. Many, I would think. Those were hours fraught with stress.

We did, however, catch the dog.

Later, after we'd found the dog, Cher and Gregg Allman's son Elijah came over to play skateboarding video games. His band Deadsy had a Sweeney connection. Here was the son of one of the men who'd stood for the photo with all of his bandmates and friends that had once, long ago, served as an example of exactly what I wanted my own life to be like. (It would be fun to say that Elijah was in the photo, but he came much later.) I'd had a crush on his mom, watching her sing "Half Breed" while seated on a horse on the Sonny and Cher show back in '73, and here was her progeny, her spawn, sprawled on DV's couch playing some skateboard game. My life was intersecting with the roots of the same popular culture that had shaped my desire to play the drums in the first place, if peripherally, and I found this strange.

That night we played a show at the Niaret club, and Ned and I had a long conversation with actor John C. Reilly about being parents. John's kid was the same age as Tabb and Adela. At the time he'd been in a few movies that I hadn't seen, like *Days of Thunder* and *Hoffa*, but Ned, Will, and I were huge fans of *Hard Eight* and *What's Eating Gilbert Grape* and *Boogie Nights*, which had been released the year before. In any case, we didn't talk about movies at all. We talked about family. We had a couple of beers. We were members of a band on the road living to gig, speaking to another working guy who was trying to just get his next job.

In San Francisco before the show at the Great American Music Hall we ate Indian food with Meegan Lee Ochs, Phil Ochs's daughter. No apologies for more names being dropped. I think it's important to remind the audience that back in Tallahassee I was running Palace Records but also still writing ad copy for sewage processing machines, was still faking my way through being a part-time college professor, was married and had a toddler, and it was in fact quite exciting for me to meet people who were on the periphery of a kind of fame, including the son of two seventies icons, Cher and Gregg, an actor like Reilly, and the daughter of a legendary musician.

Phil Ochs was a hero to a lot of the guys in the Louisville crowd, probably for his orneriness, his reputation as an anti-industry, no-bullshit kind of artist who never got his due. Meanwhile, I'd never even heard of Ochs until reading Breece D'J Pancake's short story collection *The Stories of Breece D'J Pancake* while in grad school (while a grad student at UVA's writing program, Pancake had lobbied to have the Master's in Writing degree switched to an MFA, a terminal degree, so my graduate degree, and Ned's, would not exist but for Pancake). Turns out that before arriving at UVA, Pancake taught at Staunton Military Academy, where Ochs had been sent back in the day, and Pancake had become somewhat obsessed with Staunton Military Academy's only famous graduate while teaching there. Will's friends in the pre-Slint, foundational Louisville band Squirrel Bait had covered Ochs's "Tape to California" on their 1987 record Skag Heaven, and Squirrel Bait guitarist David Grubbs would later cover Ochs's "Pretty Smart on My Part" with his band Bastro. Released in 1995, Will's song

"Gezundheit" echoed Billy Bragg's "I Dreamt I Saw Phil Ochs Last Night." Suffice it to say, Ochs was a musical hero to many of the brainy and equally idiosyncratic Louisville kids.

By the time we sat with Meegan in the restaurant, I admittedly wasn't that familiar with Ochs outside of his records *All the News That's Fit to Sing* and *Pleasures of the Harbor*, both of which had been a part of my collection for a while, and both of which I'd purchased in Charlottesville in '91 after reading James MacPherson's forward to Pancake's collection of short stories.

The Louisvillians' choice to claim Ochs and Leonard Cohen as folk heroes rather than the more obvious Dylan was typical. Dylan had once booted Ochs out of a car because Ochs claimed he didn't like Dylan's song "One of Us Must Know (Sooner or Later)," at least that's the way the old story went. After supper, we played a sold-out show at San Francisco's Great American Music Hall. It was the last show we played with the Dicks.

On the topic of sixties folk stars and the Dicks, a very short digression: In 1990 my post-collegiate roomie worked at the Museum of the Confederacy in Richmond. One morning before opening—it was early, just past dawn—my friend, broom in hand, was interrupted by a banging on the door. A man stood there, hooded in a grey sweatshirt and matching grey sweatpants. A skinny woman with long red hair that sprung out from her head in a sticky halo not unlike cotton candy stood impatiently behind the man sucking on a cigarette. He wore white Chuck Taylor high-tops that my friend noted appeared brand new, glowing there in the dawn. Also, interestingly, the man, for even though the creature was slight of frame it was clearly a man, had a white towel draped around his neck, on the outside of his sweatshirt. The woman finished one cigarette and lit another.

The museum had a problem with homeless loiterers using the bathroom, and here was another one waiting for the place to open with his cracked-out girlfriend. My friend yelled at the guy, threatened to call the cops, told him that they opened in an hour. The figure nodded and began to shadow box. The woman shook her hair; her mascara had begun to drip; she stubbed out her cigarette.

After a half hour or so the guy banged on the door again. My friend approached the door, not angry but instead wanting to settle the man's impatience, to prove to the man and woman that they'd have to wait until opening to use the bathroom. But then he knew he would open the door, because as he approached the door again, he saw that the man was Bob Dylan and he, my friend, already had tickets to the night's show at the Mosque. Dylan came inside and asked for the lyrics to "Dixie," of which the museum had the original handwritten copy. My friend showed him the lyrics on a sheet of paper in a faded folder and gave him a tour of the museum.

That night Dylan opened the show with "Dixie" but he did not sing the lyrics.

The familiar looking kid in the Supreme Dicks, the one with clean jeans and Izod shirts, wasn't a child actor but instead was Sam Dylan, son of Bob, who is now an attorney in California.

THE NEXT DAY, EN route from San Francisco to Eugene, somewhere in Northern California on I-5, a Ford Ranger pickup sped up behind me, Aram, and Ned, still in my Taurus. The truck's headlights grew huge in my rearview mirror. The driver began to tailgate us, just inches behind my bumper. There was a creamy, golden northern California sun smeared across the highway, the trees, the horizon, that did not seem consistent with the bundled rage of the guy in the pickup. I peered into the mirror and beheld the perpetrator of this act of aggression. I should not have been surprised to see that the truck was driven by an old white man with a frazzled beard and a manic halo of hair surrounding his pale and mostly bald head. Both windows of his truck were rolled down and inside of the cab little pieces of paper and detritus swirled in a mini tornado.

Traffic was thick ahead of me and to each side. There was nowhere for me to go. I sped up a little but there was a car in front of me, and anyway I recognized that for me to submit to this mouth breather's road-bullying would be to submit to an evil force of the universe. He was right on our bumper and weaving left and right then left again, trying to pass, but there was nowhere for him to go, and we were already speeding along in the eighties. Nothing for me to do. It was my task to keep my cool and hope that he might follow my lead and chill out.

It didn't work.

After a mile or so of his extremely angry and aggressive tailgating there was an opening to my right, so I eased into a small gap in the line of traffic. The guy passed us screeching and gesticulating like a madman, actually slowing down long enough to make eye contact with me as he continued his insane vituperations. Looking over at him, I decided it wouldn't be a terrible idea to flip him a bird. I shifted my gaze forward, took both hands off the wheel, lifted my left fist, the back of my hand facing him, and with my right hand pretended to rotate a crank, my middle finger on the left hand rising from my closed fist.

The word "apoplexy" in all of its physiological and medical connotations was invented to describe what happened to the man and his body when I flipped him the bird. He went berserk. By this point I'd made my way into another lane and sped up again, trying to outrun the road rager. He was weaving even more carelessly across multiple lanes chasing us, still at high speed, and every so often his head and body would disappear below the steering wheel, as if he were trying to reach something in his glovebox or on the floor of his truck…

A pistol, perhaps? A rock to throw?

I put on my blinker, carried us into another lane, braked, and we all watched as the semi-visible manic road-rager clattered and swerved up an offramp, never to be seen again. I watched my rearview all the way to Eugene, sure that we'd see our special friend again. We did not.

A few hours later in Eugene we were joined by Joe Oldham, who'd flown out from Louisville to pay us a visit. Hiking shorts, Tevas, T-shirt, trim, and as always, Joe was toting his camera. We told him about the road rage incident we'd experienced that afternoon, and Joe just smiled and shook his head, chuckling to himself. He took a bunch of photos at the show in Eugene, an odd little restaurant cum club called Sam Bond's Garage. Afterward, at a hotel, Joe chuckled when we smoked up. We offered him some; he refused, still chuckling. It was a highly aware chuckle, not at all judgmental, the chuckle of a Zen practitioner who knows that all is folly.

Joe chuckled a lot.

In Seattle the night after our final show of the tour, Ned, Aram, and I sat in Will's hotel room and opened up the envelope in which Will and Ned had stuffed the Anomoanon's cash take, and spread the money across the bed. A few thousand bucks lay in front of us. Will counted it first and came up with a number, $3,300, say. He asked Aram to count it, just to be sure.

Aram did so, tapped the stack against the covers of the bed and said, "Well, I got three thousand two hundred and fifty bucks, not thirty-three hundred."

It was my turn: I counted, the papery bills slipping through my fingers, my exhausted brain trying to tally the increasingly large number.

"Thirty-two hundred bucks," I announced.

"Jesus!" Will said.

I tried again, separating the stack into piles of twenties and tens and fives, thinking that would facilitate matters. "Er, I think Will's right. I think it's thirty-three hundred even."

Ned counted the stack. Thirty-two hundred seventy-five.

It was like being part of a magic trick, as if bills were appearing or disappearing as the stack went from one person to the next. The wonder, the strangeness, did not last long, and presently I felt a creeping doom. Four grown men, one of them an artistic genius, three of them college grads, two of them holding master's degrees, could not count a stack of money worth a few thousand bucks. Will grabbed the stack again, throwing the twenties and tens on the bed as he counted.

"Thirty-three hundred even," he said under his breath. "Like I said." He counted it again and created three piles of eleven hundred bucks on the bedspread. "Take your stacks. I'm going to bed."

NED HAD BOUGHT A plane ticket back to Birmingham in order to celebrate Jennie's thirtieth birthday, which meant that Aram and I would be in charge of driving the Taurus from Seattle back to Birmingham, where Aram's car was. By this point we were both eager to get back to wives and families, so we pretty much beelined it, fueling ourselves with gas station coffee and the odd fast food meal, something that we really didn't do when with the band. Sure, there were times when everyone was starved, we were in the middle of Kansas and the only thing was Mickey D's, but we prided ourselves on our ability to find local diners or sandwich shops, many of which, alas, were no better than McD's but at least we'd made the effort to support the local economy.

Aram and I were able to talk a lot on the drive home. We both liked the art of conversation. Perpetually uncynical and open-minded, Aram remained excited by discovering things. Music, books, movies, we scrolled through tens of titles that we'd enjoyed over the years, maybe arguing about some, agreeing on others, definitely arguing about this stupid thing or that one. Aram had been transparent from the start of our friendship about the relative infertility of the music scene where he grew up, on the Eastern Shore of Virginia. While my musical and artistic tastes had been fertilized in youth by a pretty active involvement in local music scenes—like Ned, I'd played in a middle school band that had been embraced by the older punk and new wave groups in Richmond—Aram admitted that his had been more or less a rural upbringing without any of these semi-urban or suburban opportunities for exposure to harder-to-find music or, for lack of a better term, underground culture.

As a kid in Richmond, I scoured back alleys for old books and records and electronic equipment; I loved weird used book stores (shout out to Sandor's on Grace Street, where I tried to buy the KISS comic book with their blood in the ink, to no avail!), museums and galleries and record stores like Back Alley Disc and Plan 9. I used to dumpster dive behind the art studios at Virginia Commonwealth University for pads of paper and colored pencil sets and watercolor paints, and first heard what I later identified as "punk rock" blaring from some college student's open windows in the Fan sometime in the late seventies. Aram had made it clear that Nassawaddox didn't have any used bookstores or record stores cum head shops or freaks blasting Sex Pistols on their stereos. He learned about music through classic rock radio and learned about books through school and his parents.

I'm sure we discussed existential matters, both high on caffeine. I'm sure we discussed Will and his approach to making music. I'm sure we rapped into the night about our wives, about any number of matters, our words accompanied by nothing more than road hum. We probably talked about my imminent departure for Mali, as Chris had in fact been awarded the fellowship.

We arrived at Ned and Jennie's bungalow in Birmingham at dusk accompanied by cicadas' harsh howls. The air in Birmingham was heavy and wet. It had taken us not quite two days to drive from Seattle to Birmingham. As we sat in the car preparing to exit the capsule in order to reenter the reality we shared with other human beings, I looked over at Aram. Naturally dark skinned, he was now browner than usual, this time from dirt. His hair sprung away from his head like the tines on a gumball. Around his eyes were goggle shaped, bone white. He held his sunglasses in his hands. His beard looked like it had been drawn on with charcoal. The inside of the car smelled like an unrefined natural oil gathered from the anal glands of some marsupial beast.

Ned told me later that as we limped onto his front porch, he noticed that one of my eyes seemed not to open as wide as the other, and the slight tremor in my hand as I reached for the cold bottle of beer he offered.

14

Roll Those
Laughing Bones

IN THE FALL, CHRIS left for Mali, having finished up her doctorate
coursework. Tabb and I would soon follow. We'd cleared out
of our place in Tallahassee and moved in with my parents in
Richmond. Her departure for Mali had happened so fast, with
such little forethought, that we had little time to wonder if our
decision wasn't idiotic. We had a one-plus-year-old toddler,
and everything I read about Mali indicated that it wasn't a
particularly easy place to live. There was malaria everywhere,
not to mention poisonous snakes. The country had one of the
highest infant mortality rates in the world. We'd not be wealthy
ex-pats living in a villa with servants and a pool, but instead
a family of three living on a tiny stipend meant for a single
graduate student. Originally the organization asked us to live
in a village called Kolondieba but when we learned the town
had no electricity and that it would be difficult to get to during
the rainy season we decided to live instead in the nearby market

town, a place of about 10,000 souls on the edge of the Wasulu region, called Bougouni. Chris was trying to find a house there.

Before we'd left Tallahassee, a friend of Ned and Will's in Birmingham named Mike Portera, a local musician who'd played with both Will and Ned, had offered to take over the day-to-day operations of Palace Records, so he drove to Tallahassee from Birmingham and over the course of a day or two I gave him a few tutorials, showed him my faultless system for taking orders, packing, and sending, and wished him good luck. We packed his car with the current stock and I sent him on his merry way.

My time as chief of Palace Records was over.

More interesting change was in the air: Jennie would finish medical school in Birmingham in the spring and would be awarded a residency at the University of Maryland Medical School in Baltimore, where she'd grown up. So Ned, Jennie, and daughter Adela moved to Charm City as we were clearing out of Tallahassee and prepping for the move overseas. Thus would begin a migration to the City That Reads, aka The Greatest City in America, aka Mobtown, aka Clipper City, aka Smalltimore, aka Bodymore, Murdaland, aka Baltimore, that would soon include brother Will and Dianne and, after our Mali adventure, us.

From his new home in Baltimore, through working the phones like they did in the olden days, and without the help of a booking agent, Ned was able to secure the Anomoanon a couple of great gigs that I'd be able to play before departing for Mali. We were riding a wave of good feelings, which made my upcoming departure for Mali all the more problematic. Feedback from our West Coast shows with Will had been fantastic. There'd been some good reviews but more than that, we all felt that the tour had been successful in a meaningful way.

Ned had become our primary advocate, working phones, writing endless emails to clubs and booking agencies, and generally running the Ano-show. He was good at it. He worked hard. He'd earned his bandleader status. He had become Captain Anomoanon.

First, he'd landed us on a bill with Pavement and some band that Pavement had invited along, a band no one had ever heard of. We'd be the third band on the bill, but we didn't mind, especially since the other band wasn't as popular as we were. The show was in Baltimore at the Recher Theater, a large venue fit for bands that had broken through the club ceiling and graduated to the larger halls. Pavement would definitely sell the place out, so we knew that we'd have a lot of eyeballs and ears aimed at the stage while the Anomoanon was playing, which felt to us like a continuation of the successes we'd experienced the previous spring on the west coast.

At the Recher, Bob Nastanovich, Mark Ibold, and Steve West from Pavement, touring veterans all, could not have been more welcoming to us relative rookies. Though we'd never met, West and Bob were both from Richmond and exactly my age. We talked about the glory days of Domino's Doghouse and Shockoe Bottom before it blew up, old sites of underage misbehavior in a part of Richmond that was once underground but which is now, of course, completely gentrified. Bob and I shared a few stories about our cohorts at Plan 9, one of whom was now working full-time for the Dave Matthews machine. They offered us beers from their backstage cooler and seemed excited as if this were the first night of a tour, or, even, the first show they'd ever played. I'll never forget that. Bob, Mark, and Steve appeared to recognize how lucky they were to be able to do what they were doing, driving around and playing rock music for the kids, and making some good money to boot. They asked about Will and Paul, they asked about us, and were generally the same hail-fellows well-met I'd hoped they'd be, birds of a feather.

They asked if we'd heard of the opening band. We hadn't, although we'd seen a very pale and strange-looking man and woman dressed in white and red sitting meekly in a backstage area.

As we stood there with three of the Pavement lads, Malkmus ambled past us, a glum look on his face. Charitably, I figured out at some point during the lead-up to the show that Pavement had been on the road for 320 plus of the previous 365 days, a schedule that was unimaginable to me. Sure, they had a bus, they had a driver, and apparently slept on the bus in lieu of stopping in pocket-draining hotels. As I'd heard years earlier, their bus was glammed out with TV screens and video game consoles and refrigerators. Their experience was as different from ours as could be imagined. They were on a different planet than even Will, who was still trekking around the states in a rented Ford van.

The mysterious opening band came on after our great set, and it was easy to predict within about three seconds that The White Stripes were onto bigger and better things and wouldn't be opening for Pavement much longer. I'm sure they were on someone's radar at that point but certainly not mine. The crowd response was rabid, deservedly so. Afterward Jack and I traded CDs. He got a *Summer Never Ends* and I got a copy of *The White Stripes*.

The Pavement show was also great. Even though I'd seen them before, I'd never noted how great a guitar player Malkmus was, and that night, watching him up close, I was amazed, especially considering that Pavement had once gained a reputation for barely being able to play their instruments. Later, when I started listening to his post-Pavement band the Jicks, I'd love listening to Malkmus's solos, which is a rare thing for me or any drummer to admit about a guitar player. (Listening to the Jicks was made even easier by my love of Janet Weiss's drumming). It was still disappointing that we'd caught Malkmus in such a down mood, great guitar playing notwithstanding. I think Ned tried to shake his hand at one point and was denied. It was a clear indication that the road was wearing the man down.

To make matters worse, when we tried to collect our guarantee at the end of the night, we were stiffed. This had nothing to do with Malkmus and instead was the result of a miscommunication made by someone somewhere up the corporate structure, well above our pay grade.

We were stunned. The show was sold out, and the Recher was a big house. Tons of asses in seats. Tens of thousands of dollars made at the bar, I'm sure. There was plenty of money to go around, but due to a contractual blip we were deemed an insignificant "local band" and denied our share.

IN DECEMBER, A WEEK before I was to leave for Mali, we flew to Amsterdam to play at the second annual VPRO Amstel Fest. Meanwhile, Chris had found a house in Bougouni. We were in go mode. The invitation to Amsterdam was another pleasant validation of our previous year's work, an upper after the downer of the Pavement snafu. Will would also play the festival (he'd been invited to the inaugural VPRO fest the previous year), but it was clear that we, the Anomoanon, had been invited on our own, as a separate entity from Will.

Upon arriving in Amsterdam, we ate *mature* gouda cheese and ham for breakfast, then ate some spacecakes and went to record a session at the studio, part of the deal of being invited to play the show. Writing these words decades later I feel the tickle of laughter beginning to build somewhere near my diaphragm. We were learning the Dead's "Candyman" for the set and during the very stoned recording session we could not sing the difficult harmonies during the chorus to save our lives. "Look out, look out, the caaaandy maaaaan, here he comes and he's gone agaaaaain…" I've already established that Ned and Willie were the best singers in the Anomoanon, so lay the blame squarely at the feet of me, Aram, and Jason. During the recording session, done live in the studio and thankfully without an audience, there were giggles, dropped drumsticks, and forgotten lyrics. After about a hundred takes of "Candyman," each of them ending with us collapsing in laughter after someone sang yet another bum note, I think we finally gave up. The engineer was mortified.

After a nap, the Anomoanon played a great live set in front of an energetic Dutch crowd. The engineer even told us that we'd frightened him earlier in the day with our shittiness but he was glad to report that he'd enjoyed our music. We rocked that night, even hitting the harmonies on "Candyman." I remember it well. Nice when that happens.

Also, there were Alasdair Roberts' band Appendix Out, whom Will had introduced to Drag City, in addition to Califone, from Chicago. Will closed out the night with a wonderful and moving solo show. Hearing the hits from I See a Darkness played with just a guitar and Will's voice, I was reminded that most if not all of Will's songs passed the "great song test": Can the song be played loudly by a full band and rock? Can it be played acoustically without losing any of its power? When it is played acoustically, can the listener hear more clearly those technical parts of the song that make it structurally unique: the melody, the changes in the chorus, the middle eight, the bridge? Or does the song rely too heavily on emotion and movement and speed?

In every case, Will's songs passed the test. So did Ned's. It was pretty remarkable, I realized, being in the middle of two rare talents. I was a lucky man.

15

Strong, Sweet, Bitter

Being in Mali was difficult on many levels, most of them having nothing to do with the majority of this narrative. Once we'd arrived in Mali, I had too much time to mull over my decision to leave the band while Tabb and I walked around Bougouni and Chris visited rural schools, leaving us in her dust. As the only white family in Bougouni, we were freaks. It was a good lesson in empathy toward the Other, the minority, but it did not settle my soul.

Communicating with the US was difficult in Mali. Chris and I had a laptop and access to an old dial-up server in Bamako but since we lived in rural Bougouni, the call was long distance and expensive. The phone wires between Bougouni and Bamako had been installed by the French, whose occupation of Mali ended in 1960, so it was rare to spend more than three minutes online without getting kicked off. Weeks would pass with no news from the States. We didn't find out until two weeks after the fact that Chris's grandfather had died.

I was able to glean that something had happened with Palace Records, and it wasn't good news. Back in Birmingham,

Mike was handling a lot of returns from stores and distributors. A confusing exchange of chained emails forwarded to Mali indicated that we'd had a problem with some defective product, some warped records, an unavoidable part of the music distribution business. It wasn't Mike's fault. Maybe the records warped on the way from Tallahassee to Birmingham, a three- or four-hour drive, in the back of his hot car. Maybe they were warped coming from the factory. Maybe they were stored improperly at my house in Tallahassee.

Second, a distributor has every right to return product that's not moving, and it appeared that most of the returns were *Summer Never Ends* CDs and LPs that had sat for too long on distributors' shelves. We'd sold out our first run of *ISAD* CDs and vinyl, and maybe even a second pressing of both (where the too-dark colors had been corrected as per Will's request), so the returns weren't Will's stuff, but instead The Anomoanon's. This was a difficult thing to accept on a few levels. First, why weren't people buying our records? Second, because we'd have to buy our product back, whatever meager sales we'd made from *Summer Never Ends* had just grown more meager.

We were a good band, the record was good, the songs on it were great. Why weren't people buying it?

THE ANOMOANON HAD A few drummers while I was gone, including the youngest Stith brother, Peter, who played with the Ano during an opening spot for Cat Power at Swarthmore College on March 31st, 2000. During the Cat Power set, Peter went to a balcony in the performance space, found a quiet spot to lie down and rest, and ended up falling asleep for the duration of her show. He mentioned this to Chan later, and apparently, she took it as a high compliment.

The Anomoanon made a record at Paul's, another one of Ned's literary experiments, this one setting fifteenth century

French poet François Villon's verse to Ned's music. A fantastic drummer from Louisville named Tony Bailey played the drums on the release (Tony would pass away in 2009). So far away, so separated from the reality I'd known for thirty-some years, I struggled with the idea that "we" were making a record without me, with a new drummer, and yet another record based on someone else's words.

Some good news via email: Jason and Kollette had gotten married and their wedding had been a blast.

More good news: everyone was excited about the Anomoanon's *Villon* project, and when I finally received a copy of it I understood why. It included a song, "Ballade of Villon and Fat Margot," that remains to this day one of my favorite things ever recorded by the Anomoanon, and I'm not even on it!

More welcome news: my mom, Chris's mom, and my sister would be visiting us in Mali.

Another email in the inbox, with news from Will: Johnny Cash was going to record the song "I See a Darkness."

What? Hold on a minute.

Was there some alt-country band called Johnny Cash? No? *The* Johnny Cash? Johnny Cash as in *Johnny Cash*?

The Man in Black? Recording a Will Oldham song? I let out a ripping rebel yell and showed Chris the email. Neither of us could believe it.

Will had hit the big time. All that hard work had paid off.

I longed to be home. It felt like an awful lot was taking place without me.

ONE NIGHT SOON AFTER our arrival we were invited to a show of Malian bands at the French Cultural Center in Bamako. Chris, Tabb, and I met a few friends, bought a few large bottles of lukewarm Castel beer, and took our seats.

The lights dimmed. A gaggle of well-dressed men walked self-importantly across the stage. Soon one man in an overly large pastel-colored zoot suit shooed the others off and boomed greetings into a microphone. It was all in Bamanan and French. He yelled; the crowd responded lamely. He yelled again, more loudly, more forcefully, and the crowd responded slightly less lamely.

The emcee then introduced the first band, and what followed was comparable to being at a school talent show. Members rushed out onto the stage in the confused manner of a group of middle-schoolers about to put on a play. Each musician plugged hurriedly into the backline of gear provided by the club; a small bass amp, a drum set, a box that sent the guitar directly into the house PA. Obviously having been told they only had ten minutes onstage, they counted off and began clumsily. The audience shifted in their seats as a female singer sang flat notes and as the bass player shook visibly from nervousness. The singer glared at him, annoyed as hell. A young-looking boy fiddled nervously with the wire leading out of his homemade instrument, which, I noted with a chuckle, appeared to have only one string. (I was wrong. I later found out that it had three). The singer looked awkwardly at the band members, at the audience, as the bass player reached back to adjust a dial on the lone amplifier at the back of the stage as if by turning a dial he might suddenly make himself play better.

For two entire songs it was difficult to believe that this band had ever played together before. Tabb cried out. He was sweaty and tired and bored.

I looked at Chris and pointed my chin longingly at the exit door.

"One more song," she said.

Silence. A few people clapped. The kid fiddled with the wire on his lute. I watched him spit on his fingers and twist a piece of apparently live electrical cord. A buzz burped loudly through the house system as he drew his hand quickly away and shook it in the air. The singer snapped at the bass player, whose face was blank as he smoked a cigarette with his shoulders slumped. The dancing women shifted and held their calabashes against their hips like babies. People in the audience cleared their throats. I looked again at the door and thought of making a break, but then the drummer counted off the next song and immediately there was an audible and visible shift in their onstage aura.

A union of something inexplicable occurred, and I sensed the first stirrings of an intense chemical reaction to the night, as one who has taken a psychedelic drug shivers when first feeling the effects.

The boy had been successful in correcting the short circuit that kept his three-stringed instrument from being heard and he turned and faced the audience and plucked a series of quick, sharp notes. It was what I learn later is called a *jelingoni*, a lute favored by the griots from north of Bamako and probably not unlike what a griot might've played as far back as the epic of Sundiata, which was set in the 1100s. The range of sounds the kid wrung from his three strings was astounding. The singer had gained control of her voice and sang the multi-note melodies popular among the women griots of Mali, sung high in the head with a weird nasal resonance and incredible, avian grace. Two women behind her sang and danced while tossing cowrie-covered calabashes into the air with perfect, almost eerie synchronicity, as if they were the same figure split-screened.

After a few short songs the emcee bounded out on stage, ushered the band off, and quickly introduced the next group as the singer and her band were still bowing to the now appreciative crowd. The new band wandered onstage and the members plugged their instruments into the same backline. The emcee yelled their name into the microphone and walked quickly offstage. They started playing immediately.

It was a kora troupe led by a young man named Adama Yolomba. The kora a is twenty-stringed harp held in front of the body and played with both hands. As I watched Yolomba sing while playing the insanely difficult instrument, I began to feel like some basic control of my senses was unraveling as if a spring under tension had suddenly been let loose. Yolomba's eyes were circled with kohl. He performed with the bizarre artificiality of a court dancer one might read about in Flaubert's descriptions of nineteenth century Egypt in *Flaubert in Egypt*: wide eyes, toothy, cocked smiles, birdlike movements of his head, careful but unchoreographed dance steps. Tabb still sat in my lap, leaning back into my body not with exhaustion but with something like excitement or fear. A man sat on the stage behind Yolomba, thumping an overturned gourd with the heel of his hand and his thimble-covered fingertips. It sounded like a full drum set. I was not ready for them to leave the stage. I was paralyzed by something like awe.

It was hot in the theater and sweat dripped freely down my face, and I was not sure that some of the wet I feel on my cheeks were not tears. When Tabb jumped up from my lap and disappeared into the crowd, I was unable to follow him, and could only gesture to Chris helplessly, signaling with my eyes that I could not leave. I was in thrall, hypnotized, made helpless by all that was taking place around me.

I could watch Yolomba all night and was half-relieved when he left the stage, only because then I could try to gather my wits.

No such luck.

A Ghanaian drum and dance troupe bounded onto the stage with the restrained, bunched energy of a group of gymnasts. It was as if they'd been playing and dancing for the previous hour through the streets of Bamako and had suddenly found themselves, quite by mistake, in front of a crowd in a music hall. They yelled at us as the *jembe* players positioned their drums between their legs and adjusted their shoulder straps. A leader counted off. We, the crowd, were enveloped in a whirlwind of sound and movement so intense that the only thing I could compare it to was the pure rush of adrenaline one feels when accelerating down a runway before taking flight. The drummers played so joyfully and out of control that one of the players repeatedly broke enormously thick drumsticks on a massive instrument while women dancers danced and jembe players poured sweat and attacked their drums with shouts.

They were hustled off; another band was hustled on, this one a father/son balafon group. Each balafon, the ur-xylophone, is about five-feet long, and as they were carried onto the stage the band of a hundred or so wooden keys atop them rippled like the skins of snakes. Each key must be hand carved from a blade of hard wood and then fired in a precise fashion in order to make every piece pitch-perfect. The balafons were placed parallel to one another so the father and son, as they played, were facing each other while seated on the ground. Pure liquid melodies filled the hall's increasingly close and smoky air, some strange spirit balm after the pagan celebration of the previous drummers.

I began to feel unsettled by my constant amazement. The effect was the exact opposite of numbing, and was instead a jolting, stinging, body-full catharsis. I was so overwhelmed that I suspected I might be having a reaction to my antimalarial pills or succumbing finally to the exhaustion that was always just a few steps behind us those first weeks in Mali. It was as if I was witnessing, one after the other, nothing so reductive as the "roots of blues" or the "roots of rock," but instead the ur-performers of something so huge that it was impossible to describe, encompassing centuries of human culture. Back in the US, Will and Ned and Aram and Willie and Jason were a part of the same continuum, which I'd abandoned.

In the darkened furnace of that theater I was reborn. I repeated to myself, "I've known nothing up until now." It increased my desire to return home and to dedicate all of my efforts to being in a rock band, to making other people feel like I did during that transformative show.

DURING HOT SEASON IN Bougouni, temperatures rarely dipped below one hundred, and one week spiked to 115 degrees. Even at dawn the air was still and hot. The sun would appear suddenly in the blank white sky. For an hour before lunch there'd be a few motorcycles passing by on the road, a few cyclists wobbling past, but zero cars. It was too hot to do anything. Birds screeched from the trees as if in pain. The boys driving the donkey carts would pass en route to the cotton factory, and the molten air was often split by their donkeys' strained bellowing. Small piebald dogs would walk in the shadows cast by the carts. Otherwise the town during the hot season was consumed by an amphibian silence. People would sit stock-still and breathe slowly. Ripening mangoes hung heavily in the trees.

Our home was made of cinderblock, our roof was a single sheet of corrugated tin, our windows had no screens and we slept underneath mosquito nets. We were often without electricity and sick. The antimalarials we took made us feel like we'd eaten low-level speed, and were so bitter tasting that we had to hide Tabb's crushed half-pill in a pile of syrup-saturated pancakes.

At the same time, we admired the courageous Malian spirit and found that ancient codes of hospitality and welcoming strangers were intact. Tabb and I couldn't walk down the road without being invited to sit with any number of men seated around a small fire in the shade next to the roadside, a tin pot of water on the boil, and offered the requisite three shots of over-sweetened tea served in small glasses. The first, according to lore, is strong like life, the second is sweet like love, and the third and final shot is bitter like death.

LATER IN THE YEAR, one night at a Peace Corps party in Bougouni, I heard a familiar tune echoing from someone's boombox as people danced. The sun had just set. Earlier at the party I'd seen a month-old *Newsweek* magazine on the floor and laughed aloud when I read that George W. Bush, Republican Governor of Texas, was whittling away at golden boy Albert Gore's lead in the upcoming US presidential election, which would happen a few months after our arrival home.

Good luck, Georgie, I crowed. There was no way he'd beat Gore. I couldn't wait for another term of Democrat leadership.

The familiar song on the boombox was "Gulf Shores," the song I'd played drums on, recorded on a gorgeous August day, at Kramer's studio in New Jersey, back in 1994, the day Ned and I had driven past Stevie Wonder's house on our way to get bagels. A lot had happened since then. I'd gotten married, had a son, moved to Mali. Will was becoming famous while the Anomoanon were struggling to break away from the gravitational force of the Will Oldham sun. Will had made multiple albums since then, played with scads of new musicians, had had articles written about him, had recently stood in a vocal booth with Johnny Cash. Meanwhile the Anomoanon was scuttling along like a blind crab on the bottom of a bay.

To me, "Gulf Shores" represented something simultaneously dark and light. I didn't like to think this way, but I considered, standing there in the sweltering Bougouni night, that it might very well stand as the high point of my musical career. If this proved to be the case, I thought, watching smashed PCV volunteers grind their crotches against one another as my song played—our song—it wouldn't be a bad high point.

THE DAY AFTER THE party, while Tabb ran around in the yard with his *playfriends*, I peered over our fence to watch a man, perhaps disturbed, dancing in the middle of the street. He looked like a giant spider. It was well over a hundred degrees and the sun blazed down with extraordinary ferocity. That he was in the middle of the street meant nothing, he certainly was in no danger of being run over. An hour might go by without a single car passing along the road. There was no audible music playing. Men and women walked past him as if he did not exist as the man danced to a sound in his head.

No, what was remarkable about the man, the Malian, was that he bore a striking resemblance to Will. Not only that he was Will's African twin, but that he danced exactly like Will might dance were he a disturbed man living in rural Mali.

Part Three

Destroying is better than creating when we're not creating those few, truly necessary things. But then is there anything so clear and right that it deserves to live in this world?

—The Writer, Federico Fellini's 8 ½

16

A Return

OUR NINE-MONTH SOJOURN IN Mali had been a rich and interesting one, on the main, but also incredibly difficult and often trying. Being back in the US among friends and family allowed us, for a few weeks, to be reminded of what it was like to be born again.

Chris and I floated along in a state of ecstasy much of the time, happy to be back among the bland comforts of the west. I was excited to reconnect with the band and get back to work. Our well-being was made more relative, compromised, perhaps, by the election of George W. Bush to the presidency, something that neither Chris nor I could've imagined happening when we left for Mali in December of 1999. George W. Bush and his simple-minded, right-wing Christian mush was not in the plans for our future, nor our son's, and having spent nearly a year as the other in rural West Africa, we were particularly attuned to the racist dog whistles coming from Bush and his supporters. As happy as we were to be home, to be among friends and family, there was an overarching sense of societal devolution, of having missed some epochal change in the way the United

States operated—we were different than most of our fellow Americans, it seemed, whose beliefs were opposite ours. It was a dark time.

Now that our Malian interlude had come to close, there were things that Chris and I had to take care of: getting jobs, writing dissertations, raising a toddler, making decisions about where to live, what to do.

It was easy being back in the States; it was hard being back in the States.

One day Chris said, "The only thing more pathetic than living with our parents would be to live with our parents if I was pregnant."

I didn't understand the source of the non sequitur until later. Perhaps she'd already sensed something was happening inside of her body because, of course, within two weeks we found out she was pregnant again.

We were looking at DC and Baltimore as places to live, mainly because Chris could find a good job in DC. But soon Baltimore became the easiest choice. Ned and Jennie and their daughter lived there, for one, and Will and Dianne. The neighborhoods were packed with interesting people and houses and it appeared that Robert Florida's "creative class" was really making hay in Baltimore. It was cheap, dynamic…and cheap. It would obviously be the best place to live if I wanted to jump-start my involvement with the Anomoanon and, maybe, Bonnie Prince Billy.

We moved in on the coldest day of the year, the Saturday before Super Bowl Sunday, which quite by chance featured the Baltimore Ravens versus the New York Giants. The sky was low, and seemed to sit atop the rowhouses on our street. The sun was invisible behind a mass of clouds ranging from battleship grey to deep purple. Flurries of tiny particles of ice would every so often blow sharply across our faces as we lugged beds, dressers, shelves, stereo equipment, books, records, more books, and more records into our new home. All afternoon as we were loading in our stuff from the U-Haul truck, locals draped in Ravens gear would stop and offer to help. As soon as they'd lift the edge of a shelf or dresser, they'd dramatically claim they were going to drop it if we weren't pulling for the Ravens in tomorrow's Super Bowl. "Go Ravens!" we'd yell, even though I found the Ravens a particularly unlikable team, whose defense was led by a probable murderer. A pack of homely individuals, all looking like wet dogs, stood on the stoop of an apparent group home across the street and watched us, smoking cigarettes in the frozen gloom.

The next day, our first full day in Baltimore, we set up our crappy, old style television in the basement, positioned the rabbit ears and dialed in the game, and invited over the same friends who'd help us move the previous day to eat chili and watch the Ravens vanquish the Giants. On the Avenue in Hampden after the victory we noticed that the most common means of celebration in Baltimore appeared to be hanging one's ass out of a moving car window while people on the sidewalk screamed and tried to hit the bared booty with a full can of beer. Cops were everywhere but outnumbered by bare-assed revelers.

Soon, Ned organized a recording session in Shelbyville with Paul for our next batch of songs, which would comprise our first proper full-length of original songs. *Summer Never Ends* had been a mini-album, and of course the *Mother Goose*, *Robert Louis Stevenson*, and *Villon* projects were all Ned's music and someone else's words. Our new record would be called, simply, *The Anomoanon*. The full band was there at Rove: Ned, Aram, Jason, Willie, me, plus Paul. Will came out for a couple of nights to do some backing vocals. I cannot describe how excited I was to be back in the fold of my band. I'd missed them while in Mali, and understood on a fundamental level how important the Anomoanon was to my sense of self. And unlike a lot of bands, who put up with one another for no other reasons than they're in the same band (see the Rolling Stones, etc.), these were, undoubtedly, my best friends. It was easy to imagine us hanging out even if we weren't in the Anomoanon. It was my opinion then, and remains so to this day, that we were unique in this regard.

Both Willie and I'd written songs to be considered for the record, but the established pattern of Ned being our primary songwriter remained. I would learn later that most bands would go into the studio with twice as many songs as were needed and choose the best for the record after they'd been recorded, but we didn't have the time to spend writing or recording more songs than were needed for a single release, so we showed up in Shelbyville with just enough songs to cover two sides of an album.

My song was an uncomfortable and rather painful pastiche of the British folk rock I'd enjoyed for a few years, like Fairport Convention, Shirley Collins, Steeleye Span, Pentangle, and Planxty. This was a rich vein I'd continue to mine in the coming years when it was a rare Anomoanon tour that wasn't accompanied by CDs I'd burned featuring Mellow Candle, Synanthesia, Fairport Convention, Richard and Linda Thompson, and the like. I'd soon disappear down a wyrd-folk rabbit hole and collect CDs by bands like Fresh Maggots, Trader Horne, Comus, Incredible String Band, These Trails (from Hawaii!), Malicorne (an excellent French band), Spyrogyra (not the goofy fusion one), Trees, Vashti Bunyan, Extradition, Anne Briggs, C.O.B. (especially *Moyshe McStiff*...), Roy Harper, Bread, and Love and Dreams. In any event, my song, titled "Mermaid's Womb," has not been listened to by me pretty much since it was recorded. Passive tense purposeful, by the way.

Not long after we finished recording basic tracks for *The Anomoanon*, Jason left the US to become a Peace Corps volunteer in El Salvador with Kollette, his wife, with whom he'd one day buy a farm in Hawaii and live in a yurt and raise a few bairns. If this feels like a massive plot twist clonking into our narrative without much warning, then I've succeeded in portraying how I felt about Jason's sudden departure. We knew he'd applied for the Peace Corps, knew it was a real possibility, but I'd succeeded in convincing myself that the time for Jason's leaving the Ano-fold might never arrive.

Jason had been a fundamental part of our little band for its entire life and was, just like that, out of the Anomoanon and on a plane to El Salvador for two years. Jason would play the odd show with us in the coming years but that was pretty much it for old Selma's involvement in Ano-music. He and Kollette were off to do their farming thing, something they're still doing today. *The Anomoanon* was the last record he played on.

We'd miss Jason terribly, but we soldiered on without him. There was no time to fret his absence. We had lost our keyboard player and multi-instrumentalist, and Willie became our full-time bass player.

IN OCTOBER 2000 WE set out again on yet another short tour with Bonnie Prince Billy, joined by Paul's band Speed to Roam. The soundtrack to this tour was the collection of bootleg tapes I'd brought back from Mali. Will had recently released another great record called *Ease Down the Road*.

The songs were fantastic, as I'd come to expect from Will, filled as they were with plenty to think about, to enjoy. The record included allusions to being reborn (or *reskinned* as Will sings in "Grand Dark Feeling of Emptiness"), and I could empathize with the narrator's curiosity about another version of one's self, as I'd had to do multifold since becoming a husband and a father and, importantly, the "other" inhabitant of rural West Africa.

As with every other opportunity I'd had to play with Will, the invitation to play with the Bonnie Prince band for these few dates was an oft-needed reminder that my life had value outside of being a full-time father and part-time writer with no real job. Being in the band again was a form of salvation, of validation, a much-needed reminder that I had skills outside of making yogurt smoothies and changing diapers and pretending, yet again, that I was a writer. I could play the drums and pack a van and be with my friends and create a false world in which I was free when I was in the band, when in fact reality indicated that I was very much un-free. Playing music and traveling was an illusion, a temporary shadow-play, but one that I loved.

The mini-tour took us to Bloomington, then to Newport, Kentucky, to Louisville and, finally, to Nashville.

It was great being able to travel and play with Speed to Roam. Pete Townsend, who'd played drums on *I See a Darkness*, was the timekeeper extraordinaire for Speed to Roam. Paul played bass, while Jason Hayden and Dave Bird played guitars. STR lead singer George Wethington, a Louisville local, was an energetic largish bald man possessed of a tightly coiled energy who also happened to have the same pinch-throated delivery as Pere Ubu vocalist Dave Thomas, another energetic, largish bald man. Additionally, STR's angular electric rock didn't sound unlike that of Pere Ubu. I thought the comparison was not only a compliment, but obvious.

George didn't think so.

"I fuckin' don't sound anything like that guy," George said. "Jesus. I fuckin' hate Pere Ubu."

"Come on, George. A couple of Speed songs could be *Dub Housing* outtakes!"

"What a shitty record," George wailed. "We do not sound like Pere Ubu, and I absolutely do not sound like that singer, okay? Jesus Christ."

In the van we all became obsessed with a toy Will had bought in a Walmart. It was a cheap, plastic, battery-powered toy that had a number of activated pads on its surface, plus some odd little handles and wands sticking out of it that you pulled or pushed or twisted as a male voice commanded you to do in a particular order. The toy was called Bop It. The theme song was a bit of eighties pop pastiche with firecracker snare shots punctuated by a five-note melody played on a hard rock synth-guitar. "Bop it! Twist it! Pull it! Spin it!" The game required a degree of physical and mental acuity, and we played the game for hours straight, running into odd bodegas and drugstores to stock up on fresh batteries when they ran out. George would grow particularly animated as the toy's patterns became increasingly long and complicated, screeching in frustration whenever he lost, dashing the Bop It against the van seat.

In Nashville we shared the bill with Rising Shotgun, whose leader Brett Ralph had sung on the single we'd listened to with Bep, the Oldhams' grandmother, on our way back south after the tour in 1997. More recently, Will had reissued Fading Out's unreleased 1985 demo on Palace Records. Brett's early punk band Malignant Growth was one of the local bands in Louisville who the young heroes of our current narrative, mostly Ned, Will, Paul, and Willie, had watched perform at local church basements and all-ages clubs and restaurants and thought, *Hey, that doesn't look too hard, I think I can do that, too…*

THE NEXT NIGHT IN Louisville before the show, a benefit for the Kentucky chapter of the ACLU's Reproductive Freedom Project, I donned for the first time a pair of Malian hunter's pants I'd bought in the market in Bougouni the previous year and sauntered out to do my sound check.

David Pajo saw me and immediately yelled, "Hammertime!"

He thought my Malian hunter's pants looked like MC Hammer's pants. You know the ones. Tight around the legs, loose and baggy around the crotch. I peered down at myself and acknowledged that he wasn't wrong. The pants, made of a rough cotton and dyed in a semi-psychedelic camouflage pattern, were rather extreme in their statement that the wearer, if he wasn't a Malian hunter, and if he wasn't MC Hammer, and if he happened to be white, was probably only hunting for a sweet buzz and a few rounds of Hacky Sack.

Aram, Ned, Willie, and Will noted my sweet duds and joined in with Pajo's ribbing, hooting and hollering about my pants. They were joined by people I didn't even know, all pointing at my pants as I tried to make my way to the kit to sound check. There were plenty more *Hammertime!* jokes. There may have been more than one person singing "You Can't Touch This!" while *dootly-dooting* the Rick James synth bass line and dancing back and forth like a bas relief of an Indonesian dancer on an old temple.

My attempts to be the sole member of the Anomoanon to have some sartorial awareness were a miserable failure.

A FEW MONTHS LATER, Will was asked by the Los Angeles Knitting Factory to fly out there and play a one-off to honor the newly opened LA branch of the archetypal New York club, originally founded on Houston Street in Lower Manhattan in 1987. Will decided to book a second show in San Diego the following night. He invited the Anomoanon to be his band. We were joined by Matt Sweeney on guitar, which meant we had four guitarists onstage, plus our old friend Colin Gagon on keys.

Before the show began, when the club was almost entirely empty except for us and the staff, we noted a stocky figure in a hoodie with the drawstring around his face tied tightly, so that he looked like Kenny from South Park. He stood menacingly near the bar, kind of off to the side out of everyone's way, just wandering back and forth. Eventually Matt pointed over to the figure and said, "That's Jack Black, the actor. Not sure what he's doing."

Getting ready to have his nuts rocked off was the obvious answer.

That concert in Los Angeles was the single time in our history that "Mermaid's Womb," my wyrd-folk song from *The Anomoanon,* was ever performed live. It was Matt Sweeney's idea to speed it up and play it as a rock song, which is always what you do to make a crappy song sound better. It's the oldest trick in the book! I was happy Jack Black was there to hear it.

In the band room after the show an inebriated starlet kept barging past us to use our bathroom for what I assumed were medicinal purposes. Or perhaps she just had to pee a lot. Being youngish and fairly innocent when it came to the Hollywood scene, I was starstruck and fumbled my one opportunity to exchange what might pass as intelligent conversation with the starlet, mumbling something dopey about how much I'd liked her in such and such a movie. She looked past me, a vacant look in her pale blue eyes, and rushed again into the bathroom.

The truth is that I'd had a huge crush on her since a particular director had featured her in a few of his movies in the nineties. But watching her stumble in and out of the bathroom, completely uninterested in speaking to any of us, I realized that, while certainly attractive, she was no more beautiful than ten other women I knew back in Baltimore, including my wife, and maybe less so. There was something reduced about her; the projection of herself into the public sphere was diminished in reality, not the same as on film. Perhaps it was the swollen cherry-red area under each nostril or the watery eyes as she and her friend careened yet again into our bathroom, but she appeared less holy, less goddess-like, decidedly more normal than I wanted her to be.

Seeing her much later in another movie, on the big screen, I was again in her thrall. She glowed with an unearthly, delicate but somehow wise and experienced beauty, her voice a liquid stream of emotion, her eyes sparkling with a brilliant and movingly supra-human light. It was impossible for me to think it was the same woman I'd seen in the dressing room. The representation of her on the screen was capable of almost moving me to tears.

It was true: The camera loves some people better than others.

And, I guess that's why they call it acting.

That night back at DV's we ate made us all bagels, with cream cheese and bacon. I think by that point he'd gotten rid of the dog.

THE NEXT NIGHT WE played a show at San Diego's Casbah club. We'd rented a couple of hotel rooms, downtown next to the airport, and after the show a crowd gathered in one of the rooms. A bearded bear of a man whom I thought was a fan of Will's followed us back to the hotel, and there offered me the tail end of a roach he'd been smoking, handing me the tiny drenched thing with the warning that it was some killer Santa Cruz bud or something equally ridiculous, and that I needed to be careful. I took the pathetic little roach and sucked on it as hard as I could, staring the kid down as if to say, "Dude, I'm a pro." In my mind, I was. Who was this young California hippie telling me to watch it with something as wimpy as freaking weed? I was smoking Tennessee skunk while this little kitten was still sucking his mommy's titty.

It was only five minutes later when my heart was battering my ribs and I was haunted by anxiety-induced death visions that

I reconsidered what he'd told me. My mouth was so dry that my tongue, my lips, and my teeth felt like external organs such as fingers or ears that had suddenly been transplanted into the formerly moist environs of my mouth.

He asked me what it had been like to work for Disney.

"What?" I said, rubbing my face, trying to remind myself that I was real. "When I'd done what?"

"When you worked for the Disney corporation, what was that like?"

"You mean Walt Disney, the cartoon guy?"

"I guess, you're the one who worked there, not me!"

"I never worked for Disney."

"What did you do there?"

"At Disney?"

"Yeah."

"Well, that's what I'm trying to say. I didn't work there."

"Sure. Did you dress up like Goofy? Did you juggle?"

"I can't juggle."

"So you dressed up like Goofy?"

"Dude. No. What are you talking about?"

Will spotted us and ambled over and gave the guy a hug. I tried to calm myself down and to massage my salivary glands into secreting something that would allow me to unglue my tongue from the roof of my mouth. After a minute or two, Will introduced me to the big guy. It was Kyle Field, a musician, artist, and surfer whose band, Little Wings, had released a few records on the Olympia label K Records. Will, when introducing our band during the set, had announced from the stage that I'd once worked for Disney as a juggler or something, and I didn't hear him. Do I need to state now that this wasn't true? Kyle, in the audience, believed that it was. I could not convince him otherwise and Will didn't help.

An hour later when things were beginning to settle, Colin's wife Liz began challenging us to wrestle her. Lying on our beds watching the television, me almost unable to move, I refused her challenge, Ned refused her challenge, Will refused her challenge, the rest of the guys all refused her challenge.

Then Aram, after yawning, his right arm tucked behind his head, the remote control in his left hand, mentioned that he'd once been on his high school's wrestling team. But no, he also wasn't interested in wrestling Liz, either. Hearing that Aram had once been a trained wrestler, our female challenger upped her come-ons, leaping from one bed to the next as we tried to watch TV. The more we requested that she chill, the angrier she got, especially at Aram.

"You call yourself a wrestler? Then wrestle me, you wuss! I'll whip your ass! Mr. Big High School Wrestler won't even wrestle a girl because he's too chickenshit!"

Finally, being a sport, Aram agreed to show her a move or two. He was approaching the challenge constructively, as a coach or teacher might, from an instructional standpoint. But Liz fought back with a wild, screeching vengeance, growling and trying to tear Aram's head off as he tried to show her a high-crotch takedown. She regained position, squirming out of Aram's hold, and leaping at him, keening like a banshee, grabbed his body in a death-hug, jerking herself back and forth like a dog shaking something in its teeth. Aram was smelling what was cooking and knew that Liz was taking no prisoners, so he began to fight back. Liz increased her banshee gnashings. Aram finally got her into a double grapevine, subduing her on the floor between the bed and the wall, her feet flailing around above the bed, and went for the pin.

NED AND I ARRIVED in Baltimore from the Lotus Land of Cali to find ourselves back in a harsh reality. Both Chris and Jennie were pregnant with second kids and working all the time. Jennie was working at a local psychiatric hospital, where every fourth night she was on call and had to spend the night there, while Chris was working full-time for an international organization, and spending nights and weekends finishing her dissertation.

Life was full. The kids needed to be dropped off at nursery school daily, needed to be picked up at friends' houses, needed to be run hourly, not unlike puppies, and since the gals were working so hard, Ned and I found ourselves as the primary domestic guardians of each family. Lots of time spent at parks, at swing sets, at open fields with soccer balls and baseballs and bats and mitts and lacrosse sticks, lots of time spent rushing through the grocery aisles stocking up on milk, chicken tenders, frozen fries, and smoothie supplies.

While Chris was waking up early and riding her bike downtown (even while preggers), I was in our freezing basement in Hampden, listening to Malian music and working almost forty hours a week on the book about our time in Mali. I was excited about the four hundred or so pages I'd written, which seemed on some level a display of the same sort of hubris that had resulted in my writing disappointments in the past.

However, writing this book felt different than all of my worthless attempts at fiction. Tons of fantastic, weird, and awful stuff happened to us while in Mali, so there was plenty to write about. The content was strong. It was a difficult year, sure, but also filled with beauty and joy. A lot of the book touched upon our being Western pagans in an ancient Muslim world, which gave the book a strong central point of view, that of a pagan immersed as a witness among the devout. Five times a day we'd heard muezzins calling out across Bougouni during salah, and most of our friends never drank beer or ate pork. Our Malian friends who weren't Muslim believed in ancient gods, in superstitions. They didn't believe in modern science.

I organized twenty pages of what I'd written into an essay, called it "You Are My Slave" and sent it to *The Chattahoochee Review*. They agreed to publish it. This was incredible, but the excitement lasted about twenty-three hours. I was paid $200 or so, which was fine, but soon afterward the glow disappeared. I'd spent months writing and editing the piece, hundreds of hours, and the $200 check didn't mean anything to me. I needed something else.

DIANNE, NUMBERS, WAS HARD at work on a movie she'd written and directed called *Slitch*. It starred Will "as a mentally unbalanced surfer" according to Drag City's promo. Will and Pajo, billed as the Continental OP, were doing the soundtrack. Ned was doing press for our upcoming *The Anomoanon* release. Every one of us was working hard on a project, dedicated and focused on filling the world with art and good deeds, and without sounding too sappy about it, I hope, we were also trying to offer love and support for one another's dreams—many of these dreams overlapped, of course, so each of us had a vested interest in each others' success.

SINCE ARRIVING IN BALTIMORE, we'd met some great young musicians like Dave Heumann and Walker Teret, who circulated in and out of the Heumann-hosted Anti-Folk Night at the Ottobar. Anti-Folk night was a monthly gathering where a few musicians showed up at the Ottobar and offered their own interpretations of what folk music might be. It wasn't uncommon for Ned or Will to call and ask me, Dave, or Walker to join him onstage.

Sometime around the new year of 2001, me, Ned, Heumann, and Will went to a studio in Baltimore's Pigtown neighborhood and recorded two Kate Wolf songs, "Early Morning Melody" and "Brother Warrior." The first ended up on Shellac's *All Tomorrow's Parties* compilation while Brother Warrior ended up on a split 7" with a band called Rainywood.

I'm pretty sure both songs were one-take wonders.

"Early Morning Melody" remains one of the favorite things on which I've ever played. We'd been listening to a ton of the live in-studio songs compiled on Bob Marley's *Talkin' Blues* and had played a show at the Ottobar's anti-folk night where we covered Marley's "Kaya" and "Soul Rebel." A reggae groove felt appropriate for the wintry afternoon, where the streets outside the Pigtown studio were glazed with a thin layer of ugly ice. Did we plan it out that way? No, I'm pretty sure that two seconds before Craig pushed record Will said, "Let's try a reggae groove."

Done.

17

One More Time and I'm Going Home

In February of 2001 *The Anomoanon* was released through Palace Records/Drag City. A sense of optimism and pride allowed me to believe that this record might allow all of us, finally, not to become rich but instead to make enough money to merit recording another record after this one. Even better, if we made a few extra bills, it might relieve some of my money ills.

I liked the record a ton. This was a great feeling. It sounded like the Anomoanon. A bit ramshackle, perhaps, but it felt alive to me, a living, breathing work of art that had been produced by a group of living, breathing, imperfect humans. It was warm, inviting, it had been a genuinely collaborative project and best of all, I thought it had hits. Ned's "Window (I Can't See Past the…)" and "Flock" were both radio-ready, as far as I could tell, and if my strange wyrd-folk contribution with my clumsily plucked nylon string guitar intro was one of the weaker songs on the record, well, it didn't bother me too much.

NED BOOKED OUR FIRST Anomoanon-only tour to support the record soon after its release in February. The weather gods smiled on us, allowing us to float along the highways and byways of the great eastern capitals in the belief that we were being assisted by divine providence. Jason had, of course, run off to join the Peace Corps with Kollette, and his absence meant we were missing not just a crackerjack bassist and keyboardist, but also the Great Leveller of the Anomoanon. In all the years I'd known Jason I'd seen him lose his temper...exactly zero times. Not once.

It goes without saying that Willie was a perfect replacement, and as close to Jason in personality as could be desired. Funny, sharp, a fantastic bassist, utterly disinterested in drama, Willie was so laid-back he admitted to not really caring whether or not his name was spelled Willy or Willie. For the sake of consistency, I'm going to stick to the one with the "-ie."

And as I've mentioned ad nauseum, Willie was really the only other Ano-guy besides Ned who could sing.

And sing he could: like a bird!

FROM ARLINGTON WE WENT up to Cambridge and The Middle East club, the site of Ned's long distant lamb-shin poisoning during our Christmas Tour with the Bonnie Prince, then to Rochester, New York, for an off night. We spent it with my in-laws and feasted on bucatini and meatballs prepared by my father-in-law, a good old *paesan*. The next day we had an easy drive through snow showers to Niagara Falls, where we popped a few tourist shots with my Holga en route to Buffalo.

After Buffalo, we drove to Cleveland and played a show at the Beachland Ballroom. Afterward we stayed with a young woman who invited us back to her pad, which looked vaguely familiar, with its two oddly placed gutters meeting at a juncture in the middle of a brick wall and draining into a single downspout, the three lines forming a loose y-shape, or a peace sign. Only when I asked did she let on that it was the house on the cover of Pere Ubu's *Dub Housing*, the album that George, lead singer of Speed to Roam, purportedly hated. We then looped through the Cincinnati suburb, Newport, Kentucky and the Southgate House, then to Louisville, where we stayed with Joe and Joanne and ate fried chicken keels from Indi's, followed by a disappointing set with STR at Rudyard's. The set was disappointing because I'd assumed we'd be playing for a bunch of Ned's old pals, including the Slint lads, and that it'd be a sort of homecoming for the conquering heroes—those would be Ned and Willie, of course, not me—but instead the show wasn't too well-attended and, if memory serves, the house lights stayed on through the set, which always bothered me. We were sloppy and out of sorts. After another night at the Oldham's, and probably more of Joe's pancakes in the morning, we made the long drive from Louisville to Charlottesville for a fraternity show at UVA where we were reminded that there are worse people to play for than coked-up frat kids and their nubile dates. We finished the traveling part of the tour at a school-sponsored show at James Madison University in Harrisonburg, Virginia (a receipt Ned sent me shows we were paid $350), and finally, played our last show of the tour at the Ottobar in Baltimore.

The crowds at just about every show were good. A few shows were great, including those in new markets like Buffalo and Cleveland; in Cambridge, a big house, the show was close to selling out. The show at the frat house in Charlottesville was insane, with nutso frat kids pogoing and rebel-yelling and dancing as we raced through our set. We continued to enjoy intense rounds of Bop It while riding in the van from one joint to the next. We made a little bit of dough, which always helped.

The great Venn diagram of Bonnie Prince Billy and the Anomoanon was sure to have some overlap, but our half of the diagram was growing more distinct, larger. Still, we were aware that at least a measurable percentage of the fans had come to our shows not just expecting a Will Oldhamesque experience, but instead to actually to see the Bonnie Prince cavorting onstage with his brother's band. Yes, a few fans thought that Will was an active member of our group and asked for him as we played.

"Where's Bonnie Prince Billy?" someone yelled somewhere.

"In Baltimore," someone in our band yelled.

"Why?" someone in the crowd yelled.

"Because that's where he lives…"

IN LOUISVILLE, ON THE previous tour, Paul had given us a CD he'd burned of a local band on the rise. In what we thought was a strange coincidence, they'd also recorded their music in Shelbyville, not too far from Rove Studio. The band was My Morning Jacket, and Paul thought that the Ano and MMJ shared a kindred spirit beyond both having these Shelbyville/Louisville roots. It was hard to hear the similarities between us and them at first. The record, *The Tennessee Fire*, was altogether denser, heavier, and more up-tempo than the Anomoanon's more folk-oriented stuff. If we leaned toward folk and rock, maybe they leaned toward heavier rock mixed with southern, Muscle Shoals-soul, leavened by Jim James's high, lonesome Neil Young-like voice.

If I'd long ago viewed Will as my own strange doppelganger, then I came to view My Morning Jacket as a weird doppelganger to the Anomoanon. Even though I felt a competitive urge to dislike them when I heard them, I also believed that their apparent success meant that our success would soon follow. Their popularity, combined with the popularity of the White Stripes, allowed me to believe that there was a demand for the hybridized music we were all playing, a mixture of psychedelic rock, country, soul, and folk. That both the Ano and MMJ relied on classic rock tropes like guitar solos and long, organic jams were two more things we had in common. Classic rock bands, hated by all the punks in our generation, were undergoing an image renaissance, and many of the bands we'd loved as kids, the Dead, Thin Lizzy, Creedence, Led Zep, were being reevaluated by a new generation of rock fans. We didn't sound like MMJ any more than we sounded like the Drive By Truckers or Black Keys or the White Stripes, but all of these bands were rooted in the same soil as the Anomoanon, perhaps in different parts of the garden.

Willie had seen My Morning Jacket a few times at local clubs. If there were any comparisons to be had between us and MMJ, he said, they ended at the stage. MMJ put on a true rock show, heavy as lead, that often ended in a spasm of feedback and theatrical headbanging. Audiences lapped it up. Jim James bought a Gibson Flying V and the second guitarist a Gibson SG, iconic rock guitars of the seventies, and they spun them and tossed them around like champs.

The crowds loved it.

The stories I'd hear from fans on the road about MMJ's blistering rock shows illustrated that word of mouth, that organic pattern of fan communication that cannot be bought, cannot be planned, was spreading like a virus. It was no different than the afternoon I'd answered the phone at Plan 9 just after a barely pubescent Dave Matthews had dropped off his CDs, only to learn that fans who'd never even heard the band were calling and asking us to send the CDs to North Carolina, to Michigan, to California, obviously having heard about the band from friends of theirs who were UVA students.

The phenomenon of pop success is inexplicable. It's as if a band arrives on the scene preformed in such a way to fill an already extant void in the audience's collective pleasure center, a void that *wants* to be filled. The band arrives, its music enters the ears of prospective fans and travels directly to the amygdala, gets plugged into the willing *nucleus accumbens*, the existing female void of desire is filled by the perfectly fitting male puzzle piece of the band's music and image. Dopamine is released into the participant's bloodstream and Bob's your uncle: a popular band.

Like My Morning Jacket, our shows could get blisteringly loud as well, Aram and Ned could shred with the best of them, and I'd have put Willie and me up against any rhythm section going. But we lacked a fundamental presence that created buzz among the segment of an audience who felt the urge to proselytize about the bands they'd seen. Call it charisma. We didn't provide that transformative atmosphere of Dionysian abandon that so many bands like MMJ offered their fans. We pretty much stood there and played. No dancing. No hair flipping. No hip shaking. No leaping about.

Our record *The Anomoanon* wasn't flying off the shelves, but so what? We'd just had a good tour, the record had gotten a good review in *Pitchfork* and reception was favorable. It was selling, just not as quickly as we'd hoped. We'd seen how mysterious the marketplace was, how the invisible hand often remained invisible for longer than we liked or expected it to, but sensing that somewhere out there lurked people who might be fans of our band imbued us with a sense of mission. The void in the audience's pleasure center, that void that wanted to be filled, didn't know it wanted to be filled by us yet, but, at our most optimistic, we knew it was only a matter of time before we'd be headlining sets and getting huge guarantees.

It so happened that the Ano liked growing beards, and if there's one thing we added to the cultural vernacular during this period of our growth it'd be beards. In the early aughts beards weren't cool yet. They were still things worn by aged men, by BO-having Deadheads and homeless people who had no choice but to let a furze cover their faces in lieu of easy access to razors.

It'd be another few years before they were adopted by those cultural popinjays who wore the collarless shirts, high-waisted pants and facial hair of nineteenth century clerks.

When the final accounting of this period of time is recorded, let it be shown that the Anomoanon started the beard thing. We were the first.

18

Hell's Awake and the Devil Crows

IN JUNE OF 2001 the Anomoanon drove our Ford pickup truck into a traffic jam outside of Chicago.

This was the toddler phase in the Anomoanon's development. We'd proven during our winter tour through the Northeast that we could break even if not make money, and breaking even was the modest goal we'd set for ourselves during this phase of our growth. Though this jaunt would be the second time we were road-tested without the guiding force of Will's powers, this tour was a good bit longer so the risks were far greater.

Thinking that it would relieve some of Ned's administrative burden, we'd enlisted the professional help of a booking agency and a press agent. Evidence did not yet support that hiring a press agent put more butts in seats or sold more records, but we decided to take the risk anyway. It would also be the first time we'd learn whether or not we could carry a major seventeen show non-regional tour on our own without losing money. The longish tour would allow us to play a new batch of songs Ned had written that we planned on recording after the tour ended, and which would comprise our next full-length release.

Even though Will was not with us, we'd been tasked with carrying two cases with approximately $15,000 worth of his microphones to some long-forgotten destination. Paul was to meet us somewhere in order to take the mics to Rove Studio.

The truck was Joe's. It was a maroon late-nineties Ford F-150 with a leaky Leer cap and Kentucky farm plates that read TYT-329. The vehicle's nickname therefore became Tight 329, rather than the far more pedestrian and juvenile Tit 329, which we also, admittedly, considered. It was an "extended cab" in pickup truck parlance, which meant that even though it had front and back seats, it only had two doors, so we did a lot of climbing in and out of the truck from behind folded front seats. That got old fast. The middle bench seat in the back was positioned over the transmission, which felt like an anvil, a rounded slug of iron poking right into your fleshy ass parts, so it was duly named the Krad Seat and avoided whenever possible.

Tight 329 had carried us from a few days of practice in my basement in Baltimore up to New York for a show at the Knitting Factory, whose West Coast location we'd played with Will, Colin, and Sweeney. I'd just gotten my first cell phone as Chris, back in Baltimore, was still preggo with child number two and her due date was in the same window as the tour.

Yes, it was strange leaving the very pregnant Chris behind, not the first time I'd experienced a sort of existential mini-dread as I left the comfort of hearth and home. The increasingly strapping young Tabb, now three years old, wondered where his father was going, and why was he going to be gone for so long. Logistically it was a pain in the neck as well. We had to make sure Chris's mom and my mom could come to Baltimore to assist while Chris continued to ride her bike downtown, then work on her dissertation well into the night. Stressful, to say the least.

In New York, just as we took the stage at the Knitting Factory and I seated myself behind the kit, my brand-new phone, in my pocket, started a shrill chirping. I'm not sure I knew enough about cell phones to understand I had the option to mute it. I sat behind my kit for what felt like hours fiddling with this and that finger-pad-sized button, trying to figure out how to shut it off as my bandmates loomed over me, the crowd staring at me as if I were an idiot, waiting for us to start the show.

"Turn it off!" Ned yelled finally, his voice echoing over the PA.

"I can't!" I yelled, my voice echoing over the PA.

"Dude," Aram said. "It's the button on the side. Come on."

"Dude," I answered. "I'm sorry. What button? I'm new to this, okay? Jesus."

The show, once we'd gotten started, was actually great.

There's a better than good chance we listened to Mellow Candle's *Swaddling Songs* a thousand times on that tour, although Willie appeared less enthused about it than the rest of us.

"Hobbit music," he scoffed.

I also began to wear an old North Face down vest without a shirt underneath, earning me the short-lived nickname "Vest."

In Cleveland, at the Beachland Ballroom, we played a show with Louisville's Catherine Irwin, formerly of Freakwater and a guest on Will's *Ease* record, and Big Sand's Howe Gelb, who, watching Aram sound check said, "That kid knows his Jerry Garcia." When I told him this story later, Aram was not pleased, and I understood. Even though we all loved the Dead, Aram didn't play like Jerry, didn't have an envelope filter or a wah pedal, and even though I suppose every so often Aram might play a few of those tumbling clusters of notes that Jerry claimed were his attempt to sound like Coltrane's sax, Aram's style was a lot more aggressive than Jerry's, less Wes Montgomery and more Hendrix. Later, after our set and over a few beers, the laconic Gelb called us the Holy Modern Rounders, which I took to mean that I must've reminded him of drummer Sam Shepherd, for whom I once made sandwiches back in the HotCakes days.

In Newport, Kentucky, at the Southgate House, just across the river from Cincinnati, we played with Athens, Georgia, bands Of Montreal and Summer Hymns. Later in the tour we'd meet up with them again, staying with the group at their house outside of Athens after a nice show at the 40 Watt where we got to watch Bill Doss and the Sunshine Fix play, a real pleasure.

Now, in Chicago, we were stuck in seemingly immoveable traffic. In the backseat, Willie and I played Bop It while Ned and Aram navigated the truck into the city. Our show at the Hideout club was scheduled to begin in a couple of hours and though we had plenty of time to get to the club, we were all anxious about the start and end times of the show, only because our next show the following day was twelve hours away in Oklahoma City. We figured we'd have to quit the Chicago set a little early or to offer to open the show instead of headline it in order to knock out a few hours' drive after the show, and we definitely needed to avoid drinking or smoking too much in order to not get pounded the following day. If we decided to stay in Chicago after the show, we'd have to get some much needed shut-eye so that we might pop out of bed with vigor and efficiency in order to begin the day-long drive to Oklahoma.

The Hideout is in a section of Chicago that is now probably in a completely gentrified little urban village surrounded by high-end condos, artisanal coffee roasters, and sausage makers and bicycle shops where a custom frame might set you back seven grand, but back then, aside from a proximate Whole Foods, the neighborhood was purely industrial, at least as I remember it. Remember, this is not a history but instead a series of imperfect recollections, and this imperfect recollection is from 2001.

There was a trucking depot, maybe a garage for city vehicles close to the row of tumbledown storefronts surrounding the club, but all in all the neighborhood was filled with boarded-up buildings and vagrant hotels looking like a turn-of-the-century hobo village.

The owners of the club, a clean-cut man and his equally clean-cut wife, told us to make sure the truck was locked and that anything of value was brought into the Hideout. Including, of course, the fifteen-grand worth of microphones we were toting around for Will and, of course, the lockbox containing the envelope of cash made from our shows at the Knitting Factory, at Pete's in Brooklyn, from our shows at Pittsburgh's Millvale Industrial Center, and at Cleveland's Beachland. If it wasn't a million bucks, a bunch of crinkled tens, twenties, and fifties jammed into an envelope, it was still all we'd made thus far, and we needed it.

"I'll lock the joint up tight after closing time," the owner said, pointing to the lockable grate that he could pull down over the front door. He and his wife were both going to try to catch the evening's Anomoanon show before they left for an all-night benefit for a local art museum. "You'll stay in the apartment upstairs. Just make sure everything, and I mean everything, is inside the club. It's a pretty sketchy neighborhood. If it's not bolted down in the truck, bring it in."

A single flight of rickety wooden stairs led up to the second-floor apartment where we'd stay after the show.

Chestnut Station opened. Rian Murphy, one of the founders of Drag City, was an incredible front man as he channeled Van "the Man" Morrison and Tommy James, with maybe a soupçon of Joe Cocker thrown in for good measure. Ned and I'd once watched him playing a snare and floor tom for the Royal Trux, peering myopically from one to the other, avoiding any eye contact with the audience as if in fear that someone might point out the ridiculousness of his drum kit, and here he was front and center, leading a crack band through a series of fantastic R&B-inflected dance rock.

While Chestnut Station was packing up after their killer set, we had the soundman put on Mellow Candle's *Swaddling Songs*, and I was surprised when Dan K of Drag City said that it was his favorite record of all time. I didn't know yet, had literally no clue, that the record was quite popular, and that Steve Malkmus himself would soon record a Mellow Candle cover. I thought that I'd discovered the record, having joined a super-nerdy British folk Yahoo chat group online where I learned about the strain of cracked British folk music from the sixties and seventies that would, within the next few years, result in the birth of what became known as freak folk.

During the show a steady stream of cold beers and bourbon shots made their way to the stage, sent by our adoring fans. We'd planned to stay relatively sober, remember, due to our early wake-up time the following morning, and I recall retreating further into a brown study from my throne as I watched my bandmates knocking back the shots and the brews, knowing that I'd probably be forced to take the morning's first shift on the drive to Oklahoma. (I'll admit now that if any of us had any prudish tendencies it was probably me.) Round after round, more beers, more shots, more rock and roll, the Anomoanon getting increasingly sloppy as the audience thinned, until only a small cluster of people remained for our final few songs.

The show finally ended. My bandmates were buzzed, I mostly sober.

After the show we packed up our gear, leaving everything piled in the club as requested, including Will's fancy mics and of course the Bop It, while one of the barkeeps who was there cleaning up was trying to convince us that we sounded like Crazy Horse. I didn't think so. Like most musicians in bands, I'd guess, I hated being reduced. I thought we were totally unique, maybe too much so.

"You guys, you're crazy, you sound izzackly like Crazy Horse! I mean, *izzackly*."

The owner, now wearing a tuxedo, at about 4:00 a.m., said goodnight, shut off all the lights, walked outside, and rolled the grated door down and locked it tight. He grabbed the heavy links of the security door and shook them. "See? Solid as a rock! Sleep tight!"

By this point I'd given up on being pissed that it was late and we were drunk. We had strength in numbers. Three of us could sleep while the fourth drove. The Anomoanon was a team. We had each other's backs. There was no static between us, no competition, no grudges, no beef. We grabbed the lockbox, leaving the rest of our gear on the floor of the club, stumbled up the single staircase that led to the apartment, rolled out our sleeping bags in preparation for a very short rest, and laid down.

I have a clear recollection of being perched perfectly on that fine edge between wakefulness and sleep, that zone where lucid dreams take place, when, at the edge of my consciousness I heard a very clear and unsettling noise quite close to where we were sleeping. Right underneath our supine bodies, in fact. I waited, hoping the noise was in my dream, or nothing more than a passing car, but then there it was again, an insistent banging. I was pulled out of sleep, my heart beginning to thrum. Someone was trying to break in downstairs.

Still hoping I was imagining the noise, I decided to wait until someone else said something. Willie finally whispered from the darkness, "Errr, is someone trying to break in downstairs?"

The noises were growing louder.

We all leapt up from our sleeping bags and found ourselves crouched in a tight circle in the dark room, our knees bent and hands at the ready. Ready for what? No idea.

"Call nine-one-one on your phone!" someone suggested.

I pulled the brand-new phone from my pocket and looked dumbly at the buttons.

"But if I call nine-one-one," I whispered, "won't it go to nine-one-one in Baltimore, where I bought the phone?"

"Shit," someone said. "Yes, I think it'll go to Baltimore and not Chicago!"

"Of course, it'll go to Chicago's nine-one-one…won't it?"

"Why would it go to Chicago if I bought the phone in Baltimore?"

"Because it's a fucking cell phone."

Downstairs the breaking-in noises were now accompanied by the horrifying sounds of a very large man grunting like a bear. We could hear his harsh, rattly breathing. We were separated only by that single unlocked door at the top of the staircase. There was no escape. We were trapped.

The grunting noises stopped as he got inside the club. We could hear the thief's footsteps as he trod heavily below. Then the steady sound of something being bashed, followed by a dainty little ring.

"He's breaking into the cash register of the club," someone whispered. "And we're next!"

"Keep your voice down or he'll hear us!"

"Will's mics! Holy shit!"

"Oh, shit. The mics."

"What do we do?"

"Just call nine-one-one and see if it goes to Baltimore or Chicago, and even if it goes to Baltimore maybe they can patch us in to Chicago. Or something."

I looked at the phone. My hand was shaking. I was paralyzed.

"Do it, Vest!"

"I can't."

"Fuck!"

"Fuck!"

We could now hear him prowling around, breathing erratically, mumbling to himself, and in that moment I was visited with one of those visions that only later struck me as entirely racist and awful: an incredibly large Chi-town thug from the Gangster Disciples with an even larger gun, maybe wearing a Georgetown track suit and maybe having a mouth full of gold teeth. I don't know what I was thinking! My panic knocked this purely racist vision from some deep and awful part of my lizard brain.

I wouldn't live to see my second child born!

I looked at Ned. His eyes were distant and unfocused. He raised his two hands and placed them on either side of his head and made a face like the guy in Edvard Munch's *The Scream*.

"We're gonna die!"

He was serious.

More horrible grunts from downstairs, more horrible bashing-the-cash-register sounds, then silence as, we imagined the gigantic murderous thief began to open the case containing Will's fancy microphones. More silence as we imagined him making his way to the stairwell, wondering whether or not it'd be worth it to see who or what might be up those stairs, knowing there might be an envelope of cash inside a flimsy lockbox. We huddled together, trembling.

And then a movement from outside. Two cops walking across the street, pistols drawn. So now we were going to get shot by the fucking cops!

One of us slid the window open, we all leaned out the open window and yelled out to them, "Hey, we're just a rock band staying up here in the apartment! Don't shoot! There's a bad dude downstairs! Help us!"

"We got it," the cop yelled up to us, doing that thing where cops run with their guns drawn, arms straightened, gun pointed downward. Then I saw the preppy owner running across the street as well, having been summoned from the all-night fundraiser and wearing his tuxedo, his bow tie askew, and within a minute we heard the security grille door sliding up below us, followed by yelling and the sounds of scuffling and struggle.

After a couple of minutes, we ran down the stairs, burst through the apartment door and entered the bar, where we were greeted by the owner, who had a forced smile on his face. A scrawny man no larger than a ten-year-old was struggling in the arms of the beefy Chicago cops. He may have weighed 120 pounds.

"Smokey here," the owner began, "has figured out how to climb in through the side of the security door. He used to work here, now he just breaks in."

"Let old Smokey go," Smokey wheezed. The voice that came from his leathery body sounded not unlike that of Gollum. "I won't do it no more, promise."

DAWN WAS UPON US. We were all smashed from adrenaline and nerves so we decided just to pack up and leave. As predicted, I was the first to take the wheel as my whisky-reeking mates collapsed like bags of rice in their seats. Leaving Chicago on the dawn-empty highway, I saw a few hundred yards ahead a single black bird hovering over something dead in the middle of the road. We approached the bird and I assumed it'd rise out of our path. I was wrong. An explosive smack and a spray of bird feathers blew across the windshield. Everyone, already asleep, jumped awake and looked at me.

I shrugged and said, "We hit a bird."

They all went back to sleep.

AFTER A FEW HOURS we stopped for breakfast in what we hoped would be a friendly diner for a fortifying meal. A sign outside this diner advertised their home made "international breakfast skillets," each representing some distant country's traditional cuisine. It was just the kind of place we liked to support, local, artisanal…and international.

Which world cultures did the Anomoanon choose to be represented in their skillets, you ask? Ireland and Mexico.

What represented Ireland in the skillet, you ask? Greasy potatoes floating in shortening, a pound and a half of tasteless cheddar cheese, and underdone bacon. Mexico? A pint of sour cream, mild sweet salsa, soggy round corn chips, and, of course, canned sliced black olives. The Anomoanon's revulsion at canned black olives will return in a later anecdote. Plus, some underdone eggs in both.

The skillets were terrible. The diner's coffee was terrible. The ice water tasted vaguely of sewage. We were all in terrible, terrible pain. We were surrounded by doughy retirees in W hats who peered at us through their thick, tinted glasses as if we were envoys from Satan's lair. The day's drive was equally terrible. Tight 329 was a terrible vehicle for sleeping. I woke from a dreadful half-nap with my neck at a forty-five-degree angle to my body, a string of drool pooling in my lap, my left-hand tingling as if I'd had a stroke. We were hungover and shaky from the night of hearing Smokey breaking into the club and we found no solace in the terrible skillets. It was a terrible, terrible day.

We made it to OKC in about thirteen hours and were late for our load-in. Dusky Oklahoma City light slanted in the big windows as we lugged our gear in from the truck, shining through the gathering attendees of the night's show, and casting dramatic shadows across the floor of the club. The opening band had already played. The sound check was more or less the first song of the show.

After the show, we were invited to a pool party, where Aram and I ended up sleeping on a floor underneath someone's dining room table, my rolled-up T-shirt serving as my pillow. I'd never really bounced back from my terrible stroke-nap earlier in the day and wasn't as polite to our hosts as I should've been. For that I apologize.

Terribly.

THAT NIGHT WE BEGAN a short leg of the tour with a band from Denton, Texas, called South San Gabriel. They were usually called Centro-Matic but had chosen to be SSG on this tour, and I couldn't quite figure out what the difference was, or why the same band would invent a new name in order to perform a new batch of songs… But then I remembered that we'd once changed the name of our band from Palace Brothers to Palace to Palace Songs to Palace Band to Palace Music…*all during the same tour*. So whatever pretensions I may have blamed on the SSG lads went out the window quickly. They appeared to be good dudes, all nice college boys not unlike the Anomoanon, if a good bit younger than we. The drummer and keyboardist were crack musicians, and if I thought the lead singer and songwriter Will Johnson was a little transparent with his influences, who appeared to be primarily Will Oldham, I still enjoyed the shows with them tremendously, as well as our conversations. Good band.

Also, in Denton we began a few show run with the French Kicks, whose guitar player had gone to the school where my cousin taught near DC, the same cousin who hired me to work construction for him after my return from Europe with Palace. That was an odd coincidence, meeting a young hip musician who'd been one of my cousin's drama students in high school. Later my cousin would ask me if the guy was still a nerdy, shy, backstage crew thespian type, and I was able to tell him that no, things had changed for the better for the young lad.

The French Kicks really had something. It wasn't difficult to imagine them gaining traction and rising through the ranks as the next thing. They were all handsome lads, they knew how to dress, they danced and bopped around, and they had a band name that sounded like some kind of sex position or drug cocktail. A singing drummer set his drums up in the front center of the stage and kept his throne high in order to better peer over the audience as he sang, not unlike Randy Seol, the drummer for the Strawberry Alarm Clock.

After the French Kicks' performances, they'd be swarmed by a gaggle of cute girls, especially the formerly nerdy thespian kid from my cousin's school. I recall watching them after one show, in Austin, all seated with their backs to the bar as at least seven scantily clad women hovered around them cooing and kissing them like over-attentive babysitters, while the Kicks kids, all of whom looked barely old enough to shave, sat back and smiled.

That never happened to the Anomoanon.

As far as performance quality goes, tours, in my experience, can often be charted as an inverse parabola. Or perhaps just a plain old parabola with the values inverted. The first shows are often full of energy, if not particularly tight. Band members are fresh and well-rested. There is the frequent problem of treating the first show like a party to which one has been invited rather than a show one must put on, so inebriation is common, but the pure energy often carries the night. The middle shows in a tour, on our chart, illustrate a clear flagging of energy. Those beers and smokes and bourbons have caught up to the band members, the long drives have irritated asses, necks, and backs, and maybe there's a sore throat going around or a mild case of stomach upset. The middle shows of many Anomoanon tours found Ned subsisting on bananas and yogurt and little else. By the final quarter of a tour, everyone is looking forward to returning to some sense of normalcy. The sore throat has gone. Our quirts have firmed up. The light is visible at the end of the tour tunnel, and batteries are recharged as a result.

Accompanying this lifting of spirits is an underlying melancholy. We've been engaged in this play, these performances, for a matter of weeks (or months, for some bands), and soon the camaraderie, the sounds of the crowds, the fun, the swimming, the food (including Irish skillets), the use of balled-up T-shirts as pillows, the intense rounds of Bop It, the scrolling cast of people, places and new ideas will be replaced by the mundanity of static, domestic life.

For me and Ned, that band activity would be replaced by the almost military lock-step of parenting and work. I always looked forward to the end of tours; I always dreaded the end of tours. You couldn't win.

In Austin we went swimming in Barton Springs with an old college friend of mine, accompanied by a wonderful and underdressed young lady in a cowgirl hat, a friend of Will's who made her living, we learned, as a stripper. Four married men in their thirties, one of us, Willie, still single, accompanying a nearly naked twenty-something in a cowboy hat to a public swimming hole? Friends, that's about as wild as it got for us, alas.

In New Orleans I was met by two friends also from college, now married to one another. Poe'd been the second drummer in our college band, and I wanted the night's show in NOLA to be duly impressive to show Poe how far I'd come as a fine musician. No longer a drunken basher like we'd both been in the bad old days at Sewanee, I wanted to prove that I was a real drummer, and that our night would be spent communing with the pagan rock gods of yesteryear, with me as the shamanistic leader guiding us into the mystical spirit world. It wasn't. The stage was brutally hot and I felt like I was playing my drums underwater. Beers tasted like gooey swamp water. The New Orleans night air stank of sewage. Our sound was sludgy. Having never done quaaludes, I still felt like I'd done quaaludes. My friends left early, mouthing *"Babysitter!"* as they pointed at the door and then backed out of the club.

After the show in Houston, we met up with an old friend of Aram and Jason's from the Eastern Shore who invited us back to his house to sleep. We followed him in Tight 329, he driving some kind of fancy SUV, a Range Rover, let's say, and all of us whistled as we pulled into a neighborhood of gorgeous drooping live oaks underlit by halogen spots standing in the lawns of stunningly large mansions.

The guy was obviously making serious bank working for a huge media corporation in some capacity. Inside, he told us he'd just signed a promotional deal with my old pal Dave Matthews! He was a humble guy from the Eastern Shore of Virginia who'd gotten some scrubby job out of college but was now something of a kingmaker, having moved up the ladder at Corporation X and become a powerful player in the industry. "What could he do for us?" we may have wondered. (We did, of course, wonder that.) The dude was cutting deals with Dave, right? And we were better than Dave, at least in our opinion, if not that of the marketplace...

What would we have done if he wanted to dance with us? No idea. Did we want that? Well, why not? Would making some kind of deal with him comprise selling out? Weren't there ways to make a deal that wouldn't result in our entire souls being sold, instead maybe just one little part of our souls? A part that we could easily grow back, like a salamander's tail? Wouldn't it be nice to make enough money to buy a house in the fancy part of town, and to go Range Rovin' with the cinema stars?

Yes to all of the above, I often thought. So, sue me.

Remember, back home I was jobless and my wife was about to give birth to our second child. You're damn right I was thinking about signing deals.

But there was something strange and joyless about the friend's mansion, something soulless and empty about how he avoided our questions about what exactly he did for the corporation. A huge television screen was bolted over the mantelpiece, an overstuffed pale sofa beneath it, a few darkened rooms on the first floor appeared unused. The friend didn't appear too excited about his newish job, either, padding around in flip-flops as he reached into a gigantic fridge for another round of Bud Lights.

"It's a living," he sighed.

In Chattanooga, people stood in a long line on the sidewalk in the waning afternoon heat and watched us as we lugged our gear into the club. This was exciting. The promoter approached us.

"Hey, listen, y'all got any problem with opening up? Playing the early spot?"

"Uh, I suppose not," Ned said. "Why?"

"I was lucky enough to book a local band," he said. "They're real popular right now."

So, all of those kids were there to see the local band, not the Anomoanon.

After our set, which went over very well, we stayed to watch the popular local band. It was a jam band. As in, post-Dave Matthews limp-funk noodling.

A local restaurateur who Ned knew took us back to his restaurant, after the place had closed and opened up a few bottles of great wine, made us cocktails, and pulled some snacks out of the kitchen. It was a reminder that there were always fringe benefits to being in a band, even one that was having trouble putting butts in seats.

That night I piloted Tight 329 up Lookout Mountain, one hand over my right eye, my foot pressed to the accelerator for fear that if I let up, we'd tumble backward into the Tennessee River.

As we were setting up for the Chapel Hill show, the final show of the tour, it was difficult not to notice that the crowds weren't exactly rolling in. In fact, we were alone in the club, accompanied by a single dude watching TV behind the bar. We inquired, politely of course, whether the pre-show sales had been any good, or whether there was any local buzz, maybe a blurb in the free weekly? He took a break from watching Seinfeld reruns long enough to tell us that some big indie rock show at the Cat's

Cradle was where everybody was that particular night and that we shouldn't worry too much about it.

People would probably roll in a little later, he promised.

On the poster for the show we noted there was no local opener, which was good and bad. If there'd been an opener, maybe a few of their friends might've shown up, and while the opener played, we'd have another hour or two to hope that more warm bodies wandered in from the street. No such luck. A solo bill.

One could cut this pie a few ways, but the method I was using to cut it, to process the evening, was that the club basically wanted us in and out as quickly as possible. Not a very tasty piece of pie. We took our buyout from the bored employee (he had a brown mullet, was wearing leather half gloves with circles over the knuckles, like driving gloves, and wore a leather jacket even though it was summer) then grabbed a bite nearby. After our meal we headed back to the club, hoping that more people might have arrived. Nope. Still empty. The lone employee with the mullet and leather driving half gloves was still watching TV.

By the time we took the stage there were four people in the audience. Four paying members on a door deal at probably seven dollars per guest. Do the math. Just before we started, during an onstage huddle in front of my drum kit, Willie suggested that at least we could play for ten minutes and cut out and hit the road. Getting the hell out of Dodge sounded like a good idea to me. These four poor bastards in the "crowd" would probably make it through three songs before bailing and going to check out the shitty indie rock band playing at the Cradle.

During our first song I watched Mr. Knuckle Gloves from my drum throne. He was seated in the next room at the bar still watching television and eating popcorn. Not even standing behind the bar pretending to want to sell drinks! Every so often he'd throw his head back and laugh at Elaine or Kramer or whomever.

This was shaping up to be an epically miserable finale of an epic and strange tour.

Then I noticed that the four people who were watching us weren't just watching us but were actually dancing. Wait. Why were their lips moving? Were they singing along? They were. And playing air guitar? Ned looked over his shoulder at me, at Aram, at Willie. Excuse me, but what the heck? Were they actually throwing the sign of the horns while not even singing but yelling the choruses to our opener? And leaping on one anothers' backs in what appeared to be ecstasy? It was true. They were doing all of these things.

After the first song ended Ned asked them what their story was. They said they'd driven from Missouri to North Carolina just for our show. They were Anomoanon super fans, quite possibly the only ones in existence. In fact, I'll go ahead and posit that there was no "quite possibly" about it: we were playing for the biggest Anomoanon fans on the planet. All four of them. They knew every word of every song we played, even the old ones, and danced and sang along with gusto in the entirely empty club throughout the show. They appeared to enjoy the brand-new songs we'd soon record. They interrupted the bartender's TV watching and bought us a couple rounds of beers, then we bought them some bourbon shots.

So, we played our full set, all two-plus hours' worth, and a couple of encores, pretty much playing every song we'd learned for the tour. For four people. And it was true: we didn't make a red penny that night and probably lost money after paying our bar tab.

Do I even need to add that it was worth it?

AFTER THE CHAPEL HILL show we drove through the night to an eighteenth century plantation called Onley Farm in Onancock, Virginia, owned by the Stith's old friend Pooh, arriving at the ghostly mansion at four in the morning. I wish I could write that it was the first plantation I'd ever visited, but the fact of the matter is that if you grew up in Richmond in the seventies you knew at least five families who'd somehow held on to ancestral piles that had once contributed to the evil tobacco empire that had once built our tainted country, most of them located in the Tidewater. In fact, my own grandfather had purchased one for peanuts in the early twentieth century, so my own childhood had been shaped by regular visits to Eagle Point in Gloucester, Virginia, built in 1795.

As we bumped down Onley's oystershell driveway, the moon low over the pines, the scent of salt marsh drifting in through Tight's open windows, it was impossible not to think of my grandmother, of my childhood, including the memory of learning from an older cousin how to hold a firecracker close to a blue crab, who'd inevitably reach out with a single claw and grab the firecracker. Then, with a fireplace match, you'd light the firecracker. Hijinks would ensue. And also animal cruelty.

In the morning we woke, drank coffee, set up our instruments and got to work. As usual, we didn't have much time to lay down the tracks. I think we'd given ourselves three full days. The plan was to record all of the new songs we'd been playing the entire seventeen-show tour. It had been decided that Palace Records would not have anything to do with this record. Ned had spoken to Jeremy DeVine, head of Temporary Residence records, and he'd agreed to put out the record we were about to record. Of course, Jeremy had put out Will's *Travels in Constants* in 2000 so maybe Will had recommended Jeremy as someone who'd be good to work with.

In either case, and as we'd learned already, and would continue to be reminded of in the future, it was becoming more difficult to figure out who was dealing with the Anomoanon because we had something to do with Will Oldham, and who was dealing with us because they actually liked our music or saw some commercial potential in our band.

WE WERE A PRETTY well-oiled machine by this point, and it was fun working with Aram and Jason's old friend Pooh. Pooh's house had a great feel, the room sound was wonderful, and since we'd played the songs so many times the tracking was a piece of cake. Pooh was also a great cook and good company so nightly we sat down to delicious meals of softshell crabs and fried sugar toads and oysters and multiple bourbons and bottles of wine. From the kitchen ceiling dangled a mold-covered Virginia ham, a photo of which ended up in the packaging for the next record. (A few fans even got the visual pun: old ham.) We celebrated July Fourth nearby at the Stiths' house where Aram and Jason had grown up—their parents were fantastic hosts—and spent the next two days adding tracks to the tape.

We'd really been working hard. The tour had been a blast, and we made a little money. As usual, we'd met some great new people like the guys in South San Gabriel and the French Kicks, gotten to visit some old friends and go swimming with a nubile young stripper. Poor Smokey didn't kill us or steal Will's mics. I was heading home to a pregnant wife, a three-year-old, and no job. Sitting outside of Pooh's house with a cold drink and peering over the marshes of Onancock Creek, seeing the Spanish moss-draped oaks and hearing the cicadas and nightbirds squeak and howl as great blue herons floated prehistorically over the water, it was easy to fall into a reverie and to think that our time was coming. Everything was falling into place and the natural spirits of the world agreed. They were winking at us from the woods, from beneath the surface of the salt creek, whispering encouragements.

When I listened to the tracking versions of *Asleep Many Years in the Wood* at the time, I was convinced beyond any shadow of a doubt that this would be our breakthrough. It was the most complete record we'd made up to that point. I recall laughing aloud when I heard songs like "Kick Back" and "Bluebird of Happiness" and "Sadie and Rudy" and "Tongue and Heart" during playback, having the same weird premonitions I'd had back in '94 when we were at Kramer's listening to the early mixes of Palace's "Gulf Shores" and "West Palm Beach." Ned had just absolutely crushed it when writing these songs. They were brilliant. This new Anomoanon record was our first classic record and would be remembered for the ages. There was no way "Kick Back" wouldn't become a hit, with its unironic use of a cowbell, for Christ's sake, and its unsubtle referencing of The Modern Lovers' "Roadrunner" there at the end. It was a perfect record, I thought, one that I'd listen to even if I wasn't in the band.

Asleep Many Years in the Wood wouldn't be released until 2002, but I was sure it would be the record that would establish the Anomoanon in the musical firmament.

19

Tongue and Heart

A MONTH LATER, ON August 11, 2001, our second son, named Maxwell, was born. His older brother loved holding him and patting him on the head like a small puppy. Ned and Jennie's son Sam would be born three months later.

Chris, still not finished with her dissertation but working full-time downtown, spent late nights at the computer in between breast feedings. Maxwell filled our house with a new and welcome energy.

In desperation, now the father of two young boys, I'd sunk so low as to agree to help cut grass for a property owner I'd met, which is how Tabb, then almost four, ended up straddling the hood of a green John Deere as I guided the tractor across someone's lawn in Boring, Maryland, at one of the suburban properties my new boss owned outside of town. While Tabb and I cut grass, infant Maxwell slept in the car seat in the Taurus, the same car that had carried Ned, Aram, and me across the country, while Chris worked after recuperating from her second caesarian. At lunchtime I took Max out of his car seat and put him in the Snugli while Tabb and I took a break and ate Mexican leftovers from the styrofoam container, leaning against the back of the car. After our shift ended, we all took a dip in the pool.

Dylan had once said, "What's money? A man is a success if he gets up in the morning and gets to bed at night, and in between he does what he wants to do," and if I didn't really want to be riding a lawn mower between morning and night, there was no question that I enjoyed not answering to anyone. I was not joining the great rigged game that so many of my friends had joined, those who were now lawyers, doctors, and finance wizards, and instead was living a life based purely on fundamental humanist terms: I was raising two boys. I had time to continue to work on the Mali book. I had time to play music with friends. I had tons of time to hang out with my wife, and to take my two boys to the park, to the Baltimore Zoo, often accompanied by Ned and his kids, and one afternoon by Will. Yes, I struggled with the idea that I was cutting grass for a living, but things could've been worse.

The simple truth was that Chris and I were nearly broke. And now with two sons, my struggles had taken on a new and daunting shade of bleak. I was finding that the extremes of life were more pronounced. The highs with the band, children, and family were far higher than any I'd yet experienced, which was an incredible and joyous and life-affirming rush, but the lows were that much lower. Remember that sense back in Florida when the first kid was born that I was dying as fast as the kid was growing? Square it. I had to make money, and not just a little bit, and I'd illustrated thus far in my life that making money was not one of my strengths. It was easy to sense that the adventure of being a performing artist and a pretend writer was coming to an unceremonious end.

I'd been listening to a lot of electronic music for the previous few years, pretty much since I'd gotten back from Europe with Will back in '94 (I liked listening to music with no words while

I wrote my bad short stories in our basement hovel in DC, which began a lifelong love of electronic and classical music), an obsession that really picked up when I started working at Vinyl Fever in Tallahassee with all the cool rave deejays. Autechre, Oval, Mouse On Mars, Flying Saucer Attack, a lot of Warp bands, Aphex and Richard James projects, Boards of Canada, plus a lot of dance 12"s. Will knew of this interest. One day during a phone call he asked me if I'd ever listened to much Nine Inch Nails. In fact, I hadn't. Had I heard of Chris Vrenna, drummer from NIN, who'd started a project called Tweaker? No. Will had just collaborated with him on a record, he said. He'd actually flown down to Austin and recorded it with Vrenna and Paul Leary of the Butthole Surfers.

It was yet another curveball in Will's arsenal of trick pitches.

What would Will do next? This question was never far from my mind.

I'D FINISHED A DRAFT of my non-fiction account of our Mali adventure, and through Sweeney had met an agent in New York, who seemed optimistic that my manuscript was good enough to sell to a publisher. This was a good balance to my ego-destroying stint as a lawnman, and gave my life shape, gave me something to hope for. I was, in fact, an artist who was supporting my desire to write with the more tangible and marketable skill of playing the drums in a band that was fortunate enough to be able to make records and to play with popular musicians like Will Oldham, in addition to the skill of being able to handle a riding mower, a chainsaw, and a weed-whacker. The book had been difficult to write but rewarding, and the finished product, influenced by Paul Bowles, Bruce Chatwin, and Graham Greene, was, I thought, very good. It was as perfect a narrative of our bizarre time in Mali as I could imagine, and again my confidence got the best of me.

The book would sell, I'd make some money, and go on a book tour. Like Jimmy Rabbitte, the main character in the Alan Parker movie *The Commitments*, I could already hear the interviews I'd give to Terry Gross: "Well, it was hard, Terry, living in rural Mali with a toddler, but the Malian people really accepted us…"

ONE AFTERNOON IN LATE August, just home from cutting grass, a large box appeared on our doorstep in Hampden. I dragged it into the house and sliced it open with a kitchen knife, finding inside a brand-new Lionel train set. There was a note in the FedEx envelope. It was from Sweeney. He'd met Neil Young's manager through Billy Corgan, with whom he'd just started a new band called Zwan, and was able to send the young Carneal lads a train set through this interesting connection (Neil was a big train fan and had been part of an investment group that saved Lionel from bankruptcy in the mid-nineties).

Ned, Will, Aram, Willie, and I had talked smack about Sweeney's joining Corgan's new band. Will was particularly disappointed in his two old friends. I argued that that was what gigging musicians did. They played with those who hired them. A true rocker would never turn down an invitation to make some money, even with Billy Corgan. I reminded him that one of the holy Slint dudes had played with Jimmy Eat World.

Jimmy Eat World!

Will looked at me, obviously disappointed at my defense of selling out. In this regard, he hadn't changed. He would never compromise those same ideals fostered as a young punk rocker in Louisville. The Corporation was the enemy. It was the enemy now, it would be the enemy in the future. It would always be the enemy.

I'd learned that a musician, an artist, was in many ways no different than any other professional: the goal was to move up the ladder, to do better, to attract more paying customers, and to make more money. That one wants to make more money doesn't mean one wants to become rich, but instead one wants to be able to fund their own future explorations. More money meant more music. As I saw it, this often meant aligning one's self with someone with whom one might not want to be aligned (like Billy Corgan or Jimmy Eat World), or to cut deals with people whose interests in you might not always be the most helpful or supportive. Little compromises had to be made along the way.

The more difficult question, as always, was how to go about the process of making a living without allowing those necessary compromises to ruin your sense of selfhood, or taint what drove you forward into life with confidence. And by "you," I meant us, but mostly Will. *Fame* was an arbitrary and capricious beast, I assume Will knew this far better than I did. In the complex equation of *success*, *fame*, and *talent* were variables F and T, completely unrelated to one another. Plenty of talented people would never become famous, and plenty of famous people, the majority perhaps, had no talent, but instead they possessed an unalloyed desire and ambition to be *famous*.

In the winter of 2001, I took Tabb to the Senator Theater in Baltimore to see the first installment of Peter Jackson's *Lord of the Rings: The Fellowship of the Ring* and was moved to tears by the nearly perfect evocation of one of the landmark books of my book-filled youth. Perhaps Will's literal walking away from California in the early nineties was comparable to Gandalf's realization in *The Fellowship of the Ring* that he, Gandalf, would be unable to carry the One Ring to Mount Doom, even though he was the most powerful wizard around. The Ring, like fame, was too powerful, it spoke too deeply and directly to the darkest parts of Gandalf's nature. Standing in Bilbo's house near the fire, Gandalf knew that carrying the Ring would lead to his death.

Will was Gandalf, fully aware of the destructive powers of fame in a way that I couldn't yet know.

The flacks of the music industry? The Nazgul, of course.

After unpacking the Lionel box, I set up Sweeney's gifted trains in our cold Hampden basement. My elder son would soon spend hours down there, watching the trains loop around the track, while Chris and I sat on the futon with the babe nuzzling against Chris's breast, the odd smell of ozone and the haunting train whistle coloring many of my memories of that time.

Thoughtful acts like Matt's reminded me that my *Brothers and Sisters* vision, as naive as it may have seemed, was never too far off. I really was part of a broad group of musicians for whom kindnesses came more naturally than not.

WHEN I'D FIRST MOVED to Baltimore, I'd sent my résumé to a writer named Madison Smartt Bell, who taught writing at Goucher College in Towson, a suburb of Baltimore. George Garrett, a professor of Ned's and mine at UVA, had called ahead to give Madison a heads up. Madison said they had no openings at Goucher, but that he'd keep my résumé on file.

One day in late August, holding my new son against my chest, the morning light cascading in through the kitchen window, my home phone rang. It was poet Clarinda Harriss, chair of the English department at Towson University. She said a teacher had just flaked out and they needed a warm body to teach a fiction writing class that would start the following week.

"Madison gave you a fantastic review, said you'd really done a great job for him at Goucher, said you'd be perfect for this job."

I'd never met Madison and certainly had never worked for him. I was smart and desperate enough to remain silent. George's phone call had worked.

I began on a Tuesday afternoon, had class again on Thursday, and then the following Tuesday was preparing for class while feeding the babe and listening to the radio when Bob Edwards, then announcer for Morning Edition and whom I'd met a few times when I was at NPR, said something about a plane crashing into the World Trade Center. Sitting there with my new son, having taken his older brother to our neighborhood nursery school earlier, I listened to the updates on the radio all morning long.

Among a million other thoughts, all of them upsetting, I recognized that my narrative of our time in Muslim Mali, a mostly fond recollection of our Malian friends and neighbors, all of them practicing Muslims, had just been rendered worthless by the terrorist attacks in Manhattan, at the Pentagon and in Somerset County, Pennsylvania. No one would be interested in a book about a Muslim country that did not reference 9/11 on every other page. The project was dead.

20

There's a Contrary Breeze A'Blowing

ONE EARLY AFTERNOON IN June of 2002 we began to practice in Will's front room in Waverly for a very short series of five shows that had grown out of the popularity of Heumann's Anti-Folk night. The tour was billed thusly:

The Anomoanon featuring Paul Oldham
with Will Oldham Blokbuster lineup!

Part of that Blokbuster business was musician Cass McCombs, who was a fixture on the Anti-Folk stage (as was Ned) and who'd written some great songs that I really liked. He was gaining traction. I'd played a local show or two as Cass's drummer, and he'd babysat the boys once or twice, maybe more, so it seemed natural that we'd all help him out. The

Anomoanon would be the main band onstage. We'd play some Will songs, some Ned songs, and some Cass songs.

THE BLOKBUSTER TOUR ALLOWED the Anomoanon to promote *Asleep Many Years in the Wood*, which would not be released for another few months, in November, 2002. There were questions about why we were touring to support a record that had not yet been released, but any opportunity we had to play with Will was justifiable in our minds. At the very least we'd make some money and increase our visibility in preparation for the record's release, which you'll recall was, in my mind, stellar and would be the one that would catapult us into the charts. Since we'd played the songs on *Asleep*...the entire previous tour, we had them down to a fine rocking science.

To use the vernacular, we were tighter than a tick's asshole. We were all excited to be out on the road supporting *Asleep Many Years*. The songs Ned had written for the record pulled the best out of us as a band. We were a rock band, not a folk band, not an alt-country band, but a simple rock band, and Ned's latest songs were perfect encapsulations of a lifetime spent listening to a lot of great rock and roll. I much preferred playing fast rockers to the slow, downtempo 3/4 songs, so since most of the songs on *Asleep* were 4/4 rockers, this tour fit my skills. Life was good. My two boys were healthy and hearty, my wife was moving up the proverbial ladder at work, had gotten a raise or two, and I was the drummer for an absolutely kickass rock band.

On the short tour we played "Calvary Cross" by Richard and Linda Thompson and "Blues Run the Game" by Jackson C. Frank, where each of us took a turn lead singing a verse. Frank's baritone matched my limited vocal skills, so it went over pretty well, though I remember boofing my lines in Philly.

My verse from Frank's song was "Maybe tomorrow, honey, someplace down the line, I'll wake up older, so much older, mama, I'll wake up older and I'll just stop all my tryin'."

At the end of the tour, back in Baltimore, Will told us he was moving back to Louisville and that Dianne was moving to New York. I was sad to see them go.

BY 2003, I WAS largely responsible for the happiness of two-year-old Maxwell and five-year-old Tabb, which meant making sure there were always pounds of mac and cheese ready to be shoveled into their little gullets and gallons of the yogurt drink that each little dude preferred. Chris was working more than full-time—she'd head off to Kabul in a few months and spend two weeks traveling the Panjshir Valley, where she'd note the gorgeous fields of poppies, while back in Kabul the city had been razed, and men in shalwar kameezes slouched past with Kalashnikovs—while I was teaching a full-load at Towson University and life was generally rich.

I see on the internet that in '03 the Anomoanon released a four-song EP called *Portrait of John Entwistle*, who had upped and died in a Vegas hotel room in the summer of '02. Ned had put music to the poem "Cherries" by C. M. Barker, and we covered the Entwistle song "Heaven and Hell."

IN AUGUST OF 2003 the Anomoanon hit the road for another series of shows. We were finally going to be able to tour to support the release of *Asleep Many Years*, which had gotten a rave review on *Pitchfork*, a few great reviews elsewhere, but which was thus far not causing many ripples in the marketplace. This tour, I was certain, would be a raging success, after which I'd begin another semester teaching. We'd brought along a video camera to record the shows, and I had it in my mind that I might make a tour film out of the results.

The first day's footage: poorly lit interior shots of the van, blurry landscapes, us clowning at a rest stop. Unique stuff.

My agent had bailed on trying to sell my Mali book when the big houses passed on the manuscript, partly, I'm sure, because it was a book about a Muslim country and had been written before the epochal events of September 11, 2001, which rendered the domestic-oriented adventures in the book mostly moot. Or maybe they just didn't like it, who knows. I'd written a forward trying to place the events of our year there in a more socio-religious context, which wasn't misleading. We'd lived in a Muslim country for a year and witnessed first-hand the difficulties and frustrations of existing in a country that had been left behind by the first world. But without a socio-religious context as the focus, and without 9/11 as the foundation on which the narrative was built, it was a tough sell.

Our eldest son was nearing kindergarten age and we wanted to move to the neighborhood next to ours in Baltimore to take advantage of their far superior public school, another concern. We'd have to move soon.

As excited as I was about this tour, the full-on joyous and generous spirit I'd felt in the wake of recording and releasing *Asleep* was ebbing.

THE DEBUT SHOW OF the tour in Harrisonburg, Virginia, was at a house party and not a club, which did not bode well for the tour's bottom line. As we loaded in through a basement door, a steady stream of young, crusty punks entered and exited with us. We had no guarantees for this tour so whatever money we made from the show would be from the door, and the door appeared to be not a door at all but instead an open portal through which anyone might pass.

During our setup I noted that the basement had leaked in the previous night's deluge and there was a slick of greasy water underneath my drums. Termites had eaten most of the joist that held the floor above my head so when anyone walked on the second floor little flakes of joist and flooring would rain down. I rested a beer on the clothes dryer next to me while I played. The main sewer pipe of the home drained right behind where I sat, so throughout the night I could feel against my back the whooshing of toilet water being flushed from the bathrooms upstairs.

The opening act was a young hardcore band, all of whom appeared to have been taking their fashion and fitness cues from Glenn Danzig, lots of cut-off black T-shirts with skulls, lots of ripped biceps, lots of gothy devil-locks, lots of black wristbands, lots of chain wallets flying around, lots of frustrated slam dancing among the all-male crowd. When they finished the place cleared out, never fun to watch when you're the next band on the bill, but then refilled when we began. We played a great show, even if by the end of the night most of the young crusters had hit the road.

We went to get our money from the promoter who, when we approached him, peered at us as though we were visitors from a distant time and place, Bedouins on camels, perhaps. His eyeballs were so dilated it appeared you could step right into his pupils and hang out in his brain.

"Oh, man," he breathed, shaking his head. "I have no money, man. Maybe I'll send you some?"

"Maybe you'll send us some? Like what, via Pony Express?"

"Ponies," he smiled. "Ponies on parade."

"Yeah, not so fucking funny when you're trying to make a living," I said to the guy.

"Bro," he said. "Dude. Man. Chill."

Me, Aram, and Willie ended up playing Hacky Sack in a used car lot across the street for a half hour or so while Ned tried to wheedle the shrooming hipster for some gas money, who finally, and in a rather niggardly fashion, gave us a single twenty-dollar bill.

Niggardly, with malice.

IN THE MORNING WE hiked barefoot up a mountainous footpath through summer forest shadows to Paul's Creek near Afton, where we swam in the cold mountain water. Refreshed, soothed by the mountain air and the crisp creek water, we had fun despite the previous night's disappointment.

We took the video camera up the trail and got some good footage of each of us standing beneath a waterfall, the late morning light slanting through the trees. At one point, Aram, holding the camera, panned from my feet up to what I assumed might be my face, instead pausing with a snicker and lingering on the moobs I'd been cultivating since becoming a father; moobs, beer guts, double chins, a general endomorphism being the drummer's bane. Ask John Bonham, Keith Moon, and Squeeze's Gilson Lavis (RIP)! Ask former Meat Puppet Derrick Bostrom, whose tour diaries are filled with insecurities about becoming fat! Ask all the other fat drummers!

Later we drove in to Charlottesville and ate at Tokyo Rose, a sushi restaurant. During a post-prandial walk on the Downtown Mall I was overcome by a horrible intestinal tumult. I excused myself from the lads and dodged into the back door of a commercial restaurant and found myself in the kitchen, where I speed walked past a grill cook lording over a row of rubbery burgers in my attempt to find a toilet. I relieved myself, noting that a cold sweat was beginning to form along my hairline.

We arrived back at the club to find that the opening band had filled the stage with shampoo bottles, bars of soap, and bath toys—rubber duckies and the like—in addition to two small amps and a drum kit. Curious, I set up the video camera, still feeling shaky from whatever it was that had made my lower intestine unstable, and turned on the camera. We could see a cluster of excited college students standing to the side of the stage, protecting the people whom I assumed were the opening band from our gazes. The band members came on after a few minutes, all thin bookish lads with glasses. Oh, and they were shirtless and wrapped in towels, bathrobes, and wearing bathing caps, as if they were on their way to the shower. As they adjusted mics, the lead singer said, "A little bit of Iraq in Charlottesville!"

Beat.

"We are the Bath Party! Yay!"

There were more people there for the Bath Party than for the Anomoanon. By the end of our show I counted ten people watching us. This was triply embarrassing as we'd started our erstwhile careers in Charlottesville, still had friends there, a couple of whom came to the show, but just as many had decided to beg out and stay home with their kids. Our table of merch lay undisturbed.

I put the video recorder away and abandoned my concept of a celebratory tour film. In the van, the batteries in the Bop It died, and we didn't replace them.

THROUGHOUT THE NOTEBOOKS I kept during those years I find the repeated phrase, "Morgantown, another late night of bourbon and weed" or "We stayed up late and drank a bottle of bourbon and smoked weed" or "after yet another all-nighter in New York where we drank a handle of Dant bourbon and smoked a bunch of weed…" and I guess this is as good a time as any to remind my readers that we had always been a band that enjoyed that element of being in a touring band. Very rarely did we dip into other intoxicants. Nope, we were almost strictly a beer, bourbon, and weed band. Red wine, sometimes, white wine if no red was available, and once, in Morgantown, we drank a lot of Belgian blackberry lambic, which we found to be delicious. We weren't an upper or downer type of band. No blow, no pills. Nope, the boring triumvirate of weed, bourbon, beer. And to be very clear, we were always gentlemen drinkers. Never once, not a single time, did we drink before, say, 6:00 p.m. Never during the day, never while driving (at least during the day), and we always waited for an appropriate time before we deemed it cocktail hour, usually after setting up for the evening's gig.

In fact, during this tour I quit smoking weed before shows, noting that I was a lot more crisp, to borrow Dave Chappelle's adjective, if I hadn't gotten baked.

On the way into Morgantown we misread a sign for a local restaurant called "Wings Olé" as *Wimy's Olé*, and that became part of the lexicon of the tour.

"Wimy's Olé!" we'd call out randomly, like baked matadors.

At a rest stop between Morgantown and Manhattan, Aram, wearing earplugs, stood next to the van doing some yoga, and during a deep lunge let out a fart just as a small man stood directly behind him, who flinched.

"You've invented a new yoga position," someone said. "It's called the Farting Camel."

At Bereket Turkish Kebab takeout in Manhattan before the show at Tonic, we saw Mick Turner and Jim White of the Dirty Three, whom Ned had met when they were working on Will's infamous unreleased album that ended up being part of the record *Guarapero*, and whom we invited to the night's show. Chris had also driven up from Baltimore to visit a pregnant friend, who was coming to the show with her boyfriend, who happened to be the bass player for classic rock legends Santana. Alan Licht, who was booking shows at Tonic, opened the show with some treated guitar, which I loved.

The Ano's show wasn't very good, and afterward I recall the Santana bass player offering us helpful suggestions as if we were a high school band who'd just screwed up our first talent show.

"Keep practicing!" he said helpfully. "Being in a rock band is not a sprint, but a marathon!"

Thanks, dude.

After the Tonic show in New York we played a few shows with a duo called Sin Ropas, one of whom, Tim Hurley, had once been part of Chicago's Red Red Meat. A married couple, Tim played guitar while his wife Danni Iosello played drums.

In Providence after the show we stayed up super late with Bobby Arellano and his better half Jodie Jean listening to Heart records played very loudly. They were closing up shop in Providence and preparing to move to New Mexico, so the night was both a celebration of new experiences and a goodbye to Providence, where Bob had lived since the mid-eighties, and where so much of the early Palace Brothers story began.

Sin Ropas had begged off and hit the sack early, thereby claiming the home's sole guest room and its large bed. They were married, after all, so we, being gentleman, afforded them that small luxury, though we did not offer them the indulgence of a peaceful and restorative sleep, since we blasted Heart records until the wee hours. Listening to Heart's Michael Derosier's powerful drumming blasting through Bob's living room, I was reminded that Robert Plant had once dragged a bloated and depressed John Bonham to a Heart show at Madison Square Garden so that Bonham could see Derosier, the drummer whom many were claiming would unseat Bonham as the greatest rock drummer of the time, in hopes that it'd light a fire under Bonham's ass for what would become the sessions for *In Through the Out Door*. There's some great drumming on *In Through the Out Door*, including the insanely difficult Purdie shuffle on "Fool in the Rain," so I assume the technique actually worked.

That night at Bob and Jodie's we played "Barracuda" multiple times. How many times does one need to hear "Barracuda" played in row? No more than six or seven, thought we, which appeared to be five or six times too many for the no-longer-sleeping Ropas kids. Quite suddenly, they showed up in the frame of the living room door, agitated, their hair tangled and sleep deformed, eyes mere slits, our wobbly crania angling toward them like baseball player bobbleheads. They asked us to keep it down, they were trying to sleep, for God's sake, the stereo's too dang loud, and of course, we complied without complaint, pretty much turning off the stereo, closing our eyes and engaging a bodily shutting down of operations, going into safety mode before any neurons became permanently whacked by further blasting of Heart.

Alas, the shows with and without Sin Ropas were not very well-attended. And for the record we liked Sin Ropas. They were like us. Trying their hardest to put on good shows, maybe a little disappointed that the crowds weren't better. Being the Anomoanon, we were total positive face, we still had fun, we still rocked every house we played, we were still a great band and more convinced than ever of that fact. However, we appeared unable to put butts in seats.

A FEW MONTHS LATER, the first Friday in October, I flew out to Nashville to record percussion for Will's *Sings Greatest Palace Music* record. Not only had Nashville legends like Hargus "Pig" Robbins and Eddie Bayers played on the record, but a bunch of people who'd played with Will in the past, like Aram, Ned, Colin, Sweeney, DV, even Andrew Bird, who would soon establish his own career as a singer and songwriter, were also invited by Will to contribute. It was a moving and generous gesture for Will to include so many musicians with whom he'd shared some history.

At night we went barhopping with David Berman, and it transpired that the following night there was a local band show at Springwater, what is purported to be the oldest dive bar in Nashville. After a number of beers and a tour of a few of Nashville's legendary hotspots, there was some mention of me and Will accompanying Berman as his band, and that we could play a miniature set of Silver Jews songs during the band's show. Twenty-four hours later we were onstage backing Berman for a couple of classic old Jews tunes. We were joined by guitarist extraordinaire William Tyler.

The next night we went to a cookout at Bobby Bare Jr.'s house in Hendersonville, on Old Hickory Lake, where he'd grown up. Bare Sr. was a legendary Nashville singer-songwriter who'd recorded a few songs cowritten with Shel Silverstein, whose books and sensibility were hugely important to me, evoking strong memories of growing up in the strange seventies. In addition to writing epochal kids' books like *The Giving Tree* and *Where the Sidewalk Ends*, Silverstein had written Johnny Cash's "Boy Named Sue" and all of the weirdo songs by Dr. Hook and His Medicine Show, songs like "Cover of the Rolling Stone" and "Freakin' at the Freaker's Ball." At one point me, Will, Berman, and Bobby went out into the yard, where Bobby pointed at a small, single-story rancher across the way.

"George Jones and Tammy Wynette used to live there," Bobby said.

"Country stars live modestly," said Berman.

NED WAS VALIANT ABOUT continuing to try to book as many dates during our insane domestic schedules in Baltimore as was possible. If there was any desperation about *Asleep*'s relative quietude in the marketplace he didn't show it. The record was doing pretty well for Temporary Residence, but was not spreading like wildfire as I was certain it would. "Kick Back" was not being used in a Ford truck ad, in other words, at least not yet. So Ned organized another short five-show tour, inviting our old friend Dave Heumann along. The tour would begin at Tonic in New York, come back through Baltimore at the Creative Alliance, down to Wilmington, North Carolina, then to Mt. Pleasant, South Carolina, and finally to Winston-Salem, after which we'd drive back to Baltimore.

It wasn't difficult for me to cancel a week's worth of classes, though a mild but annoying anxiety began to accompany me when I canceled class and went on the road. At first I'd been able to access an obnoxious part of myself that didn't care that I was blowing off work. I was choosing art over the grind. I was sticking it to the man. But now I was liking sticking it to the man less and less. Leaving work created anxiety. I knew I'd have five times more work upon my return.

I *was* the man now.

At Tonic in New York we were supposed to play with Sweeney and his new band Cockfighter, but he called at the last minute and said someone in the band couldn't make the gig so they couldn't play, but that one of his friend's bands had agreed to fill in instead of Cockfighter.

Sweeney'd gotten the name for his new band from the Charles Willeford book of the same title, a book we'd all read numerous times, and an author whom we'd all learned to admire. There was something about Willeford's combination of stereotypical, old-fashioned manliness, eccentricity, and humility in his male protagonists that we all found comforting, for whatever reasons.

Even though he didn't play that night, Sweeney still came to the show. His time in Zwan had ended a few months earlier but he did not appear to be too upset. It was understood that few questions about the experience should be asked, he'd been forced to sign a confidentiality agreement with Corgan, so we laid off. Clearly there were things he was not supposed to say and Matt, being a gentleman (as were we all), didn't chirp.

(Right now's as good a time as any to offer to ghost-write your memoirs, Matt.)

That night we played the Malian band Tinariwen's release Radio Tisdas Sessions as our warm-up music and Sweeney loved it; it's wild to think that a few years later he'd be playing on one of their releases.

Andrew W. K. opened the show playing some weird piano music, meanwhile wearing running shoes, sweats, and wrapped tightly in a hoodie. He was unrecognizable. Could be that he thought Sweeney was going to be on the bill with him and when Sweeney backed out perhaps AWK was upset. It's true that Tonic was not exactly packed, and here Andrew had himself a big old-fashioned record deal negotiated by Sweeney and was selling out the Mercury Lounge. But tonight, opening for the Anomoanon at Tonic, bupkes.

The other band demanded to headline even though we were supposed to. As I recall, we decided not to fight city hall and let the band headline while we played in the middle spot. Which really is not a bad place to be. You finish a little earlier, for example, which leaves more time for drinking and socializing and packing up the van.

Splitting money at the end of a night for a multiple-band door show is difficult. Frequently it comes down to gentlemanly or gentlewomanly agreements. For example, if one of the bands on the bill is touring while the other bands are local, and if the show doesn't do all that well, it's not uncommon for the local bands to donate their portion of the proceeds to the touring band. At least that's the way we always did it. The touring band, obviously, has to pay for gas and food while the local bands just have to make it home to their apartments, so it's considered a generous thing to do.

When it came time to settle up at the end of the night the leader of the other band was nowhere to be found. He'd met with the Tonic moneyman unbeknownst to us and convinced him to hand over the largest portion of the night's take, then left. We were skunked.

After the show, over a few beers at Tonic's bar, we asked Sweeney what he thought we could do to try to gain more traction in the marketplace.

"Change your name," he said, without even thinking about it. "No one can even begin to pronounce it, it doesn't mean anything. So, step one, get a normal fucking band name."

"But it rhymes with phenomenon," we reminded him.

"Yeah, well, you know that and I know that, but no one else knows it."

It was true that pretty much every fan who ever spoke to us before or after a show either mispronounced the name or asked us how to pronounce it. And yet it was Sweeney who had to tell us the name might be part of our lack of traction.

Aram, Willie, Ned, and I talked about it later. We didn't take his advice. In fact, we didn't really even think about it at all.

THE FOLLOWING DAY, BACK in Baltimore, during the afternoon before the Creative Alliance show, Maxwell, now almost four, was invited to attend one of his older brother's friend's birthday parties. As young as he was, Max was already more coordinated than most ten-year-olds and had no problem hanging with the big boys. The party was at the local YMCA and during a basketball game he got trucked by one of the bigger guys, knocked ass over teakettle. The dad of the birthday boy called us to give an injury report.

"Says his hand hurts," the dad said, "might be a little swollen, nothing bad. I think he jammed a finger."

After picking him up at the Y, we squirted some liquid aspirin in Max's mouth and plunked him down in front of the TV and went back to preparing to head over to Highlandtown in Baltimore where the Creative Alliance was located while we waited for the babysitter.

Chris had been looking forward to this show for weeks. She was excited to hang out with her old friend Jennie and the rest of the band members, excited to have a few drinks and let loose while the babysitter hung out with the boys. Just as I was leaving to meet the band members at the Creative Alliance I decided to check on the lad and his sprained finger and found that his hand had ballooned to twice its normal size. He looked up at me with one of those longing pained looks, holding up his hand, his puppy dog eyes brimming with tears, his lip quivering.

At the emergency room Chris learned he'd broken his hand and would have to be put into a cast. There was no way she'd be able to attend the show. That was disappointing. Meanwhile, just before taking the stage I was worried about my son in the hospital, having to deal with doctors and pain. It was another reminder, as if one was needed, that having kids is hard.

The owner of the Creative Alliance, whom we'd once considered one of our biggest fans in Baltimore, was, we learned that night, more of a Will fan than an Anomoanon fan. This was a surprise. An unpleasant one. Every question she asked was about Will. *How's Will doing? When's he coming back to play here? I've called him but he never returns my calls! I'm so bummed he doesn't live in Baltimore anymore. We make a loooooot of money when Will plays! Tonight's show isn't close to sold out! I wish Will were here playing with you guys tonight! We really need a boost! Did I tell you yet the show's not close to sold out?* (Theatrical sad face.)

Anyhow, it was true: we had a good crowd that night but it was not sold out. The fans who were there were treated to yet another great rock show put on by the Anomoanon. A highlight among all the lows: my sister Ann Barron and her husband Ted dancing with abandon as the rest of the crowd watched and listened. Between getting screwed in New York and having to deal with emergency rooms and broken bones and the grumpy director of a nonprofit arts organization openly blaming us for not selling the place out, it had been a weird few days.

THE NEXT DAY, A brutally long drive to Charleston. We played our show in nearby Mt. Pleasant after a long meal with far too many bottles of wine at Aram's house. Most of the guests of the show had been at Aram's house beforehand, so the vibe in the red-hued club (that's mostly what I recall through the dim haze of memory and too much red wine, that the club was bathed in a red, neonish light) was jovial, loud, and maybe a little too loose. As in, a drunken mess.

The tour wasn't very relaxing and I had too much time in the long car ride to worry about things. I'd noted of late that my normal life, my non-band life, was so busy that I frequently became overwhelmed by the stimuli. Chris and I had two sons and no money. I was stressed about going back home to the stack of ungraded papers and student emails. I also knew that the chair of the department was probably growing tired of my absences even though she was too cool to let me know that.

The final show in Winston-Salem was fun inasmuch as we got to stay with an old friend of mine from college and his wife, which really, when looking back on these tours, was what made them all worthwhile even if we didn't make a bunch of dough. They had two young twins, my friend had to get up and go to work in the morning, but still we stayed up late on their back porch drinking beers and talking and laughing until my friend, a borderline narcoleptic, fell asleep in his chair and began snoring.

21

The Dire Wolf Collects His Dues

BACK IN BALTIMORE, NED continued to work the phones in an attempt to sell the Anomoanon to a wider audience. It was a full-time job. His hard work was rewarded: a label based in Spain called Houston Party reached out to Ned to ask for permission to distribute a CD version of *The Derby Ram* in Spain and parts of Europe.

Aram, Ned, and I had recorded *The Derby Ram* in Ned's basement over the course of one or two days the previous year and it turned out great. The dirge-like epic "Derby Ram," purportedly George Washington's favorite song, was counterbalanced by a series of playful, up-tempo rock songs, including Aram's "Little Birdy," and Ned's "Ding Dong Bell." It was one of those recording sessions that goes so perfectly, so smoothly, that it's difficult to recall much about it so many years later.

When I heard the final product of *The Derby Ram*, I was overjoyed that the record had a clean, airy, and casual sound. It was a perfect encapsulation of the clean, airy, and casual feel of the recording sessions. *The Derby Ram* had already been released in LP-only format by a German label, September Gurls, and Houston Party, from Spain, was pressing an CD version. So I didn't understand why we couldn't find an American label to press both CD and LP, but by that point we realized that we were not in the position of choosing such things, and instead were just beggars.

Houston Party had licensed a lot of popular indie rock bands like Death Cab for Cutie, the Posies, the Shins, Superchunk, and Iron & Wine for Spanish distribution. All of these bands had found the proverbial traction in the marketplace and sold well. So it was a big deal for the Anomoanon that Houston Party agreed to press the CD and to distribute *Derby Ram*.

Will had recently released his *Sings Greatest Palace Music* record. Aside from being a great record, and aside from it selling like crazy and ending up on the front page of just about every website I checked with any regularity, in addition to being reviewed by major newspapers around the globe, along with all of this other stuff, *Greatest Palace Music* stood as the most powerful symbol yet of Will's success: a greatest hits record, of all things, recorded with industry veterans and his brother Ned and old friends and representing a decade's worth of success and hard work. You might consider that the Anomoanon would be jealous of Will's success, particularly in the face of our struggles. You'd be wrong. It was great that Will was doing well. The Anomoanon was not into schadenfreude. We genuinely wanted everyone around us to do well. Bringing bad vibes into a scene was psychologically unhealthy, we thought. It was better to be positive in hope that the positive energy would come back to us. Karma, and all that.

Houston Party invited us to perform a few shows in Spain to promote *Derby Ram*, so we asked Heumann to come along to play keyboards and sing backup.

The invitation presented yet another job conflict: I'd have to cancel another week's worth of classes. I spoke to my chair.

"Wow," she said, shuffling some papers on her desk. "Spain. Well, how exciting for you."

I enjoyed teaching. My classes filled. My ratings were sky high. I was doing something right. I was often a jester, a performance artist, who'd show up to class unshaven with hair a greased mess, and who might assign Frederick Exley's *A Fan's Notes* or play "Sister Ray" in its entirety at high volume and ask the students to write their reactions. When angry, I kicked chairs and gave students crappy grades. When lazy, I gave out undeserved A's. Back then, I often decided what I was going to do in class that day on my bike rides to work. In my skewed but ultimately harmless opinion I was doing what needed to be done to these mostly suburban middle-class sleepwalkers—that is, taking their dull, internet-obsessed imaginations by their shoulders and shaking them into action.

I was excited, sort of, to go to Spain but knew that leaving class for the week would create exponentially more work when I returned to the grind. I was caught on the horns of a dilemma and recognized that I'd have to choose to be a great professor or an okay drummer. I was spreading my energies too thin.

The existential crisis I'd been undergoing since the early nineties was ongoing. Something would have to change.

THE FIRST FULL DAY in Barcelona we caught a bus out to the shore and spent the afternoon swimming in big strange swells in a slate-colored sea under a similarly slate-colored sky. Parts of Barcelona were hallucinatorily beautiful. After swimming and showering back at our hotel we made our way down alleys and found La Rambla, where we tried to eat a meal at 7:00 p.m. or so but all the restaurants were empty and waiters were still folding napkins and taking chairs off of tables. We were told it was too early to be served. Way too early.

The next night we played at the BAM!04 music fest at an old, formerly grand theater in Barcelona. It was a nightmare. The crew at the venue were all on smack (or wishing they could score) and nothing was getting done. After a couple hours' wait, we finally were able to sound check. I asked for adjustments to my monitor, convinced after a while that the soundboard wasn't actually operational, it was pretend, or, more likely, that the nodding soundman did not know what he was doing. I finally told the soundman that everything sounded great even though it didn't. I just wanted to be done with the painful sound check. I realized my mistake a couple hours later when the show began.

As mentioned, we'd brought along our friend Heumann, an extraordinarily gifted singer and musician who, in the few years I'd known him, having shared a stage or two, I'd learned often turned his amp up louder than anyone. Ned and Aram were both also guilty of turning their amps up louder than they should've. Dave was playing a keyboard with a particularly piercing, treble-heavy sound, and was also turning his volume up every chance he got, which resulted in that stage in Barcelona basically sounding like living inside of an explosion.

Throw in obnoxious clashing cymbals and clattering high hats and you have a dangerous brew of sound slop, which is exactly what I was hearing. Heumann put on his deaf guy act whenever I asked him to turn it down, either acting like he couldn't hear me or, when he did pretend to hear me, also pretending to move a dial but not actually moving it. Like our first Lollapalooza show in Chicago so many years before, I was adrift in this sound explosion, and like a pilot suffering from night blindness, had no way to tell how to get back to Earth. The result? The most onstage screwups ever in the history of the Anomoanon.

OUR HORRENDOUS SET WAS followed by a European dance rock band with bass and guitars that performed live over top of a prerecorded thumping and twinkling electronica track that was controlled by a guy in the sound booth. We were standing next to the booth as the guy moved a mouse around on a computer screen and, clicking away, he bopped along to the beat as the band played their instruments on stage. Ned, already upset about our terrible show, grew apoplectic as we all watched the soundman control the electronica while the crowd whooped and danced.

"They're not even playing!" Ned yelled. A group of kids danced nearby. Ned turned to them and yelled, "This band is not even playing that beat that you're dancing to! How can you like them? Jesus Christ. It's like Milli fucking Vanilli."

The kids laughed at us and kept on dancing. If I'd spoken better Spanish, I probably would've been able to translate the words they threw at us into, "Shirrup, you old, over-the-hill guitar-playing farts. Where's your laptop? Go back to your folk rock."

I was reminded that as much as Ned knew about music from the past, far more than I, he didn't listen to much music being made by our contemporaries. Tons of bands played along to prerecorded tracks, not just rappers or deejays but normal rock bands. For better or worse, it was nothing to be ashamed of. P. J. Harvey had opened some shows for U2 in 2001, and had told Will that there was a huge black cube-shaped booth underneath the stage where the prerecorded content that accompanied the U2 lads while they "played" was controlled. PJ claimed that she wandered too close to it one night, only to be accosted by a burly guard, who told her to get lost.

The festival show in Barcelona was miserable, a disaster, and not only because of the super popular band's prerecorded beats. We had not done a great job of rocking for our fans. Ned was understandably upset. I was upset because I was the cause of many of the flubs. We were all upset. The wild crowds dancing along to the electronica made us feel like dinosaurs.

At some point I made the mistake of checking my work email from a cyber cafe in Barcelona only to learn that my teaching request for the spring term had not been turned in. I'd not been awarded any classes, which meant, as an adjunct, I'd lost my job. I'd have to finish out the current semester and then find something else to do in the spring. As tiny as my salary was, we needed it, badly. Now it was gone.

A crushing sense of failure and depression seized my soul, mainly because I'd sensed that something like this might happen. I blamed my being spread too thin on my forgetting to turn in my teaching request, and the band, and this tour, was a huge part of the sense that I was just not focused on the things that were best for me and my family, namely being a professor of English who got a paycheck from the State of Maryland every two weeks. We played another show at a club in Barcelona, which was poorly attended. I recall having a conversation with myself while onstage. The conversation was a variation on the theme of "this blows donkey dongs."

I descended into a deep funk, barely able to raise my head to look at the Alhambra. Depression resulted in a severe state of juvenile passive-aggression, a forced incuriosity about our tour, about Spain. I was done with it. I didn't even write in my journal. At some show in some nameless club in some bland Spanish burg I did something I'd never done before and haven't done since: put on a freak show, bashing my drums miserably, letting my head flop around on my neck as if on drugs, moaning and otherwise trying to sabotage our music. I hope, now, that this scene comes across as comic, but I fear that it may not. It wasn't particularly funny then. Let's just pretend that it was, and that my wonderful bandmates, ever-kind, ever-understanding of the complexity of the human spirit, forgave me. Not much was said about it, which made it even worse.

IN MADRID WE WERE invited to film a television segment for a pop show. Inside a pastel-colored set with a low stage we found twenty to thirty teenagers gathered from central casting. They were obviously kids who hoped to get some screen time on a television show in order to advance, or begin their "acting" careers, and stood in front of the stage excitedly as we set up. Teenagers with baseball caps flipped backward, cute girls with off-the-shoulder blouses and bleached hair, cute kids in hip-hop gear like high-tops with the laces untied, graffiti-spackled T-shirts, black jeans.

There was a decidedly Mouseketeeresque vibe to the proceedings. The boys and girls were all cute, all bubbly, many of them jumping up and down and clapping their hands in front of their chests while others adopted a hip-hop cool. I often wonder what exactly those poor future Disney wannabes thought when the Anomoanon came out and began our set with "Down and Brown." Or "Summer Never Ends." All those scrubbed teens stopped clapping and hopping and instead stared at us dumbfounded. A few of the game ones tried to dance, awkward little bunny hops, some lame breakdancing. Didn't work. Meanwhile cameras on dollies swooped in and out as Ned, Aram, Willie, Heumann, and I tried not to look at one another for fear of laughing.

AFTER A LONG FLIGHT from Barcelona to New York, then an all-night drive back to Baltimore from LaGuardia, I had to be ready to roll at six thirty to get the kids up and fed and to school. Chris had taken off a couple of days from work while I was gone but had to report for duty the morning after our arrival, which meant there'd be no sleeping in, no adjusting back to east coast time after a week in Spain.

She was gone when I got out of bed two hours after lying down. In one day she'd depart for Indonesia for two weeks. I was, put mildly, a bit wobbly myself, existentially.

There were some okay times in Spain. But not many. Crowds were tiny, uninspired. I was haunted by the increasingly likely notion that the Anomoanon was just not capable of gaining the traction among its fans to really last. I was haunted by the idea that I was sucking as a professor, that I wasn't treating it with the seriousness that the job deserved, and that I should have been paying a lot more attention to having my bread buttered by Towson University and not the Anomoanon.

Spain was the first tour where I felt the cart wobbling in a way that felt dangerous.

THE CART CONTINUED TO wobble throughout yet another mini-tour in November, from Baltimore, to Asheville, North Carolina, to Morgantown again and finally to Haverford College outside of Philly, where the drunk undergrad who promoted the gig failed to find us places to sleep after the show, assuming, perhaps, that we'd just drive back to Baltimore, which is what we should've done. Instead we played a great show, well-attended by appreciative college students, packed up our gear and drank the rest of the beers we'd been given as the show began. The young woman kept saying she'd get on it, she was waiting for another call from someone who had an apartment, but then it was three in the morning, we were at an incredibly awkward party at some undergraduate's room on campus, and I wanted to crash. Ned and I were both fathers of two, happily married and in our mid- to late thirties, and there we were drinking warm vodka and Kool-Aid out of stadium cups with twenty-year olds.

Should One Gyre and Gimble?

DURING A RECORD-BREAKING HOT fall after the Spanish tour and the regional mini-tour, Willie and Aram came to Baltimore for another recording session.

By this point in our narrative Chris had finished her PhD and was clocking sixty hours per week working in DC, with frequent two-week trips to such far-flung places as Cairo, Baghdad, Tunis, Rabat, Kabul, Afghanistan, Colombo, Sri Lanka, Amman, Jordon, Beirut, Sanaa, Yemen, Jakarta, and elsewhere. Most mornings she was up at 5:30 and out the door by 6:30. There were, in fact, awesome times during this stretch, filled with family gatherings, with beer-soaked cookouts, with songs and music and laughter. Ned was a fantastic cook, an expert on the grill, and many were the evenings we'd hang out in their backyard eating pulled pork and drinking rosé wine while the kids played in the yard. We may have even had a little competition going, as I fancied myself a damn good grillmaster, so there were numerous weekends where we'd ping-pong back and forth between their house and ours, and everyone in our families, plus friends and neighbors, would be treated to an array of grilled meats.

The competition was never particularly heated, we were too cool for that, but now, with humility, I admit that Ned is a better griller than I am.

Domestically, Ned and I continued to lead similar lives: We'd wake the kids, get them dressed, make breakfast, shuttle the youngsters to daycare, older ones to elementary school. We'd be the ones who'd get the call if one of the kids puked at school, we were responsible for restocking the larder when it ran low, we'd be the ones waiting in the pickup line with the moms, we'd be the ones making lunch, then trying to get the younger ones down for a nap while helping the older ones with homework, or taking the whole lot to a nearby park. We were on the hook for making suppers as well, most of the time.

The differences between my life and Ned's were subtle in most cases, but extreme in one: I'd been able to argue my way back onto the adjunct faculty at Towson University after the disastrous discovery in Spain of having lost my job. Not only had I been given back the job but I was teaching a full four-course load, so on top of all of the domestic responsibilites and the recording responsibilities, I had to deal with job crap as well. As happy as I was to have a job again, and as happy as I was that I had a loving, successful wife, loving and successful friends, I noted, upsettingly, that an overwhelming exhaustion accompanied just about everything I did and, in retrospect, I'm not sure I wasn't on the edge of a nervous breakdown when I slowed down enough to think about it.

One morning on the way to class, stopped at a red light, I told myself it would be perfectly acceptable to take a fifteen-second nap, so that's what I did, entering the sleep zone, relaxing, then opening my eyes just as the light turned green. I hadn't even put the car in park. One afternoon after rushing from class in order to hit the grocery store to restock supplies, then rushing to one school to pick up the younger kid, then rushing to another school to pick up the older one, I arrived back at my car to find that it was running. The doors were unlocked, the key still in the ignition. I'd forgotten to turn it off. It had been running for the better part of a half hour.

As usual the songs we planned to record in Ned's basement were great. But I was still on that knife-edge of being a youngish father with a job, whose wife also worked full-time and spent measurable amounts of time in far-flung locations in developing countries, and also who was supposed to play the drums for a recording session for the new Anomoanon record. I was not crisp, and instead quite flimsy.

I remember hurrying home from work and picking up Maxwell at nursery school, then running behind a jog stroller, trying to get Max to fall asleep so that I could record a track, while Aram, Willie, and Ned waited for me back at the studio. It was a blazing hot fall day and I was wearing jeans, and came home to Ned's drenched in sweat, my son not even asleep, probably even more cranky and red-faced and out of sorts than when we'd set out. I can't listen to *Joji* without feeling cold sweat building on my neck, and the sense that any second I'm going to hear the pealing cries of a three- or four-year-old just awakened and moist and crabby from a nap. It's impossible for me not to long for one or two more takes of the drum track in "Down and Brown" or "Wedding Song." In "Mr. Train" I speed up as we're heading into the first chorus, and my drumming in "Leap Alone" is so bad I sound like I'm playing the song for the first time. Truth is, I did learn some songs in Ned's basement, pretty much recording as I learned them, and the results, to me, sound it.

The guitar playing by Ned and Aram? Great. The songs written by Ned and Aram? Great. Willie's bass and singing? Great. My drumming? Fecking horrendous. Of all our records, *Joji* is the one I just cannot listen to, and it's my own fault. Still, music writer Amanda Petrusich, in a review on *Pitchfork*, absolutely loved *Joji*, gave it a great rating, our highest yet, so I stoked the embers of hope and waited, still excited even in my increasing unease about everything band-related, to see what might happen, and hoping for the best but expecting something far less.

One night Chris and I were watching a movie called *Junebug* that our local video rental store had recommended and suddenly there was Will on our TV screen. I'm not sure I even knew he was in the movie until I was watching it. He was quite funny. Like, really funny. He was Will but not Will. He was Will but also someone else.

WILL AND MATT SWEENEY had put out *Superwolf* in '05 and were touring to support it. Will asked us to open for them for four regional dates, in New York, Philadelphia, Swarthmore College, and Charlottesville. It'd be a great opportunity for us to break out the songs from *Joji*.

The straight-ahead electric Superwolf record was garnering smashing reviews and no wonder; it was, as I saw it, a brilliant blast of rock music. It was so good, so clean and free, that I recognized I was, again, expecting Will to leverage the success of this more commercially viable record for some kind of major deal. I honestly thought that was still among Will's goals. I could not have been more wrong, of course, but my expectation that Will might one day move up from Drag City to the next rung on the ladder continued to inform my fundamentally conservative mindset about careerism and my friend's professional desires. The goal, as ever, was to become more comfortable, wealthier, and more popular as a result of your hard work; I don't think Will would've disagreed with this goal necessarily, but he was going to achieve the dream on his own, without the help of a large record label.

(Remember: The Corporation is the enemy. Never forget this. Will certainly hasn't. That said, the heroic Mekons did release their records through A&M for a few years, so I supposed

I always considered that Will might do the same sort of thing. He didn't, and still hasn't. As of the writing of these words in 2019, Will is still releasing his records through Drag City.)

A bit bruised by our recent Anomoanon-only tours, we happily agreed to play the opening gigs. The Superwolf shows were all along the I-95 corridor, relatively close to Baltimore (except for the Charlottesville show a few hours south) and I could arrange it so that I didn't miss any classes at Towson. Aram and Willie came in for a day or so of practice, and we packed ourselves and our gear into Tight 329 and went north to New York, excited to see the Superwolf kids, excited to watch them play these brilliant songs.

At the sold-out Bowery Ballroom in Manhattan, we opened our set with a few bars of "Fearless" from Pink Floyd's *Meddle*. The SRO crowd went nuts for the Anomoanon. Hope sprang eternal! In Philly, the Theater of the Living Arts, capacity one thousand, was sold out. After the Anomoanon's opening set I found myself swept up by the great masses of hooting and hollering frat-rocking white boys in cargo shorts, golf shirts, and ball caps screeching like prepubescents when Will and the boys took the stage.

From one extreme to the other: the next show was just down the road in the leafy bower of Swarthmore College, just outside of Philly. Instead of yobbos in cargos we were met by two thoughtful young women in flannel shirts, one with a pierced nose, who offered us yogurts and water. In the hospitality space next to the hall where we'd play, an art major had built a gigantic modernist teeter-totter out of plywood and painted it in seventies Germanic primary-school red. The teeter-totter was composed of two solid wooden seats opposing one another on each edge of a large semi-circle, a sort of U-shape with the seats positioned on the ends of the "u" so that when two people sat in it their knees would be close to touching as they faced one another. Paul and I jumped up on it first, sitting in the seats, knees pointing at knees, finding it uncomfortably teetery. We leapt off before causing any bodily injury; Sweeney and tour manager Jessie hopped on, whence the hyperactive Sweeney and the oft-mellow tour hustler Jessie started going at it NY-style, trying to bounce one another ass over teeter. Bodies were flying.

In all the excitement Will had a yogurt explode in the pocket of his yellow fleece.

The show that night was full of the same kind of manic but focused energy. A high point of the mini-tour, to be sure. And another reminder of the potential for joy.

Another return to Charlottesville. Ned, Paul, and Will's uncle, a pilot, had flown a number of Louisvillians to the show, including Joe and Joanne Oldham, plus Willie's mom and sister. At the supposedly fancy restaurant we ate at before the show, Bonnie Band drummer Pete went out on a limb and ordered the "kalamata salad." The salad arrived tableside and we all shivered as we espied a hand formed baseball-sized clod of rubbery black olives from a can resting on about three big spinach leaves.

I felt clumsy and slow behind the kit and wasn't hearing things right...I blamed the sight of Pete's olive salad.

IN CONTRAST TO THE recent Anomoanon-only tours, the four shows we played with Superwolf were sold out. The audiences were rabid, with mad applause and wild, tear-thick shouts of joy and insane rebel yells greeting the end of each song. We were back to being the Dionysian priests leading the maenads and satyrs through another ritual of dancing and joy. Even if it hadn't become clear to us recently that Will was going decidedly in one direction and the Anomoanon the other, with his trajectory continuing to point skyward while ours very much remained on Earth, this tour proved beyond a shadow of a doubt that the only way we'd play in front of a real crowd was if we were opening for Will.

Our grand experiment of being a working band that could succeed on its own merits was coming to a close. The dream we'd had since '94 when we first became the Anomoanon, The Band to Will's Dylan, was pretty much done.

You're Going to Know That It's True

On a gorgeous early June Sunday afternoon in Baltimore in 2006, Chris, Ned, Jennie, and I were entertaining a guest from France at the neighborhood pool. Maxwell had just learned not just how to leap off a diving board but how to actually run and bounce at the end, unlike Matt Sweeney. He even sometimes pulled into a can opener or tucked into a cannonball. Sam, barely younger than Max, was there as well, leaping off the board with abandon. The older kids were playing sharks and minnows in the deep end. The sun was out but a cool Atlantic wind was blowing, epic blue skies across which an incongruous and impotent purple cloud might periodically bluster past.

There was no cell phone reception at the pool so it was pleasant to sit there in the sun and converse with friends and not have to worry about checking texts or emails or getting any phone calls. Ned told us that he, Will, and Paul were going to play some shows in New York billed as the Brothers Oldham, in

August. The show had been suggested to Will by Louisvillian Nathan Salsburg, a musician and folklorist, who thought it'd be a great thing to get Will on board singing some traditional songs; Will suggested the three brothers band together to sing them, instead of just himself. Or something like that; remember, this is not a historical record of things, but a loose approximation, and it's important to note that even as Will's star was rising, he was still interested in collaborating with Paul, with Ned. That sense of musical community established so many years before had not changed, even as much else about our lives had changed. After an hour or so in the pool, Jennie decided it was time to check her phone, so she excused herself to go to the car.

In a few minutes, Jennie came back from the parking lot holding Ned's cell phone. Someone had called Ned four times, from Louisville. Ned looked at the number on the phone, a comically exaggerated look on his face.

"My mom, of course!"

He walked out to the lot where there was better reception while we went back into the pool.

Back inside the pool we drifted into conversation with our friend from France. We were eating sandwiches from Eddie's. The kids continued to leap off the board, their cries ringing in the summer air like bells. Who knows how those moments pass?

Ned came back into the pool.

"My dad just died," he said.

LATER IN THE WEEK, at the Oldham house in Louisville before the funeral, there remained a sad pervasive sense of Joe: the hiking boots next to the door still green and flecked by the grass he'd cut Saturday, the day before he died on a bicycle ride with his friends; his bikes were still hanging from the garage ceiling, waiting to be ridden; all of the photographs he'd taken of Joanne, of the brothers, of his grandkids were hanging everywhere in the house. Joe's camera was still on the dining room table. Joanne was still referring to him in the present tense.

Standing in the home, surrounded by our extended musical family, I realized I couldn't count how many times I looked up from my drum throne to see Joe standing among a crowd of disheveled youngsters, his huge smile visible from the stage as he held up his camera and took photos. When I'd see the pictures later it was easy to see that Joe wasn't interested in the fans as they peered up at Will or at Ned, he wasn't interested in artsy shots of the clubs' decrepit bathrooms. No, he was interested in us. He was extraordinarily proud of his sons, proud of all of us, and his photos reflected this. The Brothers Oldham shows in August were suddenly instilled with something greater than they had been only days before, and became a ceremonial coming together, an honoring of Joe in a way he would've appreciated. He loved to watch his boys play music.

A rare bird, Joe was!

From my notebook, Saturday, July 22, 2006, a few weeks after his funeral:

A recent dream about riding one of Joe Oldham's bikes. The front tire had a jointed mechanism that allowed the wheel to roll in multiple dimensions, to what end I'm not sure but to some great advantage. I reached down; the tire was underinflated.

"That Joe," I chuckled.

TWO MONTHS AFTER JOE died, Paul, Will, and Ned played The Brothers Oldham shows at Joe's Pub in New York, a.k.a. Bonny Billy and Captain Anomoanon with Paul Oldham. Each of the brothers sat on a stool, each played an acoustic guitar, and they sang the traditional songs suggested by Salsburg. No drums, no electric guitars, no keyboards, just the voices of three brothers, Ned, Will, and Paul, and their acoustic guitars. What I would've given to be in that audience with a cold beer in my hand!

Even though the Brothers Oldham shows had been planned well before Joe's death, and at Joe's Pub, no less, it was easy to think the shows were a ritual organized in the spirit of honoring the idea of family, and honoring Joe, whose loss was still a hole in the heart of the fabric of the musical family we'd been building for almost twenty years. Instead, it was all coincidence.

Paul has made many appearances in this narrative, but I've probably failed to establish how he was in many ways the unsung hero of so much Bonnie Billy and Anomoanon music. The Anomoanon would never have existed if it weren't for Paul and he certainly facilitated the creation of a lot of Bonnie Prince Billy music as well. He was a foundational part of our band even if he didn't play with us a lot. Because he was less well-known as a performer or bandleader, the shows in New York were really about the interplay between Ned and Will's voices, their guitar playing, their both being interpreters of traditional folk music, but the inclusion of the youngest brother, equally talented but in a different way, was a powerful symbol of solidarity.

During this busy period of time, Ned and Jennie decided to sell their house in Baltimore and move back to Charlottesville where they'd first met as undergrads at UVA, and where Ned had first met me and Aram and Jason. Jennie had been offered an interesting professional opportunity in a small town outside of Charlottesville, and Ned had been offered a teaching job at a local school.

Chris and I, and the boys, were sad to see them go. At the same time we were all happy that they were embarking on a new adventure. Anyhow, with Will long gone from Baltimore, and now Ned, I pretty much gave up on the idea of ever playing drums with anyone again.

I'D BEEN GIVEN A promotion at Towson University from adjunct professor to salaried lecturer and offered a living wage for the first time in my life. Chris had landed her dream job, which allowed her to work with some fascinating and super-smart people who were dedicated to making the world a better place. Like the cast of shady Ibizan characters who inhabit Welles' *F For Fake*, a movie I often screened in my classes, I was learning something I'd never learned in the band—that I could inhabit the role of a professor in a way that felt comfortable, creative, fluid. Like Will in *Junebug*, I could be me but also someone else. I recalled Steve Martin's claim that teaching was another form of show business. It struck me as odd that I couldn't inhabit a rock star persona as drummer for the Anomoanon, which actually was show business. I'm not sure why I approached being a drummer with such earnestness, but I did.

Still, the lectureship, as much as I loved it, was challenging. As a lecturer, I was contracted to teach four courses per semester, one course of which I'd never taught before. Because I taught writing courses, I'd soon spend hours and hours reading thousands upon thousands of pages of students' drafts, and viewed it as my duty to make sure I read over the drafts carefully, perhaps too carefully. If in class I remained something of a showman, enjoying the performance aspect of teaching, in my office and at home I took the reading and responding to student work very seriously. No longer was I the bearded, beclogged bozo with dirty hair who played "Sister Ray" and who'd figure out what to do in class on my morning bike rides to the campus. I'd gone straight. Teaching was no joke. I'd also volunteered to be a coach for both boys' little league baseball teams, so I'd gone from being a guy who might write in his journal *another late night of bourbon and weed* to instead musing on the value of teaching a ten-year-old how to throw a split-finger fastball.

One day I realized that, like all great poetry, the Mekons' line about destroying one's safe and happy life had morphed in meaning as I'd grown older; what had once served as a sly criticism of my desire for domestic stability had been turned on its head. Being a family man with a full-time job was exponentially more difficult than being a rock drummer.

The safe life was that of the road.

24

Everybody Needs
an Angel

EARLY IN THE SUMMER of 2008, Will and Ned were on the phone when Ned suggested an Anomoanon/Bonnie Prince Billy show in Charlottesville, in August, and Will agreed that it'd be a great opportunity for a *hoedown*. The Ano hadn't played together in a while, since before Ned and his family left Baltimore, so it'd be a fun reunion, I suspected. As far as I could tell, the show was nothing more than an opportunity to play with one another, to visit, and hopefully to make a little cash. It was, to me, another beneficent gesture by Will, to agree to play with the Anomoanon. Will didn't need us at all, having recently played with some excellent musicians in Emmet Kelly and Dawn McCarthy and Alex Neilson and Michael Zerang, to name a few incredibly skilled players that Will was working with, and, well, why would he play with the Anomoanon if he could play with just about anyone in the world? Will looped Boche Billions in on the negotiations and within a few days we were scheduled to play two shows at the Gravity Lounge, a small club on Charlottesville's downtown mall. Paul would join us from his home in Louisville, Aram and Willie would join, and I'd drive down with Chris and the kids from Baltimore. Will suggested we play a bunch of Anomoanon songs, plus a few selections from Will's latest record *Lie Down in the Light*. At some point in the set Will, Paul, and Ned would sing a few of the Brothers Oldham tunes.

IN THE LEAD-UP TO the weekend, via phone, via email, no one seemed particularly excited about the upcoming shows. I was teaching three summer courses, one of them online, and felt emburdened with reading papers. I remained puzzled as to why Will would want to play with us. Speaking for me and for no one else, I was looking more forward to seeing everyone, to hanging out by Ned's grill with a cold beer, to catching up with Jennie, with Aram, with Paul, with Ned and Will and Willie than I was in actually learning a bunch of songs and playing them on a stage. I thought a group hike in the mountains around Charlottesville would be nice, bring the kids along, maybe find a swimming hole, Paul's Creek in Afton, for example, where Aram had once taken the video of my man boobs during one of our tours.

I remembered that when I was in middle school, I was in a band that was sort of popular, with my friends David and John, with whom I'd gone to the Boston concert and whom I often pushed down David's driveway on the banana skateboard. We were called the Illusion. We were awkward twelve-year-olds, I was a sort of tubby prepubescent before I hit my growth spurt, and John's voice began to change during our bandness, like Peter Brady's, leading bassist David and I to sing the Brady Bunch's "When It's Time to Change" whenever we saw John in the hallways at school. We became the pets of an older new wave band, The Rage, and opened for them a bunch at Richmond's Kosmos 2000 club, all sold-out shows.

Not sure why it had taken me so long to remember all of this, but, as a kid, with the Illusion, I hated playing onstage. I loved playing the drums with my friends but hated being up there in front of the Rage's fans. It wasn't even that I was nervous. I just didn't like it. After one show one of the Rage's twenty-something year old female fans, dressed up like one of the cats in *Cats*, told me that I was a lot shorter when I wasn't sitting behind the drums. Weird that these memories dominated my thoughts as the Charlottesville shows approached.

THE NIGHT BEFORE WE were to meet in Charlottesville for practice, my otherwise hale and healthy seventy-something year-old father rose from his computer in Richmond, where he was researching riding mowers on the internet, caught his foot on an oriental rug in his office and fell, breaking his hip. I drove Chris, Tabb, and Maxwell to Charlottesville from Baltimore, then drove to Richmond to see Dad at St. Mary's, where he'd soon undergo a hip replacement. I missed our first day of practice. He was more embarrassed than anything else, but seeing him in his hospital bed, and talking to him about the upcoming surgery, I had one of those awful premonitions that things would never be the same again. I wasn't wrong. It was an odd way to start a rehearsal weekend.

IN CHARLOTTESVILLE WE PRACTICED at the club during the day, grabbed slices of pizza for lunch at a joint around the corner, practiced some more.

Lie Down... was my favorite record of Will's since *Superwolf*. I loved how explicitly the record dealt with themes of accepting mortality. I found much of it extraordinarily moving, particularly with my previous day's experience of seeing my father in his hospital bed in Richmond. The Anomoanon's set list as written by Ned was wide-ranging and career-spanning, which was head-spinning. Ned's songs charted my adult life. Each song elicited important memories but also reminded me, as if I needed to be reminded, of how quickly time was leaving us. We had to relearn songs we hadn't played in ages, songs from most of our releases, and it was great fun, and something of a challenge, to practice so many songs from such an array of our work.

Still, the practices felt like work to me. It was always fun playing with my friends. Always. Never not fun. But I was sensing in some overarching way that, as pathetic as it may sound, I was getting too old for playing the drums in a band. Or just that something had shifted internally in my own perception of myself, of my role in the world, of my reason for being; I liked being a professor better than playing in a band. I wondered, not for the first time, if the drums weren't kind of a stupid instrument, and if I wasn't kind of stupid for playing them. So clumsy, so graceless, so noisy, so...dumb.

After afternoon practice at the club ended, we went to Ned and Jennie's home on the outskirts of Charlottesville to rest and grill burgers. As the kids were running around the Oldham's yard, a dog, a skittish Aussie, got worked up and snapped at Tabb, toothing him on the face. Tabb was okay, there were no punctured eyeballs or lacerated cheeks, an obvious relief, but it was jarring hearing the dog growl and yip, and then seeing Tabb drawing back, his hands covering his cheek, underneath his right eye. Like some Greek myth, portent upon portent began to stack—my father's fall, Tabb's close call with the dog, my weird middle-school anxiety about the shows.

When I called to check in on Dad, I was relieved to hear he was in great spirits after his surgery. He was proud of himself that he'd already gotten up and walked around with his new hip. I could hear it in his voice. He was happy I was in Charlottesville to play music with my friends. It made me happy that he was happy. I wasn't too worried about him, but as the strangeness of the weekend began to build on itself, my father's operation, his growing old, the close call with the dog, it all began to weigh me down.

WE PLAYED OUR TWO sets, an early show and a late one. The shows were damn good, as usual. I'd totally given up on wearing earplugs so played all of the practices and both long shows without them, a mistake, and I ended the second show barely able to hear through the piercing, glassy shrieking in my ears. It was miserable. A local singer named Sarah White got on the bill and we played a few of her songs, which I enjoyed. She sang the female parts from two songs on Will's *Lie Down in the Light*, "You Want that Picture" and "So Everyone." Addie and Tabb came to the early show and ran our merch booth, helping sell a fair amount of product and reaping a fine little commission as a result of their hard work. For both shows, the place was packed, so packed it was hard to get to the bar, to the bathrooms. Some friends of mine came up from Richmond, including the guy who'd long ago sent me the Jesco White tape. Each of us made a few hundred dollars for a few afternoons' work. Still, the weekend ended with a strange deflation, at least for me. Packing my car the next day, I realized they were good shows but some awful force had superseded my excitement to play rock and roll with my friends, one of those imps of the perverse that sees fit to remind you, even at the best of times, surrounded by friends you've had for decades, that nothing is ever easy, and that it all ends, often painfully.

ONE WEEKEND IN THE spring of 2010, during my spring break, Chris, the boys, and I drove from Baltimore to Rehoboth Beach to see Will and his bandmate Emmett Kelly play an unamplified show at Dogfish Head. We met Mike Fellows there in the afternoon and took a long walk on the beach before the show, catching up. At the venue I saw Will for the first time since the Charlottesville shows almost two years before. We spoke as if no time had passed. We drank a bunch of Dogfish beers with an organic farmer and his father who'd come to Rehoboth from Pennsylvania to see Will play. They loathed Amish farmers, whom, they claimed, used three times more chemicals in their crops than anyone else, but hid behind their little chin beards and horse-drawn buggies just to trick everyone into thinking they were buying some special organic product. We visited with Sam Calagione, who'd been such a great host so many years before, doling out the delicious tuna while we listened to Boston. Dogfish was now a Rehoboth institution. It still is.

Down in Charlottesville, Ned had started a new band with some local musicians called Old Calf. They were great. Minus Aram's ripping lead guitar and my clodding drums, the band was a purer expression of a lot of the British Isles-influenced folk that had always, in my opinion, been the foundation on which the Anomoanon built so much of our music.

That night onstage with Emmett in Rehoboth, Bonnie Prince Billy was back in fine fettle, flirting with the audience, dancing, singing, chewing on the scenery a bit, hamming it up, rolling around on the tiny stage, surrounded by adoring fans who hung on his every word, his every movement, his every expression of being some validation of our shared life force.

He continued to bear his burden, in addition to ours. He was the jolly troubador trying to lighten our load.

THROUGHOUT THESE YEARS, POSTCARDS would often arrive in our mailbox, often addressed to Tabb and Maxwell Carneal. I'd recognize Will's handwriting, see that the postmark was from

Spain, or Sweden, or France, flip over the card and be met with the sight of a scantily clad beauty from some distant country. He never forgot us. Never forgot our kids, even as it was obvious that we were all slipping away from one another.

IN 2011, OUR FRIEND from Baltimore, filmmaker Matt Porterfield, asked Ned to play the character Bill in Matt's movie *I Used to Be Darker*, and in a roundabout way this role was the initial flapping of the butterfly's wings that resulted in the final time Ned, Will, Aram, Willie, Paul, and I shared a stage.

Ned and I had played as a duo years previously at a benefit for *Hamilton*, Matt's first movie, which he'd shot on film in and around Baltimore. When we first agreed to do the benefit for *Hamilton*, I thought we were doing some poor film student a favor to allow for his crappy student art film to be completed. But during the benefit a few reels were shown, and I immediately noted that this was no crappy student film. The opposite, in fact. This was a stunning piece of film artistry. A few months later, *Hamilton* was being praised in *The New Yorker* and *The New York Times*.

I Used to Be Darker is about a former touring musician who's given up performing and instead runs a successful business. His wife, played by Kim Taylor, an excellent singer/songwriter from Cincinnati, from whom he's recently been separated, is still touring as a musician. They are visited by a pregnant niece, who's run away from her Irish family and ends up in Baltimore after a summer working at Ocean City. The movie's narrative touches on the constant struggle between the life of the road and the life of domesticity. It was strangely resonant, reflecting many of the experiences I'd had as a performing artist over the previous two decades, offering the possible flipside to my naive Allman fantasy: being a working artist is, by nature, to oppose domesticity, to embrace instability.

In the movie, lives are, if not destroyed, then highly compromised by the devotion the woman, played by Kim Taylor, has to the touring life, to her art. Bill is hurt by her choosing touring over him. One of the many questions the movie asks is whether or not a domestic life is even desirable. Perhaps most human growth is fertilized by struggle, and if one wants to grow, to become enlightened, then one must struggle.

When Matt asked to film the movie in my house, he and his writing partner Amy decided to write in a small role for me to play, which allowed me and Ned to play a few short musical sequences in the film.

AFTER THE PREMIERE OF Matt's movie in Park City, Utah, at the Sundance Film Festival, Ned and I played a rocking duo show at the High West bar. Do I even need to write how thrilling it was to be able to watch the premiere of the movie at Sundance with my old friends Ned and Matt, then to play this killer, wine-fueled show? The film was great, but more than that, from a personal perspective, I thought Ned had done an excellent job in portraying Bill and I was proud of him. My own role? Seeing myself onscreen wasn't unlike hearing the single songwriting contribution I made to the Anomoanon's catalogue, the song "Mermaid's Womb" that Sweeney had rearranged for that show in LA. My reaction was one of horror, even though I'm on-screen for about three seconds. Not sure I need to see myself on-screen ever again.

The next day, Chris and I hiked out into a snow-covered valley nearby, and later spent the afternoon skiing at Deer Valley. The sun was brilliant, the sky vast and clear, and the last day I joined Ned and Kim Taylor for a few songs, a rather more subdued mini-set than the one at High West. Unbeknownst to them, Ned would call young stars Hannah Gross and Deragh Campbell onstage to accompany us for a version of eighteenth century folk song "The Cruel Mother" (Child Ballad #20), teaching them the choral singalong on the spot, "Oh, the rose and the linsie-o / Down by the greenwood sidey-o." Hannah and Deragh played along for the first few rounds but bailed after it became clear that none of us except Ned really knew what we were doing.

After the show two young African American women were following me and Chris around, whispering as we walked up and down Park City's main drag. They were trying to spot some stars. I had a long grayish beard and uncut, shaggy hair. They were getting closer and closer, and at a certain point we realized they were whispering about us. Chris finally turned around and asked them what they wanted. They giggled and tittered into their hands.

"Are you the guy in *Django Unchained*?"

"Uhh, Jamie Foxx?" I answered dumbly.

"No, the white guy."

After realizing they had not mistaken me for Jamie Foxx, I realized they thought I was Christoph Waltz.

"No," I laughed. "That's not me."

IN JUNE OF 2013 Ned and I flew to Louisville for a screening of *I Used To Be Darker* at the Flyover Film Fest, which will be where this narrative ends. Fret not, the ending comes softly, painlessly, with no harsh words, and with some natural sense of closure, of the clicking shut of the door to our shared past. There again, I'm oft reminded what Faulkner said about closure and the past: *The past is never dead, it's not even past.*

Ned and Willie had organized an Anomoanon show at a local club called Zanzabar in conjunction with the screening. Paul and his wife Amber had recently moved to California but happened to be in town visiting Joanne. Will and Willie lived in Louisville, so it was easy to let Willie organize the gig, easy for Will to join us. A band Willie was playing in, a prog-surf band called the Flyswatters would be the opener, then the Anomoanon would play a set afterward, with Paul on third guitar and vocals. Amber would hop onstage at some point and we'd play a few of the great songs she and Paul had written and would soon record in Los Angeles as Lucky Eyes. Then Will would join us for two songs, "Horses" and "The Wanderer."

Aram drove up from Charleston, a long drive, to play the single show with us. It was a clear illustration, if one was even needed, that Aram's loyalty to the band was noble, movingly so. It was a sacrifice for Aram to leave work and to drive all the way to Louisville. We'd probably get paid nothing for the Zanzabar show, and Aram would be taking a loss on gas and sundries. Still, he knew the Anomoanon had transcended any careerist goals and had completed a full circle, back to playing for the sake of friendship and fun, and nothing else.

I HOPE IT'S NOT too annoying to skip ahead in time a few months to the fall of 2013. We'll go back to Louisville and the Zanzabar in a minute for what will be, alas, the climax of this tale.

But before we get there, let's zoom forward into the fall of 2013. When *I Used To Be Darker* had its New York premiere in October of 2013 at the IFC Center theater in Greenwich Village, me, Aram, Ned, and Heumann, minus Willie, played a weekend's worth of shows in New York that distilled the entire existence of the Anomoanon into two succinct nights: the first show, at Brooklyn's Union Pool with the mighty Endless Boogie, took place on a gorgeously clear fall night, and before the show, we were reunited with Dianne, our lovely first road manager, the unshakable Numbers, who'd gotten a series of great teaching jobs in New York since leaving Baltimore. In fact, Dianne had just been named the Assistant Dean of the School of Art at the Pratt Institute. She was also working on a stop-motion short called *The Itching*. Things were going pretty well for Numbers.

Chris and Jennie had accompanied the band to New York. Chris hadn't really seen Dianne since she'd left Baltimore, so we all drank beers outside the club and talked and laughed before the show. To think that our friendships, our marriages, our partnerships, could now be measured in multiple decades was moving, exciting, and deepened the joy of visiting with Dianne, but also served as another stunning reminder of the brutal passage of time.

That night, Endless Boogie was fantastic, and in spite of my own sense that drumming was in the rearview for me, our own set was an explosive, sold-out blast, where we communed via the magic of rock with an insane audience engaged in the Dionysiac abandon of the young. It was a special night, one where music and friendship and performance and expression and memory come together in a single stream of powerful sensations that allow us to proceed with excitement and hope, even though we're all headed toward the grave. And isn't that the role of art in our lives, to remind us of this continuum?

The second night's show was the polar negative of the previous night's brilliant-hued Kodachrome slide. It was a reminder that the grave is often closer than one would like and that the continuum ends, abruptly and with malice. The show was at the Living Room in Manhattan, and from the start during our load-in I'd knew it'd be trouble. It was an acoustic-only club, or mostly acoustic, and we were definitely not an acoustic group. As we brought in our drums and amps, the soundman went white…whiter than he already was, in any case, which was to say, from the pasty hue of too many hours spent in a folk club to the blue-white hue of cake icing.

"What are these?" he asked. "These big ugly things that look an awful lot like…*amplifiers and drums?*"

During our sound check, the soundman kept telling us to turn it down. He illustrated zero awareness that the problem—a rock band being booked at a folk club—was the fault of whomever booked the band, and not necessarily the fault of the band itself. Perhaps there'd been some miscommunication, because Ned and Kim Taylor had played a set or two as an acoustic duo, but we all thought it had been made clear that this show would include electric instruments. Perhaps we weren't clear enough. The soundman didn't appear to have much respect for non-acoustic instruments, and after placing the mics and taking his spot behind the soundboard and asking us to bang around a bit, he commanded again and again that we TURN IT DOWN.

Aram, Ned, and Heumann, looking like chastened teens, slumped noncommittally toward their amps, placed their fingers on the volume buttons, and pretended to move them, then played a palm-muted chord softly in an attempt to trick the soundman into thinking they'd actually moved the knobs without having done so. I was told many times that I was hitting my snare too hard, and did I have a set of brushes I could use? A lot of bands might respond to such requests with obnoxious rockstar 'tudes, but not the Anomoanon. We wanted to please. We didn't see the point of creating bad vibes. We were positive face, to the end. So even though the guitarists were constitutionally unable to turn down their amps, and I had no brushes, we tried to play more quietly than we might've otherwise, which was a mistake. You can't rock while walking on eggshells.

There were a few flubs. During a duet between Ned and Kim on Gram Parsons's "Love Hurts" (I preferred Nazareth's version), I completely screwed up the dramatic ending. The bad ending, in turn, screwed up the song, which in turn allowed the awkward show to end on the most awkward note possible.

The rock godz giveth, the rock godz taketh. A continuum, indeed.

ARRIVING AT ZANZABAR, ARAM, Ned, and I got a beer, found Paul and Amber, caught the last minutes of the Flyswatters, who were great to watch, and noted from the size of the crowd as we took the stage it was clear that no internet rumors had spread about Bonnie Prince Billy playing onstage with his older brother's band. Aside from a few of Willie and Ned's old friends, it was hard to tell if the people standing at the bar were there to see us or, I assumed, there for a normal weekend night to get a few drinks with friends, to hang out and see what might be going on at the neighborhood joint. My memory of this night is not as clear or as pure as I'd like; by the time we'd made it to the club I was more interested in hanging out with Aram, with Paul and Amber, with Willie and Ned and Will. The instruments we were playing, and that we were playing a show, felt invasive somehow, interruptive of some other process that seemed more important to me. Whatever happened that night wouldn't be a spectacle, nothing more than a band playing a few songs together, nothing more, nothing less. Another middling to good night for the Anomoanon, well short of a sellout. After a quick sound check, I counted off and we began.

AFTER PLAYING A FEW Anomoanon songs and Paul and Amber's Lucky Eyes songs, Ned called for Will, who shouldered his guitar and made his way to the stage. A buzz went through the small crowd.

Will stepped onto the stage and plugged in his guitar. I counted off a simple four to lead us into our first tune, "Horses." "Horses" is the song that began this memoir in 1994 at the Fri-Son Club in Fribourg when Will spat in the man's thinning hair. It was the song that The Mekons had played when I brayed from the audience that the Palace version was better. We'd been playing the song for nineteen years, and over time it had emerged as a fan favorite, and even though I'd played it dozens of times since then, if not hundreds, I still loved listening to the song as I played it. It had taken on an iconic place in the Will Oldham pantheon (even though he hadn't written it—remember that we have Mekons Sally Timms, Jon Langford, and Brendan Croker to thank for that), and is filled with the iconography of early Palace Brothers, things like death's head rings, horses, angels, and devils. And no matter how many times I'd played it, I still felt the same excitement licking up my spine as we barreled into the first chorus.

Everybody needs an angel
But here's that devil by my side...

AFTER "HORSES" WE PLAYED Ned's song "The Wanderer," featuring Ned and Will singing in harmony. Savor the simple things, the grizzled narrator implores, community-based things, family-based, love-based. And since I'd long considered us a musical family, and that our musical family had grown through the decades, and that something felt final about this show even though we couldn't have known that at the time, "The Wanderer" seemed an appropriate song to play.

During the song, as the brothers sang, beautifully as always, those genetically matched voices twining around one another like vines, and as the audience watched, I noted from my throne that Will wasn't just looking over at his older brother as they sang, but was instead staring at Ned balefully. Puzzled, trying to hang with the song's rollicking ¾ beat while watching the brothers sing, I initially assumed Will was trying to get Ned's attention so that they could hone their harmonies. But something else was going on.

Maybe I was reading too much into the emotional evening, but Will looked angry at Ned, at us. He'd agreed to sing Ned's song to make a point, and the point was being made, only it appeared I was the only one seeing it. And what the point was was too complex and mysterious for me to comprehend then or now.

I'm a wanderer
So I may not be fit to advise you
In the summertime
I go north and in winter go south
I have no family nor any friends
So well may you wonder
How I can say what I'm about to
Honor your father
Listen to your mother
Help your brother
Care for your sister
And your grandma, grandpa, uncles, aunts, and cousins
Love them all;
Husband, wife, daughter, and son.

As the final notes of the song ended, the audience whooped and clapped as Will removed his guitar, gave us one final half-smile, and leapt off the stage as if he was in a hurry. He disappeared through the crowd as the applause grew louder, more intense. The crowd wanted more music. More Will.

And more Anomoanon, I like to think.

I looked at Aram, at Willie, at Ned. We all looked at one another, looked at the door to the other part of the bar where Will had disappeared, waited a beat, two, three… No Will. Ned shrugged. Aram shrugged. Willie took a sip from his bottle of beer. I took a sip from mine. Seemed there'd be no encores with Will. I counted off the next song and soon we called it a night.

AT THE END OF the night the barkeep gave us more money than I thought we'd make, a couple hundred dollars or so, maybe even two fifty. He really appeared to appreciate the Anomoanon and thanked us profusely as he wiped the bar down with a white rag. Country music played on the house system and if there weren't neon beer lights casting a red glow on the bar as the barkeep wiped it down, then I'm mistaken. And if it wasn't country music on the house system, something by Mickey Newbury, perhaps *Looks Like Rain*, then I'm also mistaken. At the end of things, this is my story and no one else's, and my memory is no better than yours. Mistakes have probably been made, and I can only hope those mistakes don't hurt feelings. My intention has never been other than wanting to tell this story, to share these fond recollections, but I now know that's a lot more complicated than it sounds.

In the bar people sat around darkened tables in the glow of the beer signs and finished their drinks. Some looked at one another sadly, others with laughter in their eyes, and still others with lust. A busboy carried a load of glasses from the bar and they clinked and rang as he shifted the rack that held the glasses. Maybe there was no bar back, maybe there were no racks of glasses, and maybe the barkeep washed all the glasses in the small sink behind the bar. It doesn't really matter.

The barkeep offered us a bourbon shot and a few more beers, but by that point my thirst, for drink, for music, for the performing life, had been quenched. Instead, I asked for a glass of iced water. I longed for the bed at the local hotel where the movie fest people had put us up, Ned and I, each in our own room. I was ready to wake up early and ride out to the airport and to get back to Baltimore the following day. I was teaching a summer course and had to read student stories before the afternoon's class meeting. It was a creative writing class and I'd allowed the students to write fantasies, science fiction if they wanted, and a few of the early drafts were far better than

I expected. A few were far worse. So it goes. My sons had baseball and lacrosse games that I didn't just need to watch, but wanted to watch.

Maybe on the weekend we'd load up the minivan with the boys and their friends and Chris and me and drive down to the Chesapeake Bay house my parents lived in during the summer. Down there we'd sail, fish, piddle around on boats, try to avoid being stung by stinging nettles. Maybe my sister and her husband Ted and their kids would come down, and maybe we'd shoot off some fireworks we'd bought along the roadside. It would be hot during the day. It always was down there on the Piankatank. My mother would make big salads from vegetables from her garden while my dad and I would grill steaks while I drank beer and while my dad drank one of his nasty caffeine free Diet Cokes in the copper-colored cans, he having quit drinking alcohol in the eighties.

The room cleared out pretty quickly as we lugged our gear out to Willie and Aram's cars. Aram was going to wake up early and get on the road, a ten-hour drive, at least. Outside, people stood on the sidewalk and smoked cigarettes as we said our goodbyes. I hugged Aram, hugged Willie, hugged Ned, hugged Paul and Amber, manly hugs all, as my ride pulled up to the sidewalk. Standing there in the dark Louisville night outside of the club as we packed the cars, Ned decided to give all the money we'd made to Aram to defray his gas costs. I certainly didn't mind. I didn't much need the money and it was a long drive back to Charleston.

I knew, waiting for my ride to the hotel, that I didn't even want to watch TV and was instead ready to stretch out, maybe read a few pages of my book before entering the disorienting sleep state I often experience in hotels, where I frequently wake in the middle of the night, wondering where I am, often seeing a sliver of bright light peering in through the slit in the drapes like some giant reptilian eye, reaching around for Chris, finding an indescribable happiness, of safety and all being right with the world when my arm lands on her warm body. Without her in the bed that night in Louisville, I knew I'd hardly sleep.

Acknowledgments

THANKS TO ALL AT Rare Bird, Dan K, Dan O, and Rian at Drag City, Peter McGuigan at Foundry Media, my mother, Ann Carneal, and to Sorrel King for editorial advice and moral support. Last, this book is written in memory of my father, Drew Carneal, and of David Berman.